The Gift of Coac

The Gift of Coaching

Love over fear in helping conversations

Erik de Haan

Open University Press

Open University Press
McGraw Hill
Unit 4,
Foundation Park
Roxborough Way
Maidenhead
SL6 3UD

email: enquiries@openup.co.uk
world wide web: www.openup.co.uk

Executive Editor: Eleanor Christie
Editorial Assistant: Zoe Osman
Content Product Manager: Ali Davis

A catalogue record of this book is available from the British Library

ISBN-13: 978-0-3352-5198-8
ISBN-10: 0335251986
eISBN: 978-0-3352-5199-5

Library of Congress Cataloging-in-Publication Data
CIP data applied for

Typeset by Transforma Pvt. Ltd., Chennai, India

Praise page

Integrating more than two decades of research and practice, this immense resource offers deep insight into the theory and nature of coaching. Finding meaning in the intersection between love and fear, De Haan takes a forensic look at what it means to nurture another person's experience and in so doing produces an essential and immensely powerful book.

Marina Cantacuzino MBE, Founder of The Forgiveness Project

In Love over Fear, *Erik de Haan has reflected on and shared more than 25 years' of both academic and practical experience gained from his coaching sessions as well as study. Erik opens a window into his deep learning which will be of significant benefit to both new and experienced coaches and is up to date in acknowledging more recent developments coaches need to pay attention to, such as team coaching and our planet.*

There is a wonderful combination of almost ethereal and practical wording used in describing how the initial awkwardness and fear at the beginning of a coaching session can give way to both letting go of the fear of not knowing and allowing natural curiosity and exploration of not knowing take its place, thus allowing love to replace fear.

Gina Lodge, CEO, Academy of Executive Coaching (AoEC)

What an amazing book! Why should anyone ever again try to write a book on coaching? I am afraid that no few words can do it justice but here is an endorsement you can use:

This is a tour de force of coaching. de Haan wields concepts like love, humility and quality of relationships like a maestro inspiring an orchestra. As one of the most highly published scholarly authors in coaching, he has provided a rare book with deep intellectual foundations, prolific empirical evidence and engaging stories. He has left little room for future authors to add more than he has already said about coaching.

Richard Boyatzis, PhD, Professor, Case Western Reserve University, USA

Erik continues to enrich the coaching space with his insights and his commitment to the maturation of the field and its practitioners. He asks some important questions about our role in these times that are well-worth the read.

Dr David Drake, Founder and CEO, The Moment Institute

The Gift of Coaching is a compendium of coaching research, wisdom, and case study examples. But this is no staid treatise. It's a download

of Erik's brain provided through the provocative lens of the powerful human emotions love and fear. Erik masterfully weaves this knowledge into one—or both—of these emotions in order to illustrate the potential for each element of coaching.

Joel DiGirolamo, VP of Research and Data Science,
International Coaching Federation

A refreshing take on coaching from a well informed source! Erik is well known for his groundbreaking contributions to coaching research. While research is crucial for growing our profession, it can objectify the core purpose of coaching – helping others. Erik takes us back to the essence of coaching by illustrating the importance of trust, love, fear and humility through case studies, research and his own vast experience. This is a worthy contribution to our continuous search for understanding the building blocks of our profession.

Dr Nicky Terblanche, Head of MPhil in Management Coaching,
University of Stellenbosch, South Africa

"Love is the aspiration for communion and solidarity with other souls, and that aspiration always liberates the source of noble activities. That love is the supreme and unique law of human life, which everyone feels in the depth of one's soul. We find it manifested most clearly in the soul of the infants. Man feels it so long as he is not blinded by the false doctrines of the world."
—Leo Tolstoy, *Letter to Mohandas Gandhi*, 7 September 1910

For Carmen, who suffused my fearful life with love and let me have the week off to complete this book.

Contents

Contents

Foreword by Carine Metselaar

It is often said that sustainable relationships are hard work. They require that one does not give up when things get difficult and that both parties continue to communicate about their personal needs, pains, hopes, and desires. Obviously, the basis of every romantic relationship is love, and no one will probably deny that fear plays a huge part as well: fear of losing your loved one, to be left by them, or to experience betrayal. It would therefore be tempting to think that this book, with *Love Over Fear* as a subtitle, might contain insights and reflections not only about coaching relationships, but also about ones that can also be applied to other relationships. And, yes, this could be true to some extent. Except for one major difference: as coaches we are paid to be in this relationship. With this transactional element, whether we want it or not, a need to perform creeps into the process. Unfortunately, as also mentioned in the introduction of the book, 'love does not sit so well with business coaching when coaching is all performance-driven'. This tension is discussed in Chapter 6 in relation to the growing application of NPS ratings, which take the feedback outside of the relationship that matters. Back to the analogy with romantic relationships: talking *with* your loved one usually works better than talking *about* them, to say the least. In this book, alternatives that do more justice to the coaching relationship, based on love instead of fear, are discussed. However, in my view, we should also accept the imperfections in this process as leadership performance has never been and never will be a clearly defined concept. Can we accept a little messiness in the area of (leadership) coaching in relation to performance feedback? With love over fear, we might.

This is just one of the many tensions thoughtfully explored in this book. After all, managing tensions, sometimes appearing to us as paradoxes, is at the heart of our work. In Chapter 1, which contains a plea for attending to the basics of our profession, we encounter the paradox of the complexity of simplicity, and the many layers of 'just' listening, engaging, and understanding. In many leadership development programmes these are presented as coaching skills that can be mastered; yet, the behaviours are far from simple, most of all because they go beyond the mastery of a skill. We may think we conduct an intervention, but basically, we *are* the intervention, even if we don't do anything. According to Erik, even before we enter the room. Of course, becoming aware of this produces fear and sometimes even panic, especially in novice coaches, who enter the profession with a certain confidence that they will be able to master new skills, yet feel vulnerable when realizing that nothing we do guarantees the success the paying client might hope for. Yet, we know that, generally speaking, coaching brings results that do contribute positively to the performance objectives set out at the start. But how do you trust the process if you cannot yet rely on your own experience? Dealing with the tension between providing psychological safety while at the same time minimizing structure in order to stay with your client and keep your focus on wondering about what is going on, continues to be a huge challenge because we are part of what we try to 'manage'. In this regard, I like the concept of minimalistic coaching that is used in Part A, as it reminds me of my early introductions as an adolescent to conceptual art and minimalistic design, when I began to realize the relevance of *less is more, but never simple*. Maybe there is as much art to coaching as there is science, which makes me think of another paradox: participants in our postgraduate programmes usually deliberately opt for an academic institution to professionalize as an executive coach, expecting a thorough, science-based approach to coaching amidst a world full of 'bogus coaching'. However, whereas there is a growing body of research into coaching and cumulating evidence of its effectiveness, so far, there is no scientific evidence for favouring one approach over another. If we are serious about our humility, as this book is and as it becomes a red thread through the third part of the book, we should not consider certified practitioners to be superior to the non-certified. Yet, we know certification contributes to developing reflective practitioners who tend to explore and inquire, and are willing to keep their doubts fresh and alive, rather than impose knowledge and methods upon their coachees. The well-established Dutch Rietveld Art Academy mentions on its website: '*We are not a school. Schools expect the right answers; an art academy, by contrast, expects good questions, that stretch the limits of expectation and perception. We train students to master the tool of imagination, which makes them specialists in sensory intelligence: an essential asset in society.*' So maybe there is a bit of art to coaching after all; I can imagine *Love Over Fear* would apply to the arts in many ways as well.

Back to humility, the core of Part C. When complacency enters a profession, we all lose, as this jeopardizes the quality and safety of our work. It has been demonstrated that coaches can have a view about what they actually do in a session that differs from what coachees have observed or experienced, so there is reason to be humble about what we know about our own interventions. As emphasized in Part A, we need to suspend or defer our judgements regarding inquiry itself and what it is yielding. Chapter 2 talks about the liberating effects of not knowing and relates this to the early work of the sceptics in ancient Greek society. I here interpret 'liberating' as getting rid of fear, releasing or unloosening what is holding us back and thus freeing up fresh energy and liveliness. Yet, our hypotheses, however open, are also guided by our theoretical assumptions about human nature and are therefore by definition also potentially restrictive. Therefore, the best we can do is to be fully transparent about what guides our thinking and what drives us as professional coaches and human beings. This book does this in a candid and convincing way. I hope it will inspire many of us to follow this liberating example with love over fear.

Amsterdam, April 2022

Introduction: the eternal theme of love over fear

This book tries to capture what I have learned in over 25 years of coaching leaders. How many times have I said to myself, 'I must muster the love that I can feel for my clients, and not worry so much about what will happen next, as what will happen is not up to me, and even entirely unpredictable.' I have always felt doubts and insecurities in doing this work, and when I did not feel such doubts and insecurities, I found I did my worst work as I was far too certain and convinced of my approach.

In contrast to my two previous books (De Haan, 2019c and 2021), this work is not a statement of the fruits of research. Here, my hunches and fondness come to the fore, rather than general knowledge. I want this to be a book full of experiences and ideas which can be helpful in practice, rather than the facts and models that have been tested or the findings from research programmes.

Time and time again, two themes were triggered within me, both equally helpful if we are open to them and accept their influences: fear, doubt, and insecurity, on the one hand, and love, gratitude, and respect, on the other – insecurity about myself and my feeble talents for helping others, and respect or awe for the nature of this work and the person of my client.

Doubts in coaches have emerged in my research and my writing as well, and so has love, in the meaning of *agape* … fondness, charity, friendship, respect, loyalty, devotion, commitment, fidelity, trust, hope. Love has many names. And so has fear.

It is interesting for me that love and fear, however much they are in opposition – many writers say that one cannot be present where the other prevails – also have something very important in common, which is perhaps where they meet and fuse. Fear and love both bring you to the present moment. They invite you into forgetting past and future. Raw fear brings you in contact with your love of self, and you will do anything to get out of the danger you are in. Nothing else matters but the present moment and its existential, glaring crisis. The same for love: true love makes you forget about the past and the future; and brings you fully into this blissful, shared, present moment.

For me, there is a founding myth of the helping professions, a story about love and fear, and it is linked to the irresistible lightness of being. Here is my formulation of it. Herk the manager discovers that every time he solves a problem, every time he is right about a solution and gets his team on side with a proposal, there is a lift in his step, and he rises in the workplace. He has noticed this happening over a couple of decades, and he now floats upwards to the sixty-first floor without using the elevators. When he glides into his corner office and he answers a couple of emails with firm replies, there is a lightness in his head which has become intoxicating and is difficult to do without (such as when on vacation). Herk sits on a high horse in the workplace and he is often right, whether it is about the strategy or the people or the savings that can be made. Others, who are increasingly in awe of him, suffer slightly from his superiority and his righteousness, which he calls being 'driven'. Now what Herk has not noticed so well over the years, is that coming back down the stairs has become a real effort. He is often tempted to stay on the sixty-first floor longer than is necessary, just because the downward path is so hard. Instead, because he needs more time to focus and come up with those solutions, he often goes up to the sixty-second floor where the view is even better still and where there are many unused 'board meeting rooms'. One day when pondering the longer-term market capitalization, his dreamy eyes come to rest on an old whiteboard where a 'corporate challenge' is written – and he notices his initials written there too. When he reads the challenge, his face turns white and he falls to the floor. It feels like a punch in the stomach, and he gasps for air. Suddenly, he realizes that there is someone in this vast office building who holds the key to the future of this business. But who is it? Who has written that? And when? He now becomes so restless that he cannot spend time anymore on this floor and he realizes he no longer belongs on the sixty-first either. He needs to come down. But when he takes the stairs down, every step is a huge effort, the soles of his feet feel as though they are burning, and he has to hold on to the handrail. He cannot even reach the floor below, the sixtieth floor, not with the knowledge of the challenge he has just read. So, he flies back up to the sixty-first and pleads with the first person he meets, a receptionist, to go down with him. The receptionist knows he ought to stay in post and at his desk, but the despair in this executive's eyes mollifies him and so he goes along with him. That decision turns out to be the beginning of a helping relationship. From now on, Herk can only visit lower floors when escorted by the receptionist. Moreover, it takes several months to find the employee who wrote the challenge. On his search Herk meets many interesting characters, including ugly characters, very loud characters, sinister characters, and doubtful characters. He discovers that on lower floors some windows are open, they have no permanent aircon, and one can breathe a different, much fresher air. Interestingly, the receptionist also markedly improves with the walks and the fresher air. Both are finding new oxygen, literally as well as figuratively, although that still does not make it easier for Herk to come down and off his high floor. He continues to need help with making that journey, for much longer than he initially realized.

In this little myth, the manifold 'characters' stand for Herk's fears and the fresh breeze is love. Looking at the myth, I might have subtitled the book 'Love Under Fear' instead, as it is only when we come down and wrestle with our demons that on the lowest floors, or even under the waterline, where we may connect with earth, grass, trees, and ponds and all sorts of little creatures, we find new love for our colleagues, ourselves, and our challenges. Coaching at its most profound is a journey from crippling anxiety, fear or hubris, towards a sense of knowing what to do and towards love for ourselves and our fellow humans.

This book is intended to be a homage to a great existential writer in the helping professions: Irvin Yalom, who wrote a book with the title *The Gift of Therapy*, in which he similarly purviews his own learnings from a long and varied practice.

I am not going to apologize for using the word 'love' in the subtitle even if I know this will invite a strong response. I have long felt the role of love in the workplace has been ignored and under-explored. Is it too frightening a word, perhaps, an experience too much linked with fear – the fear of loss, the fear of rejection? What with all the existing stresses and work pressures, do we now also need to think about 'love'? Do we now need to admit that there is a lot we do not understand about basic friendship and commitment? Yes, I think we should: many workplaces do not carry friendship well – they make friendship and love exclusive and volatile, transactional and shallow, noticeable only in contrast to those who do not enjoy the friendship and the support, the ones, the many, who are being judged, manipulated, and corrected on a daily basis.

Nevertheless, love, desire, and greed are behind so much of our production and our achievements, even if we prefer not to think about that. As a result, in the workplace love and friendship are often confused with exclusive privileges and unsettling relationships. Those exclusive links can be upsetting and disrupting, can be experienced as viscerally unfair. Which is why many organizations now regulate against (exclusive) love in the workplace, and understandably so.

And what about us coaches and consultants? I have felt that also on our side, in executive coaching, we have somewhat lost sight of the love that is behind 'helping', lost sight of our commitment and 'duty of care' towards our sessions and our clients, which was perhaps more central in the flower-power days of OD and in the olden days of process consultation … love does not sit so well with business and sports coaching, especially when that coaching is all about performance and results, and relationship and personal growth really do not seem to matter that much. Many coaches think of their own work as 'performance', a performance for their commissioners and the organizations that employ them, a commitment to outcomes that may be privileged over the requirements or needs of their coachees. Something I hear increasingly these days, certainly more so than I did 10 years ago, is that a coach is considering 'dropping a client' when the client does not change, or does not commit, or does not turn up, or does not move as fast as anticipated. I believe the very idea of discontinuing runs counter to the essence of helping and is certainly not something a coach should decide unilaterally.

The more I am aware of love and fear, the two core emotions present in each and every coaching session, the more I realize that we need them both and that one will always evoke the other. In a very profound way, a helper who approaches a fearful or doubtful theme-with-individual will feel a surge of love.[1] As long as you are not traumatized or hurt by the fears or doubts of your coachee, you will realize your own care and loving impulses. When you then make contact and accept that loving care, you most naturally become an attachment figure for the other, and together you begin a powerful process of fear meeting love, which is a re-enactment of the 'love over fear' founding myth of our profession. So, in a rather essential way, we need both these emotions to be present and to meet with each other in our coaching conversations.

The coaching encounter also introduces new fears, mainly because of the meeting with the unknown and the potential for something unanticipated and new. To use a topical metaphor, we meet the other without any facemasks, so the encounter throws up new viruses which then produce new antibodies. We can see this when challenge, confrontation, fresh hypothesis, or feedback come up in the session. The common initial (and natural!) response is that of shutting down and driving out the intruder, usually by explaining ourselves again or denying any relevance. However, eventually, this dangerous encounter can strengthen the auto-immune response for the future, for other encounters at work, where similar challenges may arise yet remain largely unexplored. The coachee will feel fitter and more prepared as she comes through the challenges of the coaching sessions.

The book is structured in three parts, evolving from the theme of trust (trust both in ourselves and our coachees) in Part A, to the core theme of love over fear in Part B, and then to the development of humility in our practice in Part C. If I had to summarize the book in one line, I would say: develop trust, nurture love in response to your fears and those of your coachees, and practise humility particularly as your success or 'seniority' grows.

That would be the gift to myself as a coach: ongoing humility. Only then can I remain confident of me being a gift to others.

Several chapters in this book have predecessors in the form of shorter articles which I have changed and expanded to present similar thoughts here and I would like to profoundly thank the editors of the two journals involved: *International Coaching Psychology Review* (Stephen Palmer) and *Coaching Today* (Diane Parker), who trusted my ideas and collaborated on the first drafts by reviewing and improving them. I have asked for permission from the publishers to use and rework these published articles. Chapter 2 was based on De Haan (2014), Chapter 3 on De Haan (2011), Chapter 4 on De Haan (2012), Chapter 5 on De Haan (2019a), Chapter 6 on De Haan (2020), Chapter 7 on De Haan and Metselaar (2015), Chapter 8 on Shohet, Birch, and De Haan (2018), Chapter 10 on De Haan (2006), Chapter 11 on De Haan (2018), and Chapter 13 on De Haan (2019b). I would like to thank close colleagues who were co-authors on earlier versions of these chapters, in particular Annette Bienfait, David Birch, Carine Metselaar, and Robin Shohet.

In the more than thirty formal case examples of coaching featured in this book, I have carefully disguised client identities and their context. I have asked permission for as many case examples as I could, certainly for all of those that appeared in *Coaching Today* as that is the editorial policy of that journal. Nevertheless, it is possible that individuals in some of the cases may recognize themselves, but I trust that they will also know that outsiders or their colleagues will not be able to do so. I am well aware of the ethical implications of publishing real-life case material; however, I also believe it is impossible for us coaches to continue in our learning if we cannot do so on the basis of written authentic case material.

Note

1   Lou Andreas-Salomé, the psychoanalyst, wrote about this in a letter to Freud, dated 15 February 1925: 'In my eagerness to understand her completely and to help her I become more and more well disposed towards her. I know of old this gentle increase of sympathy in myself; it constitutes for me one of the most heart-warming and joyous experiences. For left to myself I am a cold fish who is fond of only a few people.'

Part  A

Trust your coachee knows how to change

In this part of the book, I wish to return to the fundamentals of coaching and restate them in my own words. Those fundamentals help to ground my practice in contributions that I believe matter the most to my coachees. Ultimately, coaching is undertaken to have a positive impact on the coachee's fortunes and challenges. Therefore, the coachee and the coachee's capacity for change need to be central to our work as coaches. All we need to do is partner well with our coachees to realize (as much as possible) that capacity for change. That's why this part of the book explores what such a helping partnership means.

From my own experience as a coachee, I have always felt that coaching works for me and that I do not need any statistics to prove that: once I fully commit to coaching, I tend to feel helped, strengthened, and inspired. Whether other clients also feel helped seems irrelevant for my own experience. Yet as a coach it is reassuring to know that many clients do feel helped and seem to benefit in objective terms as well. Quantitative research not only shows this, it provides information on what it is in coaching that yields those outcomes, and how coaches can optimize or fine-tune their interventions to different clients and different needs.

The basic helpfulness of coaching is in the midst of being confirmed by hundreds of empirical studies in the field (see De Haan, 2021). In the first chapter, we will briefly review the building blocks of effectiveness and the fundamentals of helping conversations, to remind ourselves what it is that we have come to learn about the expected outcomes of coaching. Chapter 1 briefly summarizes, in lay terms, a treasure trove of research in the helping professions (in mentoring, in psychotherapy and counselling, in managerial and in health coaching), ending on 'ten commandments' for coaches: ten contributions that we now know are effective, or at least have some evidence to support them.

In the second, third, and fourth chapters, we look at where some of that magic of coaching may be coming from, by reviewing three fundamental building blocks of effectiveness that are also three expressions of kindness, care, and love. They are, simply put, attention (or listening – Chapter 2), relationship (or engaging – Chapter 3), and empathy (or understanding – Chapter 4). Together, they ensure that clients can truly participate in the simple experience of 'having a conversation about what matters', 'being listened to and being committed to', and 'talking things through with care and attention'.

In Chapter 2, we look at the basic stance of 'not knowing' that underpins all listening. How can we let go of all the things we already know or think we know, and become curious again and open to new information?

In Chapter 3, we think about what happens *between* coachee and coach. What are the aspects of the emerging and evolving relationship in the coaching room that we can take on board and work with to improve our coaching? This means revisiting Freud's concept of transference and gaining a solid understanding of its origins and contributions to coaching relationships.

In Chapter 4, I offer a 'model' for coaching, a grounding to base our empathy on. This is the model of attachment theory and the proven links between 'secure' attachment and a coherent reflective stance, sometimes called mentalization. This is probably the only 'coaching model' in the book, and even this model was not originally a coaching model. It describes our minds and our sense of security more than our approach or interventions during sessions, and is by no means confined to coaching. Coaching models are often too coach-centric, and for that reason they do not play a major role in this book.

I guess that what I am trying to say in this first part of the book is that I am convinced that we will become the best coach that we can be for our coachees, if we truly and deeply trust our coachees to do what is right for them. In other words, we can reach the highest mastery if, paradoxically, we dare to practise very simple tasks such as listening, engaging, and empathizing. I will also show that although these offerings to the coachee are simple and straightforward, there is always more that we can do to improve them.

Take 'listening' as an example. I am convinced we can always listen better. We tend only to receive (some) overall impressions, somatic (felt) information, words, voice inflections, gestures, facial expressions – but there is always so much more that goes on within our coachees. We know this because it is true for ourselves. Even if we are sitting quietly in a meeting, we are still thinking lots, we are feeling more, and we are even entertaining feelings and thoughts that we do not know anything about, feelings we may discover later. There is always an internal world behind our quiet (or busy) presence. Some of this internal world is available to us: our conscious thoughts, aspirations, feelings, doubts, anxieties, and so on. The same is true for the coachee who sits there with you: a myriad of data, considerations, intentions, and concerns are developing right in front of you – and there is only a tiny proportion that you will be able to notice and listen to. Hence it makes a lot of sense to continuously improve our listening skills. And it is worth knowing more about how to 'empty our heads' more deeply, detach from our own state of mind, calm ourselves internally, while we sit down with our coachees. I will talk about such aspects of listening not only in Chapter 2, but again in Chapter 10.

The same with 'engaging' and 'understanding': we can always do more of them, provided we do not impose ourselves or stand in the way of our coachee's creative thought processes and developing curiosity. There is a theme running through this part of the book, namely that coaching works, and its workings are even (deceptively) simple: we only need to be present for the other and fulfil very basic, core conditions. However, when we start thinking more about what that means we encounter deep and only recently (somewhat) understood mysteries of personal learning and growth.

In summary, the two main questions to you in this part of the book are:

1 Can you dare keep it simple, trust your coachee, and leave 'your' coaching session to the coachee?
2 What do you contribute when you are being present while getting out of the way for your coachee to develop?

1 Back to basics: what evidence do we have that coaching works?

So, what can we really know about our coaching? I used some of the lockdown due to coronavirus in 2020 to make an inventory of all the quantitative coaching research that I could find. After checking an array of sources and references, I identified 160 independent coaching outcome studies, 35 of which were randomized controlled trials. I summarized these in terms of what they show about effectiveness, about the 'ingredients' of effectiveness, and about the possible outcomes of coaching (De Haan, 2021). This chapter is a brief summary of what I have learned through that exploration.

We know that statistical research is important, as it provides the only 'general' knowledge about coaching that we have. Any significant patterns found in quantitative research, however small, are predictive and are thus a reliable indication for future contracts and sessions. They can therefore legitimately inform coachee/stakeholder decisions regarding whether to invest in coaching, and what type of coaching to invest in.

My new learning from the past year can be summarized by five main themes as laid out below.

1.1: Mounting evidence that coaching works

I believe that scholars have now gathered enough evidence to confirm that coaching is an effective intervention. At Ashridge, we have undertaken a meta-analysis study comprising 34 of the 35 randomized controlled trials identified, including seven recent ones (De Haan and Nilsson, 2022). We found that the overall effect size of these studies was 0.62, with a prediction interval that barely includes zero, so we can say with 95% confidence that coaching will produce a palpable effect over and above a non-intervention control group in exactly the same circumstances (an effect size greater than 0.5 is substantial). We can even argue that coaching is better researched than a lot of related fields such as mentoring, consultancy, training, and management development – some of which are harder to research because the interventions have fuzzier boundaries.

That is powerful information, and all we need to know when considering whether coaching is worth the investment. It tells us that real, palpable change is likely to result from engagement with coaching. The only problem with this strong result is that it is mostly supported by coachees' self-reported scores, although if we take the few studies with more objective measures like work results or 360-degree ratings into account, the effect size is still of a similar magnitude. Therapy has a higher effect size (recent estimate 0.73; Cuijpers *et al.*, 2020), but the prediction interval for therapy is wider, so the spread of effects is more pronounced.

In this regard, I am often asked about the differences between coaching and therapy. We can make very fine distinctions as to these differences. But we must never forget that our clients will not make the same distinctions. If they trust us, they will feel free to bring any and all information to a session, whatever feels relevant, whether work-related or highly personal. Hence, we must remain open to therapeutic material, not cut it off, and gently come alongside to think how this material might fit into the coaching contract. Usually, the new, personal information can help shine a new light on the (work-related) coaching objectives. For these reasons, my answer to that question about differences between therapy and coaching has increasingly become 'there is no difference', unless it is to confirm that the coach will try to understand all material from the perspective of the coaching goals and contract, which by definition are work-related. It is no surprise to me that therapy research shows the same or very similar correlations and dependencies as coaching research does, and that no major differences have been found between the two fields in terms of (indications for) effectiveness and active ingredients.

Having said this, it is also important for all of us coaches to know our limitations and be open about them, and we will come back to this in Chapter 12, when we look at coaching ethics. When you are hired to provide coaching, you need to be a qualified coach, or at least working towards your qualification (and be transparent about your 'unqualified' status to your clients). When the needs of your client increase beyond coaching (when highly personal dilemmas or conflicts are at stake), it is important to open up the conversation towards these increased needs. You may conclude together that there is an underlying case for once-a-week or still more intensive psychotherapy, in which case you might help to find a suitable therapist. I would always try to involve the client's GP in that referral, as a doctor can check for any underlying medical or general health indications. While you support your client in the search for a suitable therapist, it is important to remember that you are still bound to the coaching contract. You would not want to add any hint of rejection to what is probably a very sensitive period for your client already. For this reason, I have found that it is most helpful to offer to work alongside the therapist, albeit at a lower frequency and focusing on the coaching goals, but also checking with the client the expected improvements in the more personal areas of concern. I would never end the coaching contract just because overwhelming material has crept into this contract or come to the surface. This is what I consider my 'duty of care'. In my own case, I have a dual qualification. I am qualified for coaching as well as once-a-week psychoanalytical psychotherapy, so I am sometimes able to propose to my clients a once-a-week arrangement. However, when it comes to needs that go beyond that, I help as much as I can to find a suitable, qualified, and preferably local psychotherapist.

1.2: Coaching really flexes around objectives

My second most intriguing finding was how diverse the demonstrable out-comes of coaching were. Although the randomized controlled trial invokes the medical model, coaching does not behave like a simple 'pill' that enhances or dampens a very specific function. Quite the opposite: coaching has been demonstrated to be effective for a wide range of goals, ranging from efficiency savings (call centre times, numbers of units of production per day), to effect-iveness improvements (sales conversion rates, service levels, precision sur-gery), quality improvements (in sensitive meetings, improved health, improved safety standards), and career transitions (higher rates of return to work and of job retention), to name a few (De Haan, 2021).

For me personally, the most fascinating finding about the 'range', is actually the 'depth' of some of these outcomes of coaching: several studies show that coaching has a positive impact on a leader's personality – assuaging neuroti-cism, anxiety and fears, impostor tendencies and emotional volatility. These may be early results, stemming from three recent studies only; nevertheless, they begin to confirm what many coaches and coachees report from their coaching sessions, namely that coaching helps us to rebalance, stabilize and offset the risks of leadership derailment.

1.3: Evidence for an uncanny meta-understanding between coach and coachee

The next finding is just as intriguing. I have seen evidence in the coaching out-come literature that coaching may be as effective as it is, *irrespective of the total number of sessions*. Stiles *et al.* (2015) show similar results in psychother-apy, namely that for patients who attend any number of sessions between three and twenty, the clinical improvement observed is broadly the same. What does it mean if coachees achieve the same overall outcome regardless of the number of sessions they negotiate? This could mean that somehow, between coach and coachee, an 'appropriate' number of sessions is negotiated for which they will tend to achieve the 'normal' outcome (which is that, on average, a coachee does better than some 72% of the control group). Or, whatever the number of sessions allotted to the coachee, the coachee will use that precise number to achieve what they can. This is counterintuitive, since one normally thinks of the num-ber of sessions as the 'dose' of the treatment, and one would expect the effect to go up in line with the 'dose' rather than remaining flat across any number of applied doses. In my view, this finding points to a particular form of 'placebo effect', where coach and coachee implicitly negotiate, or accommodate them-selves towards, what feels like the 'right' number of sessions. If that continues to be shown to be the case, then it is very heartening for our profession. It means we can trust our coachees even more than we already do, based on demonstrated effectiveness, as summarized above. To be precise, we can trust coachees regarding the 'number' of sessions – that is, they will generally do well irrespective of the number of sessions they agree to attend.

1.4: The quality of the relationship matters, but not in the way we thought it would

Research exploring the ingredients of successful coaching has found the quality of the coaching relationship to be of great importance. Whether described as 'rapport', 'trust', or 'working alliance', the relationship usually emerges as the strongest predictor of coaching outcome. We have known this to be the case in the helping professions for some time (see, for example, Wampold, 2001). However, it was only very recently that longitudinal trials were conducted, where the impact of the coaching relationship was measured from session to session, and the results were very surprising (De Haan *et al.*, 2020). It turned out that although the strength of relationship (i.e. the working alliance) correlated strongly with outcomes, there was no indication that the alliance also correlated with outcomes *per session*. In fact, we found in our own research that there was no link between an increase in outcome after the first session, and any measurements of the working alliance that we made after each of the six sessions of coaching. This means that working alliance is an independent variable, nothing to do with the sessions themselves, similar to the coachee's overall self-efficacy or resilience. Alliance may not even be related to the quality of the relationship as experienced, or as could be observed by an outsider. This means that we must now go back to the drawing board in terms of measurement of the relationship or of relational coaching in the moment. And the link between alliance and outcome has become a lot more tenuous, even controversial.

1.5: Some evidence that the youngest coaches are the best coaches

In the course of my research, I came across an article by George *et al.* (2020), who undertook a retrospective study to determine which external coaches of nurses for safe childbirths in India had been the most effective. Demographics were collected for ten coaches and (observation-based) practice-adherence criteria for their coachees, in the course of observing 1,052 child deliveries. A highly significant ($p < 0.0001$) inverse relationship was detected between the coach's age (or experience) and the nurses' adherence to the practice checklist. So, it seems, at least in that special context, younger coaches were more effective than older, more experienced ones. The effectiveness of the coach seems inversely related to both the coach's age and years of experience, presumably – according to the authors – because young and relatively inexperienced coaches were less directive.

Many novel research findings have been reported in the literature. Having summarized all the new data after the recent boom in coaching research and having noted many surprises in those results, I was also able to confirm most of my own summary of the main findings from many years previously (De Haan, 2008a), which was based not on coaching research outcomes but on the psychotherapy outcome literature at the time.

1.6: The evidence from psychotherapy outcome research briefly summarized

Let me end with a review of how I summarized my understanding of psycho-therapy outcomes in 2008 in the shape of ten 'commandments' for coaches (De Haan, 2008a), and how I chose to amend only the seventh criterion in the light of the most recent research.

1. *Do no harm.* This commandment comes from medical lore, where *pri-mum non nocere* is usually followed by *in dubio abstine* – i.e. if in doubt, it is better to do nothing than to carry out an intervention that may be harmful. Coaching will not work if the commitment is not there and if the coachee is not volunteering or at least giving it a chance.

2. *Have confidence.* If you follow tried-and-tested ethical principles and your honest intention is to help your coachee, there is a good chance that you *are* helping. Coaching interventions are moderately effective, by all accounts – this is confirmed by a recent meta-analysis (De Haan and Nilsson, 2022).

3. *Commit yourself heart and soul to your approach.* Although we cannot demonstrate that there is one specific approach that works better than others, it *is* possible to show that your commitment to an ideology and an approach, to which you gear your interventions, will contribute towards your effectiveness.

4. *Feed the hope of your coachee.* There is such a strong placebo effect in the helping professions that it is worth strengthening the coachee's (self-)motiva-tion where you can. If the coachee has a strong belief that the process will help, that will ensure about half of the effectiveness of coaching will be guar-anteed, i.e. half of the effect will be achieved and half of the work will be done.

5. *Consider the coaching situation from your coachee's perspective.* The working-alliance scores which the coachee provides correlate strongly with outcome in coaching.

6. *Work on your coaching relationship.* Even if the working alliance is per-haps only an overall predictor and therefore more of a coachee characteristic

than we ever thought, it is still the best predictor that we have for a good outcome overall. In other words, our efforts to strengthen the relationship as much as we can and regularly review it are probably not in vain.

7. *Make good matching part of your practice.* Because of the general importance of the working alliance from the outset, it is good practice to give the coachee the choice as to which coach he or she wants to work with. Thus, the best form of matching occurs when meeting in person and checking if there is sufficient chemistry to move on with the relationship. This matching process does not need to involve a lot of coaches, since all we need is a 'good enough' coach. So, it is best just to meet one qualified coach and, if the 'click' is there, then work together; if not, meet up with another coach and see if that works. If at any point the relationship is working less well or if the coachee's needs change beyond coaching, then it might be better to suggest continuing the work with another (helping) professional. It is important to realize in such circumstances that a referral also puts the relationship under pressure and may be experienced in part as a rejection or a loss, so perhaps we need to be somewhat restrained when recommending another coach.

8. *Look after yourself, to keep yourself as healthy as possible.* There are many aspects of coaching that make it work. It is not just about the coachees and their motivation, about a conducive organization and an equally conducive coaching relationship – it is also about the coach's own personality, or in any case the coach personality as perceived by the coachee. What role the helper's personality plays is not yet at all clear, but it seems to be a significant one, and it seems to make a difference in a positive sense if the coach comes across as competent, stable, healthy, happy, attractive, empathic, warm, and trustworthy.

9. *Try to stay fresh and unbiased.* Applying pre-determined procedures and protocols, with often carefully considered and ingeniously devised interventions, appears to have little impact on the outcome. Indeed, it seems to have an adverse impact as it makes the coach a lot more central to the work. It thus appears that a coach who meets the coachee with a fresh, unbiased, and friendly or sympathetic approach will achieve better results.

10. *Do not worry too much about the specific things you are doing.* Overall, psychotherapy and coaching outcome research shows that specific techniques and interventions make much less of a difference than the more general 'common factors' (De Haan, 2021).

I hope I have been able to show you how research is leading our understanding of executive coaching, and of helping conversations in general. I, for one, cannot wait for new, rigorous outcome studies in the very near future.

Chapter summary

This first chapter summarizes the research literature in the helping conversations. It highlights important findings in coaching outcome research, as well as in quantitative research into mentoring, psychotherapy and counselling, and even managerial and health coaching. The chapter covers the main aspects that are really worth remembering in my view, and that can have a meaningful impact on our confidence and on how we conduct ourselves in coaching conversations. The *ten commandments for coaches* reported here are an attempt to summarize all the findings in lay terms, suggesting ten contributions by coaches that we now know can be effective, or at least have some general evidence to support them. In short, these ten commandments say: have confidence, stay hopeful and feel free to use any trusted technique, within any approach or philosophy, provided you maintain allegiance to your approach, and you remain fresh and receptive, while you pay attention to understanding and strengthening the emerging and evolving coaching relationship.

2 Back to basics: listening[1]

This chapter is a homage to the simple and yet mysterious practice of observation. From the first moment we meet a coachee, we observe and begin to notice things about them. Yet our observations often start well before we meet them for the first time. When we get a referral, a few facts or impressions about the coachee are communicated to us and we start observing and begin to make sense of who this person is and what they might want to change or bring to the sessions. We gradually take in the experience of meeting our coachee, from the start we sit at the feet of experience, the experience of meeting, getting to know the coachee and what is at stake for the coachee.

This chapter delves deep into observation, simply because listening is so important and all our future work with the coachee will depend on what we observe, the information we gather, and the conclusions we come to, all as a result of listening to and viewing our coachee. The simple gift of being listened to is nurturing in and of itself, and helps change the coachee from within. There is a body of research that confirms that the simple act of taking time out for reflection and mindfulness, for just sitting and listening, is beneficial in and of itself, and benefits both the coach and coachee.

Whole schools of coaching, textbooks, and research are ultimately based on the simple practice of listening or active listening, listening with care and attention, technically called inquiry. If we want to go back to basics, we need to go beyond those textbooks and schools, back to the practice of listening itself.

What do you understand by the phrase 'sitting at the feet of experience'? Are you familiar with doing nothing other than remaining attentive to your practice as it unfolds, staying in touch with your experiences as they are? Do you know how difficult, nigh impossible even, that is? You will have experienced how easy it is to get distracted – and not realize you are distracted – even after a few moments of paying attention, to prematurely rush in and label, categorize or judge, and how tempting it is to prejudge or evaluate your experiences, even to act on them early on in a variety of ways. You will also have discovered how easy it is to get carried away by experience, rather than taking the time to just observe and be present, or in other words, without taking the time 'to just experience'. I dare say you will have set yourself a challenging task if you set out to 'just' experience your experiences and not judge them!

2.1: About the schools, their irreconcilable differences, and the limits of knowing

Of none of our future statements do we positively affirm that the fact is exactly as we state it, but we simply record each fact, like a chronicler, as it appears to us at the moment. (S.E. I.4)[2]

'Just' sitting at the feet of experience fulfils the simplest offer that executive coaches may make to their coachees. In my view, this rather minimalistic part of coaching, 'just' sitting attentively as experience unfolds, is often undervalued. Schools abound with competing ideas about what else coaches and coachees should be doing together – or what coaches should do after some initial listening:

- *Solution-focused coaching* tells us to avoid 'problem traps', look on the bright side, at what works, when problems are not there, and imagine even brighter futures based, for example, on the 'miracle question': 'How might you know that you have found what you are seeking?' (Greene and Grant, 2003).
- *Performance coaching* tells us to formalize goals first and foremost, then to establish the tension between those future goals and present reality, move on to ways in which we can reduce that gap, and finally to remind ourselves of what exactly we are going to do to reach the goals (Whitmore, 1992).
- *Rational-emotive coaching* tells us to dig into our 'false' cognitions, self-beliefs, and limiting assumptions, challenge them and adopt a stoic stance in the face of adversity, keeping our emotions as much as we can under our control (Sherin and Caiger, 2004).
- *Person-centred coaching* tells us to offer an exuberance of warmth, respect, and understanding from within, to any issues and situations that our coachees may raise. In this conception of coaching we need to be as unconditional and pure in our love and understanding as a loving parent (Joseph, 2006).
- *Relational coaching* tells us to investigate and reinforce the productivity of the here-and-now relationship from the coachee's perspective, and therefore explicitly to explore with the coachee the coaching relationship itself (De Haan, 2008a).

This is only a very short selection of models and methodologies, with the first three taken from various cognitive-behavioural schools, the next one from a humanistic orientation, and the final one broadly integrative with roots in psychoanalysis.

As we also saw in the tenth commandment at the end of the previous chapter, there is not a lot of evidence to back up these various claims about what it is helpful to do in coaching (see, for example, the overview of what we know about coaching interventions in De Haan, 2021). And even if one trusts the evidence from, say, trials that include control groups, then there are still good reasons to be sceptical about how much of that can be translated back to practice. Outcome-research evidence is based on simple digits collected after or at unique points in a long and rich coaching journey, so it cannot say very much about what happens within that journey.

To make matters worse, what evidence we do have points to an *equivalence* of all these various models and schools. 'Everybody has won, and all must have prizes'[3] – or put slightly ironically: coachees and coaches are going to get extremely busy in their coaching room trying to do all these many things that are now shown to be effective, many of which are arguably incompatible.

There is a long history in executive coaching, and more generally, in helping conversations, of presenting specific ideas, schools, techniques, and interventions as somehow 'effective' or 'evidence-based'. At the same time, many of us remain unconvinced. It is far too early for any single approach or technique to claim a unique evidence base beyond what we achieve by simple listening, engaging, and understanding.

> *The schools frequently admit only such facts as can be explained by their own theories and dismiss facts which conflict therewith though possessing equal probability. (S.E. I.183)*

As a result of this situation, which, in my view is likely to continue, it is ultimately very hard – even for experts – to say that any piece of coaching is 'good' coaching (or 'helpful', 'effective', 'adroit', etc.). In order to attest that any coaching is good, one needs to apply some criterion or criteria. For any criterion one wishes to apply, it needs to be demonstrated that the criterion is actually related to what is good in coaching, i.e. to outcome, or effectiveness (see the previous chapter). For such a demonstration, one needs to know in general terms what makes up a good intervention or a good assignment, and why. As professional coaches, I believe we should be honest and remind ourselves regularly that we remain clueless as to all of the above.

> *If, then, one cannot hope to pass judgement on the afore-mentioned impressions either with or without proof, the conclusion we are driven to is suspension; for while we can, no doubt, state the nature which each object appears to possess as viewed in a certain position or at a certain distance or in a certain place, what its real nature is, we are unable to declare. (S.E. I.123)*

Despite the lack of certainty about what works, we keep finding that coaching is generally considered helpful and shown to be effective, and that panels of experts and lay people (such as in our Ashridge Coach Accreditation Process) tend to agree remarkably well on those matters. Nevertheless, the reasons for agreement are not known and have not been demonstrated. Moreover, panels of accreditors do also occasionally experience profound disagreement in the co-assessment of live sessions of coaching.

This is yet another reason why we should step back from all the models which focus too narrowly on the coach, and focus instead on the coachee himself or herself. We need to first understand what it is to meet and be present with and to partner with the coachee really well, before we can then think about the interventions of the coach – let alone about the many schools of coaching.

I will start this book – and probably end it as well – with a 'minimalist' conception of coaching, where we 'just' sit with the coachee. We 'just' sit trying to observe what the coachee is bringing. And we remain in doubt about what that means for our own role, i.e. about what our 'helpfulness' means. We 'just' try to remain present with our experience, the experience both within the 'material' of coaching and also as emerging in the here-and-now interaction in the room.

2.2: About the real freedom and understanding one can acquire by not knowing

Having read many textbooks with good ideas about what to do in the coaching room, it can really free us up to forget about all that and suspend our judgement for a while. As in every profession, it appears to me very wholesome to try to relieve ourselves in this way of all dogmatism. Freed up from preconceived notions and dogmatic tenets, we become more aware of how little we can really know about our contribution, and we become as sensitive as we can be to what our experiences might be telling us in this very moment as we do our work.

It was Socrates who said, in defence of his philosophical way of life,[4] that the 'unreflected (or unexamined) life is not worth living'. I believe similarly that the 'unreflected coach' is not worth hiring. And to make it even more Socratic: the reflected coach is not worth hiring either. That would still make the person doing the hiring a passive 'customer' of a reflective coach. However, what is worth doing in my opinion is to engage reflectively and humbly … together with your reflective and humble coach.

I would like to describe this practice of 'sitting at the feet of one's own experience' in a few more words. The practice has many forerunners and many followers, in a great variety of traditions of thought. I will here first follow the Sceptical tradition, which is one of the oldest and seems closest to our present-day ideas about reflective inquiry, before making a link with a great Eastern tradition as well, that of Buddhist mindfulness.

In fact, in ancient Greek the word *scepsis* has a basic meaning of 'viewing' or 'inquiry', which is usually translated into English more fully as 'suspension of judgement in investigation' (S.E. I.30). *Scepsis* can also be translated as 'perception', 'examination' or 'doubt'.

Scepsis/inquiry means, first and foremost, taking leave of what opinions and views we may have and holding lightly all 'knowledge' we may think we possess. For a genuine inquiry, we need to actively open up space. This opening up of space the sceptics call 'deferring judgement':

Thus the Skeptic, seeing so much anomaly in the matters at hand, suspends judgment as to whether by nature something is good or bad or, generally, ought or ought not be done, and he thereby avoids the dogma-tists' rashness, and he follows, without any belief, the ordinary course of life; for this reason be has no pathos one way or the other as regards matters of belief. (S.E. III.235)

To open up space for inquiry, we may even need to depart from certain convictions that are important to us, about how one 'ought' to live, how one 'should' coach, or which reflections are 'better' than others. Much more room for inquiry will be opened up if we can park our opinions on the good and the bad, the effective and ineffective, even the ethical and unethical, even if only temporarily.

For the person who believes that something is by nature good or bad is constantly upset; when he does not possess the things that seem to be good, he thinks he is being tormented by things that are by nature bad, and he chases after the things he supposes to be good; then, when he gets these, he falls into still more torments because of irrational and immoderate exultation, and, fearing any change, he does absolutely everything in order not to lose the things that seem to him good. But the person who takes no position as to what is by nature good or bad neither avoids nor pursues intensely. As a result, he achieves peace of mind or ataraxia. (S.E. I.27)

We also need to suspend or defer our judgements regarding inquiry itself and what it is yielding. If we can do that, we may discover that the findings of inquiry are quite often liberating and innovative, because they really add something to our experience. They are also impossible to generalize or turn into 'knowledge' (generalizable, replicable facts or essential truths), precisely because inquiry is such a highly personal, unique, and liberating expedition.

No practice can be perceived in its purity or essence. There is the relationship with the perceiver and the present state of the perceiver that impacts on the perception, and there is also the context and the other practices in view which impact on the perception. (S.E. I.135)

Finally, complex definitions and jargon are best avoided, as they tend to close down the space for reflection with elaborate and esoteric language.

Thus, for instance, to take a silly example, suppose that one wished to ask someone whether he had met a man riding a horse and leading a dog and put the question in this form – 'O rational mortal animal, receptive of intelligence and science, have you met with an animal capable of laughter, with broad nails and receptive of political science, with his posterior hemispheres seated on a mortal animal capable of neighing, and leading a four-footed animal capable of barking?' – how would one be otherwise than ridiculous, in thus reducing the man to speechlessness concerning so familiar an object, because of one's definitions? (S.E. II.211)

The sceptics had a number of 'invocations' to help them to stay rigorously with the practice of fully and undogmatically attending to experience, which are all really helpful for us as listeners and observers (see S.E. I.107 onwards):

1 'Not more': do not attend to one aspect more than to another. Or: for what reason would this view or this perspective be more important than that one?
2 'Non-assertion': assertively non-assert that one thing is like this or like that, to remind yourself that ultimately one is not able to affirm or deny any assertion or evidence, as a counterexample may yet emerge.
3 'Perhaps, possibly, maybe': an emphasis on qualifying terms that make sure we are reminded that by simply observing we will find out more and we will never attain ultimate certainty or ultimate truths.
4 'I suspend judgement': reinforcing the basic premise which creates space to observe and to reflect, in a fresh way.
5 'I determine nothing': I am in a state of mind where I come to no conclusions and where I do not, nor would I want to, determine anything.

By suspending judgement about experience you do not deny any assertion about it while you also do not affirm it, you do not embrace the experience nor do you flee it, you do not value the experience nor do you devalue it – in short, you aim to be perfectly still and tranquil with regard to your present experience, neither moving the experience along nor being moved by it, yet infinitely attentive to it. Freud (1912a) famously spoke about 'evenly hovering attention' to make the same point, and Bion (1970) spoke about consulting 'without memory or desire'.

In modern forms of inquiry, which build on Lewin's (1946) coining of the term 'action research', there is recognition that personal inquiry can be undertaken at many levels within a coaching or organizational relationship. Executive coaches can inquire into their coachees' and sponsors' experiences; the experiences of their coachees' organizational counterparts such as colleagues, line managers, and customers; and their own experiences with their coachees. They can make use of individual reflection, co-created reflection (in dialogue), and they can gather fruits from outside reflection by third parties; in other words, they can engage in first-person, second-person, and third-person inquiry (Reason and Torbert, 2001). Finally, they can practise individual or first-person reflection entirely within themselves or reflection with others (such as their coachees) into how they are experienced by them; in other words, executive coaches can make use of both the 'inner arc' and the 'outer arc' of personal inquiry (Marshall, 2001).

Of all the many traditions of philosophical scepticism that have practised these and similar paths to inquiry-based understanding (Buddhism, Cārvāka, Jainism, Al-Ghazali, Montaigne, etc.), I would like to draw particular attention to *mindfulness* even if only for its popularity in the twenty-first century. Mindfulness signifies inquiry into the present moment, as practised in Buddhism.

Both inquiry traditions, Buddhist meditation and Pyrrhonic scepticism, are over two millennia old: one an important philosophical tradition from the West and the other from the East, and they come together in their ability to create space and tranquillity for the inquirer (*ataraxia* or peace-of-mind cum serenity in scepticism; *bodhi* or awakening cum enlightenment in Buddhism).

Among the earliest suttas of Buddhist scripture, there are instructions to mindfulness practice. They describe the liberation felt by just attending, or just noticing, in a very similar way to Sextus Empiricus. Here is an example:

> *Thus he lives contemplating feeling in feelings internally, or he lives contemplating feeling in feelings externally, or he lives contemplating feeling in feelings internally and externally. He lives contemplating origination-things in feelings, or he lives contemplating dissolution-things in feelings, or he lives contemplating origination-and-dissolution-things in feelings. Or his mindfulness is established with the thought: 'Feeling exists,' to the extent necessary just for noticing and remembrance and he lives independent and clings to naught in the world. Thus, indeed, O bhikkhus, a bhikkhu[5] lives contemplating feeling in feelings.* (Satipatthana Sutta, 29 BC)

While the sceptical tradition helps us to move away from dogmatic views and to defer our judgements, so that we can begin to attend to experience itself, the Buddhist tradition delves deeper into how it is to attend fully and how it is to inquire into experience in the present moment, as that moment unfolds. More links between Buddhist traditions and the inquiry process can be found in Bentz and Shapiro (1998).

2.3: Specific help with listening and inquiry: beyond right and wrong

The first problem for psychologists, coaches, and consultants who want to 'just' sit with experience or undertake a 'pure' or 'sceptical' inquiry, is that they will want to do it well. As with anything they would undertake, they will want to make a good job of it. Right there, at the very start, they begin interfering with their own inquiry, as they start asking themselves questions about what a good inquiry might be, which methods to use, and how to make the best use of time, models, guidance, and other resources. The idea of doing an inquiry well is a fallacy, and sets up the polarities of good and evil, and the dogmas of established doctrine, that one wants to move away from. It is possible to sit at the feet of your experience rigorously, or intensely, but it is hard to do it 'rightly', or 'correctly'. Thus, we can judge an inquiry afterwards, or at least the fruits of inquiry, if it is written up, in terms of what we infer about the quality of inquiry retrospectively, and in terms of other aspects as well ... but if we judge an inquiry as it happens, we seriously obstruct it. By judging it, we move it away from its central purpose.

Case example 2.1

I was asked by a reviewer if I could provide more case examples for this chapter, to show coaches how they might get into inquiry work and to clarify the relevance of these ideas to their practice. I appreciated this question and how such examples might enliven the chapter. Yet I had no ready-made cases to hand, and I was away from my coaching work. So, I decided to make the need for more examples a topic for my inquiry. As a result, instead of creating a case vignette, instead of putting any words to paper, I started to go about my business with this question in mind. Something helpful would surely come up, as long as I truly inquired into my question. At first I thought about several recent coaching conversations. Then I had memories of inquiry-process students and how helpless they sometimes found themselves at the beginning of their project, when they were trying to design or embark on their inquiry. I remembered how they made me feel out of my own depth as well when the only thing I could say to them was, 'trust the process' or 'just stay with your question'. I tried to do precisely that myself this time. The breakthrough came on the third day, when I realized that I could use this very request: my inquiring to think up relevant case examples. In every way it was an appropriate, lively, and relevant example, and it was right under my nose all along! This is how a new truth or a new solution may emerge spontaneously, and unexpectedly, from the mere practice of staying with your question and sitting at the feet of your ongoing experience.

The second problem one encounters is the choice of an inquiry or coaching question. A question limits space rather than opening up space. To choose a focus constrains the essential freedom of inquiry, and thus goes against the spirit of inquiry, even if ever so slightly. Strictly, it is not necessary to have an inquiry question in order to sustain an ongoing inquiry. Yet it is very hard to sustain an inquiry stance without a question, as many reflections will become diffuse, unfocused, and circular. Similarly, a coaching session may become unfocused and unsatisfying if there is no question, topic or need. An 'area of focus' might do instead of a question, as, for example, the concentration on our breathing when we engage in certain forms of meditation. Or the unfocused nature of the session so far in coaching: as soon as that becomes the topic of inquiry, the session will feel fresh and focused again. The prime example of a focus in executive coaching might be 'what the coachee brings to the session'. In my inquiry process as a coach, I might be interested just in what the coachee brings. A clear bounded area or well-defined question limiting the topic of inquiry helps to contain the experiences, to structure the work, and to measure its progress, yet such a boundary needs to be held lightly while one is engaged in the inquiry. Insight from other domains might just enter into the inquiry process and serve the process rather than distract from it. My attention may, for example, be drawn by 'how the coachee presents what she brings to the session' – and this may or may not illuminate my earlier focus on 'what the coachee brings to the session'.

The third problem of inquiry is its impermanence. A pure inquiry is like the flow of our attention or like our heartbeat: always in motion, never fixed, self-directed as well as responsive. If an inquiry stops flowing, then it dries up, ossifies, and turns into 'dogma': it stops being an inquiry and its life saps away before our eyes. On the other hand, once you embark on or ignite any inquiry process, you will notice that you enter a natural cycle. A healthy inquiry, therefore, is necessarily circular yet also has elements of freshness, more like a spiral.

It is possible to have an unhealthy inquiry as well which is circular, as when we are fretting about something or when we are navel gazing. In such cases, you have an inquiry that turns in on itself, an inquiry curious of itself only, which stops being fresh, stops taking in new information.

If you have ever tried engaging in a meditation practice, you will have noticed that your attention drifts off and then – usually once you notice the drifting – returns. Something unsettles you or distracts you, brings you out of your meditation, and then you recalibrate or re-find your meditative stance. Inquiry is exactly the same and this is why we often talk about 'inquiry cycles'. Inquiry cycles exist on many levels and timescales all at once. The smallest cycle is straightforward: take an object in your field of view and try to focus your full attention on that object. You will find that within seconds your attention has wandered somewhere else, and if not away entirely, to a detail or some abstract property of the object; then you will remind yourself, and your attention will flow back to the object. This is the simplest and briefest example of an inquiry cycle. On a larger scale, an inquiry cycle might be a particular meeting that you are going to study from a certain aspect, or even a longer experience like a journey or an entire assignment. You will try to stay with the meeting and with the focus of your inquiry for the time it takes, and you will find yourself drifting in and out of focus. At the end of the meeting or journey, that particular inquiry cycle is over because the engagement is over. Similarly, you could put an hour aside to undertake an inquiry, e.g. a short coaching session or when in meditation you set an alarm to remind you of your timing. Again, this would be a structured inquiry cycle. You would experience many cycles during the hour, yet the hour itself would also be a clearly demarcated cycle. At the end of the hour, you will find yourself in the same place, yet somehow enriched or changed by new perspectives, sentiments, experiences, all that you noticed, all that was fresh, and all that changed your initial outlook. In coaching and action research, one might make notes after the hour or after every larger cycle of inquiry.

The richness of cycles of inquiry is hard to describe, and ever-changing. There are cycles of breathing, cycles of bodily sensations, cycles of moods and emotions, cycles of thought and deliberation, just to name a few. Moreover, all these cycles are ever-present and ever-changing, whether we attend to them or not. This is part of why we will not be in the exact same place after we complete what we have demarcated as an inquiry cycle: if we sense we complete one circle, we are still midway on other cycles which are of different duration or intensity. Take the example of focusing on an object on the table: at the end of that exercise, having completed the cycle of attending to that object, your heart has beaten many cycles, your breathing has probably completed a good few cycles as well, and yet you only progressed little in the day, let alone in longer cycles on the calendar or a life-span.

Within all these manifold nested cycles there is one movement which is of particular relevance to sitting at the feet of your experience. This is the cycle of your singular, focused, conscious attention – in other words, your presence with the inquiry itself. By noticing yourself as you are inquiring, you will observe how your concentration grows and wanes. You immerse yourself in your inquiry one moment, yet you don't even think about it a moment later. These cycles of 'concentration' and 'distraction', which we could also call cycles of experiencing and reflecting, are ever present. They are like the tides of your mind, a continuing ebb and flow of offering attention, drawing it back, becoming lively, letting go, switching on, switching off, immersion, reflection, in endless cycles. In my experience, something interesting happens each time the waves of attention flood your inquiry and then flow back again. If you notice carefully, you will see that there is a small 'adjustment' every time this happens: a conscious shift of attention, a small critique within your inquiry, or a tiny assessment of what you are just experiencing. In my experience, we shift from inquiry to meta-inquiry and back during each one of these moments. We focus and then we think about our focus, and then we focus again. We cannot do both at the same time: we cannot attend *and* reflect on our attending, we cannot inquire *and* reap the fruits of our inquiry. These things happen sequentially, not in parallel. To find, learn, change, or progress in the inquiry, one needs both, one needs immersion and one needs realization. In other words, it is on the cusp of this oscillation that something new happens, or some opportunity for inquiry gets lost, time and time again.

It is not only the fruits of inquiry that change during these cycles, the questions of inquiry also change. The impermanence stretches out to the inquiry itself and to its focus. Engaging in coaching may change the question or focus of coaching, and that is fine. Indeed, often it is a good sign if the initial topic (or question) for an inquiry is changed by the inquiry itself. It is a good indication that something meaningful, something refreshing and new, may have taken place during the inquiry.

Case example 2.2

A coachee decided to send me an overview of topics for our next coaching session, a few days ahead of the session. A list of eight bullet points, which I realized was in a way pre-empting our session. Interestingly, and probably because the coachee had recently participated in many formal meetings, he had put 'Any other business' as the ninth bullet point, as if finally acknowledging that things might also be discovered during a coaching session. At the start of our coaching conversation there was a pregnant silence and the coachee said, 'Oh yes, you want me to start don't you'?. He said a few things about feeling more lively and energized recently. Then he embarked with some hesitation on his bullet point number one. When there was a pause, I decided to thank him for the list of topics and said that I was particularly interested in the 'any other business' – what might that be? We both laughed heartily at the idea of 'any other business' for a coaching session. Gradually a conversation developed which covered but also went beyond the various topics and bullet points, in a considered, reflective way. Through starting the session in an open and inquiring manner, we allowed fresh reflection to emerge early on and for existing reflection to branch out into new perspectives.

There is ample evidence from research (for a review, see Davis and Hayes, 2011) that cycles of inquiry and in particular mindfulness practices have demonstrable positive effects – such as on the ability to focus, on the ability to regulate emotions, on lowering levels of stress, anxiety, and rumination, and on heightening the capacity for empathy. This research confirms that inquiry is a loving antidote to fear. However, bear in mind that an inquiring mind, a true sceptic, would not attach too much importance to such findings even if in this particular case they bear out his or her own views. Mindfulness has gained a huge following in less than two decades, so it is to be expected that powerful research is now demonstrating the benefits of this form of focused attention and inquiry.

Here is a summary of the three challenges of inquiry, which can also be seen as three pillars one has to have in place for any inquiry:

1 We need to suspend judgement regarding the inquiry itself and hold lightly the consideration whether we are doing 'it' right or not.
2 It is helpful to find some anchor in a particular object or area of inquiry, often expressed by our 'coaching topic' or 'coaching goal'; also, we need to suspend judgement with regard to this anchor itself and appreciate its impermanence.
3 We endeavour to navigate our way through nested cycles of inquiry, reaping insights or findings of more permanence from the ever-present fluctuations, oscillations, and transitions of attention.

2.4: How not knowing and inquiry can free up your executive coaching practice

Sextus Empiricus distinguished ten broad areas to be sceptical about, or to inquire into, which he says can be broken down into three categories:

1 we may be sceptical of *ourselves* as 'subjective' perceivers;
2 we may be sceptical of the 'objective' *world* around us; and
3 we may be sceptical about the *relationship* between perceiver and the world (S.E. I.38; my emphasis).

In executive coaching, similarly, we can be sceptical about (1) ourselves as the observer-participants, (2) the other person and the 'material' of coaching, and (3) the relationship between the two partners, or the coaching relationship. So, if we follow through the same 'minimalist' inquiry as described above within our executive coaching work, we now sit at the feet of our experience with our coachees, and gently inquire into

1 our own state of mind, feelings, impressions, and in particular our 'felt' bodily sense as we are engaged in the coaching relationship;
2 our coachee and partner, and the material he or she is bringing to this coaching session at this very moment; and
3 the relationship of coaching as it unfolds and what is going on within that relationship that may shed light on one of the other fields of inquiry.

I believe the inquiry process that Sextus Empiricus recommends prepares one for a purer, more grounded and more loving stance during coaching. We may not change anything in our coaching approach, yet we develop a more reflective stance towards what we are doing. We listen out for and notice the material, our responses to the material, our attraction to certain aspects and our moving away from other aspects, our own values and judgements coming to the fore, as well as our secondary responses to these responses to the situation and the material, and so on. We try to stay as much as possible with the experience itself and our direct impressions, and hold any of our judgements, hypotheses, memories, and thoughts, which are bound to emerge incessantly, as lightly as possible.

As an example, let us look at my process notes from the first few minutes of the eighth and last encounter with a coachee:

Case example 2.3

Just before the session, I realize first that I am slightly rushed as I arrive shortly before, and then I find out that something has gone wrong with room reservations so that we are in a different room than usual. I notice my own feelings about this and some tension building up. I also notice how I am making a conscious effort to calm down. Then I am aware of my coachee walking in. I notice facial expressions, indications of mood, anxiety, energy. I notice the different environment of the 'new' room, and I find myself wondering how my coachee is responding to this room change. My coachee tells me he has asked and was granted a reduction of responsibilities in his job. I notice his delight and his confidence, and also his slight embarrassment. A memory comes up, from an earlier session; regarding the expert-witness work my coachee enjoys doing outside of his job. He will have more time for that. I notice myself wanting to make a note, apparently not wanting to lose that thought. A minute later, I venture an observation on the new arrangement. I notice my coachee finds my observation challenging. I notice tension in my chest. I keep noticing how my coachee seems cautious and slightly taken aback. I am not sure whether I have lost him here. Something seems to be brewing inside him. I decide to say something about the effect of my observation. I name an emotion which he recognizes. We are now both more relaxed. There is a similar mixture of confidence and embarrassment now between us as I noticed within the coachee right at the beginning. I notice myself wondering how the coachee wants to use this final session. I have no idea about that at the moment.

In a study of eighty-six descriptions of critical moments from coaching practice written up by inexperienced coaches (De Haan, 2008b), I found that critical moments of beginning coaches are strongly characterized by *doubts*. More experienced coaches tend to feel more secure about their critical moments, and even if they are tense and anxious in their most critical work, they have been shown to be a lot less doubtful than beginning coaches (Day *et al.*, 2008). What the inquiry process tries to do is to keep those doubts fresh and vivid, convert the hidden anxieties into more available doubts. These coaches try to keep inquiring into their lived experience in an open, fresh, and curious way, deferring judgement as much as possible. Then they try to retain this position of curiosity, openness, and doubt, which lies at the basis of every coaching contract, over a longer period of time, ideally over the full length of the contract.

Reflective, sceptical inquiry can be used on many levels. It has been used in a book by coaching practitioners writing about their practice and in the interest of the authors' own longer-term professional development as executive coaches (De Haan *et al.*, 2013). It can also be used on a session-by-session level as we offer our coachees this most basic offering of a coach: grounded, open, and reflective presence. Thirdly, inquiry will be used by our coachees as well, whether they call it inquiry or not, to deepen their reflections on their circumstances. We may at several times during coaching assignments help our coachees actively to develop a more reflective stance, by noticing together with the coachee and inviting the coachee to notice. In these terms, executive coaching consists of building up a stream of reflectiveness and doubt alongside the drivenness, convictions and action orientation of the coachee; loving inquiry meeting the adrenaline rush of business action.

Case example 2.4

I remember one board-level coachee in the telecoms industry that I worked with for several years, who radiated his executive presence and control, and quite often approached me in a manner similar to how he would approach, say, an IT contractor, letting me know about his progress and where he might have a query for me. I responded with little more than just my observations, letting him know what I had understood of his progress and of his queries, and also how I noticed his stance towards his progress and towards me. On his final feedback form he described the impact of my reflective presence: 'I think the moments where difficult questions were asked about my behaviour or honest feedback about what I have said, stand out for me. I enjoy the direct feedback during our conversations, about the job and the whole environment around it.'

There is another way in which a sceptical stance in the vein of Sextus Empiricus is groundwork for coaching. Executive coaching 'material', the stuff of coaching, often starts off in a rather dogmatic and formulaic way, in the shape of repetitive thinking about experiences which appear to be dished up to 'entertain' or 'cover' the coach and the coaching session. Coaches enter from a position of advantage here, as they come fresh to this material. By remaining fresh and inquisitive, coaches can tear down stilted thinking and rash conclusions, to open up space for new reflection on the coachee's original experiences. Sextus Empiricus has shown us the way to do this, in books with titles such as *Against the Dogmatists*, *Against the Professors*, and *Against the Logicians*.

If inquiry is the groundwork for coaching, then based on the previous section we can intuit the groundwork for this groundwork. In that section, it was suggested that the underpinning foundations of inquiry are

1 letting go of the pressure to do it right;
2 having a clear anchor or inquiry question, which in a coaching session might be to understand what the coachee brings; and
3 navigating and extracting insight from impermanence and nested cycles.

In other words, sitting at the feet of your experience means opening up space by suspending judgement, anchoring your perspective and letting go, reaping from experience and again letting go, and opening up space again, and so on in continuing cycles of experience and inquiry.

I end with the same quote and with the same reminder that the stuff of any inquiry is 'just' tentative, 'just' lived personal experience: mostly observations and hypotheses – with very few conclusions. Whenever you report back summaries or broader results of your listening, or even of a longer inquiry like a whole session, make sure that you remember this helpful caveat:

Of none of our future statements do we positively affirm that the fact is exactly as we state it, but we simply record each fact, like a chronicler, as it appears to us at the moment. (S.E. I.4)

Chapter summary

In Chapters 2–4, we look at where some of the magic of coaching may be coming from, by reviewing three fundamental building blocks that I believe play a role in the general effectiveness which begins to emerge as 'fear meets love', i.e. as coach and coachee overcome their doubts and anxieties to sit down and work with each other. Those building blocks are, simply put, attention (or listening; in Chapter 2), relationship (or engaging; in Chapter 3), and empathy (or understanding; in Chapter 4). In this chapter, we focus on our *attention* as coaches.

Here in Chapter 2, we begin with our basic stance of 'not knowing', which underpins all listening. How can we let go of the many things we already know or think we know or believe to be true or want to be true, and become curious again? How can we become really open to the fresh meeting and the new information in front of us? It is shown that we can loosen ourselves from what we thought we knew about the coachee, from our memories and notes, and also from our desires for the coachee, so that we become more available to listen right now.

Notes

1   This chapter is an expanded version of an article which first appeared in the *International Coaching Psychology Review* (vol. 9, no. 1, 2014). © The British Psychological Society.

2   Sextus Empiricus writes this at the beginning of his text on scepticism: *Outline of Pyrrhonism,* a text that I will return to several times in this chapter, with direct quotes from the Loeb Classics and OUP translations (in *italics*). I will refer to it briefly by the letters S.E. – e.g. this citation is at S.E. I.4, *Outline of Pyrrhonism* Book One, Section Four. Of Sextus Empiricus very little is known and he is usually described as a Greek physician and philosopher living in Alexandria, Athens and Rome around the year 200 AD. He wrote in Greek and drew on five hundred years of sceptical philosophy, a tradition that started with Pyrrho from Elis who travelled with Alexander the Great on his campaigns in the East.

3   The present state of affairs in helping conversations was already intuited by Rosenzweig (1936) and to sum it up he coined this phrase from the 'Dodo verdict' in *Alice in Wonderland* (Chapter 3).

4   As romanticized by Plato in the *Apology*, 38a.

5   A 'bhikkhu' is a practitioner or a monk; literally a 'beggar'.

3 Back to basics: engaging[1]

As we sit with our coachee and listen, we begin to form a relationship. Coach and coachee engage with one another. There is no two ways about this – even before the coach and coachee meet for the first time, they become a unit. As one of my teachers once said: we become a relationship just like a cappuccino – there will be no way of telling where the coffee ends and where the milk begins. With every phenomenon within the relationship, we will be co-creating and co-responsible. We will form ideas about the other person and we will begin to respond to what we observe, beginning the dance of relating which lies at the basis of every conversation.

As we have seen in Chapter 1, the relationship itself has properties of its own and contributes to the change process within the coachee. For that reason alone, it behoves us to understand relationships at a deep level; to know that what we notice in relationship has deep traces in all other important relationships that we and our coachees have ever engaged in. That is the phenomenon of transference, which is what this chapter is about.

Engaging means entering the world of transference, the world of earlier relationships which sway and re-emerge in this relationship here and now. Transference is a powerful phenomenon that underpins the importance of the relationship in achieving coaching outcomes, possibly through the impact of the working alliance (positive transference) or else through becoming noticed in other ways. Unnoticed or misperceived transference seems to lie at the root of mistakes and deterioration as reported in executive coaching relationships, such as misjudging the relationship, aggravating the status quo by collusion, the illusion of being all-powerful, or abuse of their power by coaches (Berglas, 2002). In Berglas's article, transference is explicitly mentioned as a phenomenon that is missed at the coach's peril. In short, both to become relationally more perceptive and to learn to avoid very real dangers in executive coaching, it is essential that executive coaches take time to study transference. It seems worthwhile, then, to go back to the source and study the early writings about transference, in particular, Freud's technical papers. There is something powerful and unavoidable about the story of the discovery of transference which may be re-created in the development of every coach and in the discovery process that every coach and coachee undertake together.

This chapter is about appreciating the process of discovery of transference and countertransference. The chapter enquires into what the process insights we can gather could teach us when taking on new coachees. It argues that coaches can learn both from Freud's discoveries and from the benefit of hindsight.

In many of the guides to the coaching profession, transference is mentioned extensively in the context of psychodynamic approaches to executive coaching (e.g. Peltier, 2001, Chapter 2; De Haan and Burger, 2004, Chapter 8; Stober and Grant, 2006, Chapter 5; Palmer and Whybrow, 2007, Chapter 14). Moreover, a lot of executive coaching handbooks and articles that are clearly not psychodynamically orientated still underline the importance of the phenomenon of transference (e.g. Zeus and Skiffington, 2000, p. 24 and elsewhere; Rogers, 2004, pp. 195–196). Books about psychodynamic approaches in consulting also mention transference as an important phenomenon to be encountered and worked with in practice (e.g. De Board, 1978; Hirschhorn, 1988; Czander, 1993). Increasingly, we find transference mentioned in publications on consulting and coaching, often under the name of 'parallel process'.

In the past decades, substantial empirical evidence has demonstrated the phenomenon of transference ('old issues from past relationships emerging in new relationships') more objectively (for an overview of that evidence, see Andersen and Berk, 1998; Kraus and Chen, 2010; Bressan and Damian, 2018).

However, it is worthwhile and insightful to go back to the original publications on this phenomenon starting from Sigmund Freud's famous discovery, particularly if one wants to gain a fresh understanding of the phenomenon and its various manifestations. The next sections will trace the discoveries around transference from its first mention in 1904 by Freud until half a century later: 1955, when the related term 'parallel process', and 1965, when the 'working alliance' was introduced.

3.1: Freud on transference

'Zur Dynamik der Übertragung' (Freud, 1912b) is without doubt Freud's core text in the area of transference. In it he defines transference as that part or those parts of the person's highly individual, highly personal, and largely unconscious loving impulses not being satisfied in their relationships. He states that everyone will repeat one or several of such 'clichés' regularly in the course of a lifetime (Freud, 1912b). He defines transference, therefore, as at the same time (a) highly individual in its modelling itself after previous relationships, (b) unconsciously motivated, and (c) related to thwarted libido, unfulfilled reaching out. He assures us there is nothing special about the phenomenon, except for two 'problems': (1) more neurotic people have more thwarted libido, and therefore a more intense transference; and (2) transference becomes the strongest resistance against treatment in psychoanalysis – in spite of it being originally an important bearer of healing and condition for success. Freud (1912b) argues that it is precisely that part of the resistance that becomes transference (the example he gives more than once is the faltering of 'free association', which may point to thoughts about the therapist) that is the first to come into conscious awareness. Time and time again, he points out, when pathogenic material is approached, that part of the pathology which may translate into transference will be the first in consciousness and defended most vigorously. In other words, the dissatisfaction tries to defend itself by defending itself *in* transference, by acting into transference, by becoming dissatisfaction in *this* relationship (i.e. the relationship offered to the therapist *becomes* the illness). The consequence is that conflicts with the status quo will have to be fought out (i.e. healing needs to be done) in transference, within this very relationship here and now. Victory in that conflict, Freud (1912b) assures us, heralds an enduring way forward, a 'cure of the illness'. In 'Zur Einleitung der Behandlung' (1913), Freud expands by stating that if and only if the full intensity of transference has been used up on overcoming resistances, will it become impossible for the patient to continue the illness even after the transference is dissolved (i.e. after treatment).

For Freud (1917), transference is *always the same thing* (*'immer das Gleiche'*), which will never 'allow its origins to be mistaken': it is libido streaming back from the symptoms – through heightened understanding of them – and into the relationship with the therapist.

There are for Freud (1912b) essentially two types of transference: positive, loving[2] transference and negative, hostile transference. The relationship needs to be built such that the positive transference will be strong enough to counter or overcome the hostile transference, a precursor to the subtitle of this book: love over fear. Of the loving variety there are again two, associated with *eros* (erotic transference; see also Freud, 1915a) and with *agape* (friendly transference). Transference is always there, from the very start of the cure. In the initial phases, loving transference represents the 'strongest drive to the work' (Freud, 1917); later on, it may become an obstacle as it attracts additional libido from freed symptoms, defences, and resistances. Negative transference occurs only in a minority of cases, and usually somewhat later in the cure.

The history of the discoveries related to transference and countertransference seems to be transferential in itself, as it clearly is a repetition of the process of overcoming or eliminating obstacles (again, see Freud's 1917 lecture, 'Die Übertragung' – The Transference):

Obstacle 1 (1880s): *the problem is (related to the) unconscious*, a hidden feeling or wish. Pills don't work, the effect of hypnosis is not long-lasting, arguing with the patient –when it is at all successful – only instils an idea *next* to the unconscious, and doesn't really touch it. Solution: (1) find out about the unconscious by listening closely and with dedication – see also Chapter 2; (2) discover some of the suppressed material; (3) make it more conscious. Then one can work with it more directly.

Obstacle 2 (early 1890s): remembering stops, memory does not give in or give away its treasures. At such a moment one discovers *defences* such as repression. Solution: name them and shame them.

Obstacle 3 (late 1890s): remembering stalls again as it touches on something painful, embarrassing, or contrary to morality, and the patient becomes reluctant. In such a moment one discovers *resistance*. Solution: overcome it, by guessing or intuiting it,[3] and naming it. Historically, this discovery corresponded with the start of the 'fundamental rule' of free association – as Freud's earlier technique was found to invite unnecessary resistance by its directive nature.

Obstacle 4 (1900s): free association stalls again or becomes repetitive. A heightened interest in the helper becomes apparent. *Transference* arrives on the scene. In extreme cases, we encounter 'transference neurosis', as a new re-enactment of the neurosis. Solution: (1) maintain the transference, as it 'opens up an intermediate region between illness and real life, through which the transition from the former to the latter takes place' (Freud, 1914); and (2) demonstrate how the feelings and actions do not originate in the present situation, so that repetition can be transformed into remembrance and reflection (Freud, 1917). Here what we see is that 'transference itself is used for resolving transference' (Strachey, 1934), i.e. that the force behind analysing the transference is itself transferential in origin: it is the positive, friendly transference underpinning the therapy as a whole.

Obstacle 5 (late 1900s): *countertransference*. First mentioned by Freud in 1910 as the influence of the patient on the 'unconscious sensing' of the therapist. Countertransference was discovered much later than transference, although some have pointed out (e.g. Lear, 2005) that countertransference must have been experienced without being recognized or named as such well before (e.g. by Breuer in his work with 'Anna O', or by Freud in his work with 'Dora'). Solution: for this purpose, Freud (1910) suggested self-analysis and ongoing analysis ('supervision') for the therapist in order to understand and overcome the obstacle so as to be able to return to the work.

Obstacle 6 (late 1940s, i.e. post Freud): the therapist's anxiety keeps bubbling up even if well understood. Solution: welcoming and using countertransference as an antenna to deeper listening (Heimann, 1950).

Historically, each of these developments was 'first considered a somewhat annoying interference with the work, then an instrument of great value, and finally, the main battleground for treatment' (Racker, 1968).

On the way to discovery, a lot of people were left behind: initially peer hypnotherapists, then Joseph Breuer, then Freud himself (witness the delay in publishing the 'Dora' case), and then certain earlier Freudian assumptions. This seems a path not just of discovery, but also of a gradually emerging honesty about the discoveries. Freud (1914) himself notes that 'the development of psychoanalytic therapy was probably delayed by a decade at the start, because of an erotic transference situation', hinting at Breuer with 'Anna O'. Racker (1968) surmises that perhaps according to some Haeckelian law,[4] this discovery process repeats itself with every new analyst and indeed every new school of psychoanalysis, as they struggle initially with defences and resistances, only to become more open about their own countertransference at a relatively late stage.

'Bruchstück einer Hysterie-Analyse' (Freud, 1905) is the first publication we have that is explicit about transference. There is only one clear-cut transference example in the case study, related to the first dream, involving smoke 'Dora' smells just after dreaming. The smoke is linked in the therapy to Freud, while bearing in mind that also 'Dora's' father and 'Herr K' were passionate smokers. So, in this very first book about (erotic) transference we find the full Menninger-Malan (Malan, 1979) triangle-of-person (father, significant other, and analyst) all connected around a cigar – the same cigar which has become so proverbially associated with Freud. Later on, but more implicitly, it seems to be the un-interpreted negative transference which leads to the breakdown of 'Dora's' treatment.

In the 'Nachwort' (epilogue), which was added almost 4 years after writing the case study, we find the first definition of transference (p. 279), and Freud makes a different distinction between transferences as compared with his later writing: the one between 'unchanged reprint' versus 'revised edition'. This is an important distinction: the first (unchanged reprint) boils down to a primitive displacement of one person by another, while the second (revised edition) has an element of sublimation and adaptation to it, and so, Freud continues, the content of the second is 'milder' (Freud, 1905). Freud adds that the job of guessing and interpreting transference is the 'hardest' part of the work, while the analyst has to work in a self-reliant manner, with very scant evidence and without getting carried away. This may be the first, veiled reference to countertransference, a concept that is not yet mentioned at this stage, but we can imagine and know from other sources Freud did experience strong feelings with regard to 'Dora'.

He then notes that people will judge this phenomenon as a disadvantage, and perhaps even as evidence that the psychoanalytic cure engenders new pathology – and argues against both positions, stressing first the inevitability of transference and then the converse of his imagined opponent: 'this, the biggest obstacle of the cure, is destined to become the strongest instrument of it when we succeed to guess it time and time again, and translate it to the patient'.

By the time of the 'Rat Man' case (Freud, 1909), Freud shows himself a real master of the transference. He demonstrates in some detail how crucial breakthroughs in this treatment happen after Freud is able to sustain and interpret a heightened negative transference (rude and denigrating abuse directed at Freud combined with existential fear of Freud) and to link the transference to some of the main discoveries of the treatment so far, after which the Rat Man is able to provide a host of new associations and improves.

There are clear connections between transference and some of Freud's other discoveries: resistance, repetition compulsion, and the death drive.

- *Resistance* was introduced by Freud as early as 1895 (Breuer and Freud, 1895): overcoming resistance is the crowning piece of 'Studien über Hysterie'. Is transference 'resistance' as in the expression 'transference neurosis' (Freud, 1914) would lead us to believe, or is transference rather the 'resisted', the relationship that the patient is unable to remember or express, and does not allow into consciousness (Freud, 1920)? Racker (1968) points to these two contradictory positions that Freud must have held at different times.

- The *repetition compulsion* is introduced in Freud (1914) as something underpinning transference; indeed, as something even more fundamental than the role of love, the pleasure principle (Freud, 1920). Transference is by definition a repetition, and when it is central in session after session it can well be experienced as a compulsion.
- In 1920 Freud also introduces the *death drive* as an explanation of negative transference. Before that, Freud was thinking of 'love' and 'hate' in the unconscious as very similar, almost interchangeable, as he demonstrates in dream analysis ('representation by opposites'; Freud, 1900). There is good support for the earlier explanation: both erotic and hostile transference produce very similar obstacles to treatment – so there are still many who maintain the death drive is not necessary to grasp the phenomenon of transference.

One can reconcile Freud's various positions by looking at transference as repeating ('being'), rather than remembering ('reflecting on'). This is close to the argument in Freud (1914). Transference is then an expression of the unconscious root of our behaviour which springs from earlier experience. When the task is remembering, transference offers resistance to the task. When the task is understanding or interpreting, transference comes across as the resisted: the aspects of our being here now that would complete the picture. Transference is not *a priori* driven in either direction, it is 'always the same' (Freud, 1917): that part of our relating here and now that consists of the unrequited love that we are not conscious of. It can be seen as an expression of love (Freud, 1912b), or equally as a neurosis (Freud, 1913), and it can even be an expression of hate and self-destructiveness (Freud, 1920).

3.2: The power of transference

From the earliest days, transference had struck Freud and other participating observers as a form of sublime cooperation and sublime resistance at the same time. The importance of transference for helping conversations is considerable. Indeed, in Freud's view, transference has the capacity to take over the whole treatment (Freud, 1917). Nonetheless, if one looks at the reports from Freud's patients about his technique, he rarely appears to address or interpret transference head-on (see, for example, Lohser and Newton, 1996). Other schools of therapy also teach the concept, and it has found its way into our field of organizational consulting and coaching (see the references mentioned at the start of this chapter, or Ledford, 1985).

I encounter the power of transference in coaching and consulting both early-onset and in longer-term relationships. I was first 'struck' by transference in my work in management development in the 1990s where we were wont to end a workshop with an afternoon working with trained actors. The participants would think of a conversation or a relationship that they wanted to improve, the actor would receive short instructions, and then the scene would be played out several times, re-enacting its original course and trialling new approaches. The actors would often get standing ovations at the end of the afternoon and would remain with the participants as the highlight of the workshop. Many participants remarked on how real the role-play had been for them, how it had felt like being in the room with the real person. It was similarly fascinating to observe the changes in the participants when they were in the scenes, trying to wrestle with their bosses, rivals, and clients. In organizational work, I use Searles' (1955) term 'parallel process' to refer to phenomena where both transference and countertransference play a part, acknowledging my own possible contribution to what is emerging. The terms transference and countertransference can then be limited to describe individual responses or behaviours.

Case example 3.1

A shadow consultant had just started supervising a team of change consultants working at a financial services organization. As the group session progressed, she noticed that whenever the project leader was speaking, her mind wandered and even when she forced herself to listen, she was only able to follow what was being said for a few minutes at most. When others in the team spoke, she found it easier to concentrate, but was concerned about the quality of her supervision because she had not fully followed the project leader's contribution. When the same thing happened during the second session, she decided to share her experience with the group in a way that avoided criticizing the project leader. She asked whether others felt the same way and whether this might be a reflection of their work with the organization in some way. To her astonishment several team members admitted that they too found it hard to follow their project leader's thought processes. The leader was initially embarrassed, but with the help of the group came to realize that their key client, the CEO, was isolated and remote from their colleagues, who also seemed to only half-understand what they were trying to communicate. The supervisor pointed out that the team's experience of the project leader could in fact be seen as a classic example of a parallel process, in other words a replication of what was happening in the client system.

The supervisor then helped the team think through what the project leader could do differently and how this insight might also be relevant to the CEO. This resulted in a profound shift in the team's effectiveness, as they learned to share what might be construed as negative feedback in a spirit of mutual inquiry rather than criticism. The CEO was similarly defensive when the project leader shared their observations but was astonished at their accuracy when he sought feedback from his closest colleague.

Readers will recognize the power of 'transference interpretations' in their work as coaches or consultants: the inescapable and often quite unhinging effect of feedback on here-and-now behaviour while it occurs. One senses an almost devastating power when such interpretations cut through a stuck situation just by bringing to someone's attention how they seem to initiate or respond here and now with the consultant or coach, and one is reminded of the quote 'it is impossible to slay an adversary *in absentia* or *in effigy*' (Freud, 1912b, and again, slightly differently, in Freud, 1914) – that is, of the very real power to cut through behaviour by a single hypothesis or even summary *in situ* (relating to here and now).

In contrast to the careful and slow first journey of discovery of transference, nowadays we recognize the immediacy of transference and are inclined to see 'parallel processes' everywhere, in our coachees' experiences, in our own, and in non-work relationships we engage in. Freud (1913) also gives an example of immediate-onset transference, a patient to whom in the very first session 'nothing' springs to mind while in reality he is obsessed with the treatment, the consulting room, and lying on the couch. Harold Searles writes (1955, pp. 169–170):

> ... my experience in hearing numerous therapists present cases before groups has caused me to become slow in forming an unfavourable opinion of any therapist on the basis of his presentation of a case. With convincing frequency I have seen that a therapist who during an occasional presentation appears lamentably anxious, compulsive, confused in his thinking, or what not, actually is a basically capable colleague who, as it were, is trying unconsciously, by this demeanour during the presentation, to show us a major problem-area in the therapy with his patient.

Case example 3.2

Here is a recent example of quickly developing transference from one of my own supervision groups of executive coaches. The supervisee was an English management consultant who had been sent by his English client organization to a subsidiary in Italy where he was to coach a senior manager. He described how he found the exuberance of expression and emotionality of his new coachee difficult to handle. During supervision he worked with another participant and discussed the challenges posed by this new coachee. At the end of that short coaching conversation, one of the other coaches drew attention to the fact that the supervisee seemed to have changed; he had never seen him so animated and extravert. We realized that he had copied his coachee's behaviour, particularly his gestures, and he agreed when this was pointed out. It is surprising that he first felt almost intimidated by his coachee, and then was able to intimidate someone else in the very same way. This type of transference that comes across as a modest 'repetition compulsion' can also be viewed as an unconscious learning process that helps the individual to handle new behaviour by first adopting that behaviour themselves. It is the age-old story of how the victim becomes the victimizer, until noticed and interpreted back to its origins.

In summary, the importance of transference is not only related to the ubiquity and the immediate onset of the phenomenon, but also to the myriad of possibilities and the complexity of relational patterns that are copied, repeated, partially repeated, or mirrored in transference. Transference is not only 'always the same' (Freud, 1917), but it is nevertheless an immensely rich phenomenon that plies and adapts itself to session after session, and within sessions.

3.3: Newer thinking about transference/countertransference

Nowadays the term 'transference resistance' (Freud, 1912b) is less and less heard, with the emphasis more on the associative quality of transference. As a consequence of this, Freud's (1913) advice to leave the theme of transference untouched as long as the patient's communications run on is observed less, and more therapists feel that transference can be explicitly addressed from day one (an observation also made by Racker, 1968).

Here is a brief summary of a few newer influential papers in the area of transference:

- Strachey (1934) looked into the conditions which have to be fulfilled for a transference interpretation to be 'mutative' or 'killing', as Freud called it in 1912b.
- Heimann (1950), in a short article, broke ground when reappraising the concept of countertransference. Heimann and follow-up studies such as Racker's (1968), gave therapists permission to listen more deeply to the countertransference they bring to the occasion as well as in particular their own transferential response to the patient, and to use the information contained in their countertransference for the benefit of the patient.
- Harold Searles (1955) was the next to make an important new distinction as regards the phenomenon of transference, pointing out that there are essentially two possibilities, namely that the patient either relives his/her earlier position (e.g. feeling how it felt with father, acting as they acted with sister, etc.) or incorporates the position of the other (e.g. feeling and/or acting like father). He called these two options 'unconscious identification' and 'complementary unconscious identification'. In our field they are sometimes called parallel and inverse transference (see De Haan, 2004, pp. 82–84). Freud must have been aware of the distinction. For example, see his analysis of the play of his 1½-year-old grandson in 'Jenseits des Lustprinzips' (Freud, 1920, Chapter 2), where he shows a boy who takes the role of the 'perpetrator', his mother, and thus displays inverse transference from the earlier interaction with his mother. Another example is my second case in section 3.2 above.
- Greenson (1965) introduces the concept of *working alliance* as a broadening of Freud's (1912b) 'zärtliche Übertragung' (friendly transference), which

opened up the prospect of actually measuring transference. Bordin (1979) was instrumental both in creating a 'two-person' or interpersonal description of the working alliance and in identifying three measurable aspects of it (goals, tasks, and bonds), which allowed the working alliance to be operationalized. There is now a plethora of working-alliance psychometrics available, such as the Working Alliance Inventory (Horvath and Greenberg, 1986), which has been translated for use with coaches as well (e.g. in De Haan *et al.*, 2016).

The still newer, relational school of psychoanalysis also attaches great importance to transference. It argues for:

- the idea that change happens in the relationship, and only in the relationship, which suggests that change in the transferential relationship here-and-now is a necessary and perhaps sufficient condition to bring about change outside the consulting room (Stolorow and Atwood, 1992);
- the philosophical position that we are not so much driven by libido as Freud used to think (Freud, 1917), and not so much by the internalized objects of our libido either (Fairbairn, 1952), but that it is relationship (Mitchell and Aron, 1999) that unconsciously motivates us, i.e. being in a relationship that is familiar to us and where we can thrive or continue to suffer in similar ways because we have experienced it before.

Relational psychoanalysis moves the concept of transference right to the centre of personality theory as well as of psychotherapy, where perhaps it should have been all the time since that very first case history in 'Studien über Hysterie' (Breuer and Freud, 1895), that of 'Anna O.', were it not for the intricacies of the discovery and revelation process. It is important to note that many of the innovations that the relational school claims to have made are perhaps not as new as advertised, and that much of relational thinking goes all the way back to Freud or is at least not contrary to Freud's theories (Mills, 2005).

In summary, it is safe to say that transference has become completely mainstream in psychotherapy, and that therapists are now open to a very broad spectrum of events in the here-and-now, while they work with their patients, ranging from the 'real' relationship (rapport, working alliance) to repetitions of patterns taken from elsewhere, both as intuited from their patients and as sensed from within themselves. The psychoanalytic literature gives them full encouragement to think about these phenomena and to use them to build what are hopefully 'mutative' interpretations, or interpretations that really make a difference.

3.4: Application when taking on new coachees

Freud (1917) stated that the natural emergence of neurotic transference and countertransference tends to have a rather late onset, i.e. after defences and resistance have already appeared and been noted. As discussed elsewhere, nowadays it is thought that this observation may have been due to missing earlier transference (Racker, 1968). It seems worthwhile to consider actively working against missing out on earlier transference phenomena by attending to transference from the earliest relationship with the coachee. There are two clear advantages of looking for transference earlier, i.e. taking another route than the original discovery route of psychoanalysis. First, this may prepare us better for our sessions as we will have already considered our own share in the process. Second, we would be countering a process which in itself contributes to pathology as it repeats itself largely unnoticed, against the possibility of new learning or thinking.

Let us look into such a thought experiment reversing the 'order of appearance' as discussed in the first section above, i.e. the natural and historical genesis of therapeutic discovery which indicates that the 'root of the matter' is

1   avoided altogether;
2   hidden in the unconscious;
3   defended against;
4   buried beneath resistance to the therapy;
5   transferred into the therapy room (repeated rather than remembered);
6   obscured by countertransference.

This would mean that we train ourselves to be aware of our countertransference responses first, and even, specifically, before contracting with a new coachee. We would be literally counting back from this final discovery, countertransference. And in this way, we can identify six principles to bear in mind during a coaching relationship:

[6] 'Notice your own countertransference early'

Racker (1968) suggested that there is a universal countertransference response which is oedipal (Freud, 1900) in nature. In essence and if we are completely honest, we will find that we want our coachees of one sex to love us, and we want to defeat ('murder') coachees of the other sex, even if these tendencies might at times be reversed (according to the 'negative Oedipus complex'; Freud, 1923). Not exactly an ideal situation to begin a helping relationship, which is precisely why these tendencies were not written about for such a long time and why we need to think hard about them before we commence a coaching relationship.

What we might try to do when preparing for new coachee work or for individual sessions, is ask ourselves what instinctual responses we can detect within ourselves. This can go a bit further than just liking and disliking, attraction and aversion. We can easily form a spontaneous 'image' in our minds of the coachee, even if we have not met them. Sometimes it is a glance, sometimes a posture, sometimes an action in the room – rarely is this image verbal. It is more of a sense of being-in-the-room with the other person. Once we have this sense, we can analyse it and explore how we are unconsciously preparing for our coachee: are we feeling superior, condescending, anxious, desiring, etc.? Rarely do we feel 'neutral', despite all the exhortations of classical psychoanalysis, and if we do, there is probably scope for more analysis of our own felt neutrality and what it masks.

While the coachee meeting draws closer and we gather more information and shared experience, general countertransferential patterns become more specific. The coachee will remind us of someone in particular or will prompt in us a flurry of emotion with a single gesture. Emotions that we feel during the sessions have a countertransferential component. Racker (1968) also describes how some of our outlook may change into a 'depressive' one where much of our feelings are related to our superego, and we may experience feelings of self-doubt, inadequacy, or superiority with regard to our coachee.

Later uses of countertransference include our response to perceived ruptures in the relationship. Experienced coaches and consultants learn that frustrations or interferences may turn out to be the main arena of their work. This is true both for individual coachees and for sponsors of the coaching work. Time and time again one can notice that the best and most effective consulting work is done soon after something unsettling happens, but only if the relationship survives this rupture.

When you want to work with your countertransference or any of your 'gut feelings' during a session, there are essentially two ways of doing so and they are quite different. One is speaking to it and the other is through gentle questioning. The first way is the more straightforward and boils down to disclosing (some of) your gut feeling, e.g. saying, to put it bluntly, 'I am distracted', 'I feel sad as I sit with you', or 'Do you recognize this irresistible pull to burst out laughing?' The second way of using your countertransference is by guessing the feeling of your coachee in that same moment and sussing out how it might be related to yours, e.g. 'Do you feel distracted?', 'I am picking up a sadness in your expression – am I right?', or 'Is a part of you not taking this very seriously?' In both ways of actively using countertransference, you may surprise your coachee and that may become difficult for her, as this is about what happens right now in the conversation. However, the second way, through gentle questioning, is safer. There will normally be less of a rupture if you ask a naïve question that is dismissed, as compared to when you name strong feelings that are not (immediately) recognized. Either way can be summarized as 'love over fear': loving inquiry moving in to meet rather raw and unrecognized or unwelcome emotions.

[5] 'Attend to the coachee's transferential patterns from the start'
Once we are somewhat aware of our countertransference response and we have analysed some of our feelings towards our coachee, we can begin attending to what the coachee brings in terms of transference. In

this regard, it is productive to think about the following quote: '*place yourself on the side of the tendency towards repetition, or on the side of the struggle against the resistances which oppose repetition*' (Freud, 1920; as quoted by Racker, 1968, p. 48). In other words, we can keep our empathy firmly on the side of the transference in order to try to understand its origins from within, in particular to understand some of the coachee's central conflicts through the acting out of the transference, and also the repressed memory or impulse that has given rise to this particular transference at this particular time. Transference need not be something that is developed over time between coach and coachee. Similar to countertransference, transference will always be present and start from session one and even before ('pre-transference').

It is important to work with transference in a way that is at the same time open-minded and robust; in other words, to adopt both a thick and a thin skin when responding to transference (De Haan, 2008d). A thick skin allows us to sustain the workings of transference and preserve us in the midst of pulls to respond in certain stereotypical or 'clichéd' ways. A thin skin helps us to sense and pick up subtle cues that can inform us about this behaviour and its transferential origins.

[4] **'Within the sessions notice "resistance to coaching" as an undercurrent'**
Within what we perceive of the transference towards us, we try to identify and overcome the resistance of the coachee from moment to moment. Freud (1912b) wrote that 'resistance accompanies treatment at every step' and later that 'overcoming resistances is that part of the work which occupies the most time and the greatest trouble' (Freud, 1940). Within the context of this chapter, it is relevant to note that in the last technical introduction that Freud wrote, from his last year in London and left unfinished, he follows the same order as here: he covers transference first and then moves on to resistance as the 'other important part of our job' (Freud, 1940), while in his earlier, more historically based overview (Freud, 1917), resistance comes first.

[3] **'Try to pick up cues – defences – which help to deepen the conversation'**
While spotting relational phenomena like countertransference, transference, and resistance, we continue practising our 'evenly hovering' free association to listen to our coachee both consciously and unconsciously. On this level, the information in our sessions is well captured by Malan's (1979) *triangle of conflict*, which includes defences, anxieties, and hidden feelings or impulses. Malan (1979) argues that the first of these we will notice is the defence, as defences form layers of (pre-) consciousness around more hidden anxieties and feelings. Resistance and defence are coupled: resistance can be defined as 'defence protracted into the here-and-now', i.e. as additional defences needed when the coach comes uncomfortably close.

[2] 'Follow the deepening content of the conversation: anxieties'
Being somewhat aware of the *context* at this moment (countertransference, transference, and resistance) helps to be secure enough to become more fully aware of the *content* of the session in this very moment, i.e. what goes on for the coachee underneath words spoken, issues and ideas offered, and defences demonstrated. We can see the origin of defences as a layer of protection, isolation, and/or dampening of *anxiety*, which thus becomes the next discovery in our journey of understanding.

[1] 'Spot authentic feelings and wishes beneath those anxieties'
Finally, anxiety can be seen as a consequence of an emerging desire or *feeling* which is problematic or unwelcome. This deep feeling or impulse lies at the root of many of the perspectives that went before and will only be discovered last through understanding ever better the relationship in the room, resistances, defences, and anxiety.

Figure 3.1 is a sketch of the various aspects of (or perspectives on) the here-and-now in a coaching session, without wanting to reify any of these aspects. Each of the six concepts may describe the same *affect* or emotion during a session, under various viewpoints, so all six amount essentially to one and the same 'thing', the thing that is going on at this moment, which could be called the *symptom* as it presents itself right now. The various perspectives or ways the symptom engages with us, are each always there and they are themselves multi-layered, ambiguous, and contradictory. Of these six, resistance is probably the one that is most 'objective', or best observable. All the others are usually hidden under the surface, to various degrees.

Figure 3.1

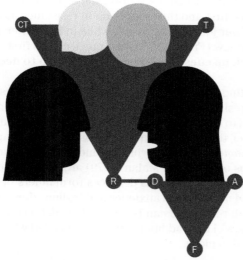

CT = countertransference, T = transference, R = resistance, D = defence, A = anxiety, F = feelings

3.5: Conclusion

Transference, or the re-emergence of past relationship patterns (sometimes called core conflictual relationship themes) within present relationships, is a fascinating phenomenon. Not just because it is so infinitely varied and rich, as the traces of meaningful relationships in our lives and careers are bound to be. Not just because transference leads to curious misunderstandings and impositions on (new!) partners in a relationship. What makes transference so fascinating is that it occurs, or at least begins, subliminally, in an area of consciousness that we do not have much access to, not even through introspection. Transference phenomena have great potential for self-understanding and personal development, as they provide us with a 'royal road' towards perceiving how previous relationships have affected us. In the realm of leadership and coaching, transference gives us the promise of access to the 'shadow side' of our leadership aspirations, the aspects of ourselves and our past that propel us forward to take up certain roles and engage in certain modes of behaving, but that are largely hidden from our own view, and barely accessible through reflection or introspection. These shadow sides may well have something to do with the frustration of our own desires and wishes (as Freud suggested), which would explain why there are such frequent indications of transference in helping conversations.

By opening our eyes to the possibility of transference, even of crossed or inverse transference where we repeat other people's roles in a relationship rather than our own, we may enrich our relationships and our lives. And as a minor concomitant, we may enrich our experience of executive coaching and enhance our impact as coaches. Studying the roots of transference as I have done in this chapter, both the historical roots and the roots in our own coaching relationships, may bring a substantial return on our efforts to find meaning and understanding.

Chapter summary

In this chapter, we think more deeply about what happens *between* coachee and coach. What are the aspects of the emerging and evolving relationship in the coaching room that we can take on board and work with to improve our understanding? This means revisiting Freud's concept of transference and gaining a solid understanding of its origins and contributions to coaching relationships. Here we follow the entire 15-year (1895–1910) history of the discovery of concepts, such as defences, resistance, transference, and countertransference and we also look at more modern understandings of these relational phenomena. It is shown that we can assume transferences play a role and we can alert ourselves to them by carefully checking in with ourselves around what we are noticing and what known patterns are being stirred up for us. I suggest we might deliberately reverse the normal process of discovery by starting with reflections on countertransference rather than come to these at a late stage or only afterwards, in supervision.

Notes

1   This chapter is an expanded version of an article which first appeared in the *International Coaching Psychology Review* (vol. 6, no. 2, 2011). © The British Psychological Society.
2   It is hard to translate the tender German word *zärtlich* but loving will do.
3   Freud seems to use *erraten* and *vermuten* interchangeably. Interestingly, Freud's original term for working through, *überwinden*, means to get through it or overcome it, not so much to work with it in any way.
4   In 1866, the German zoologist Ernst Haeckel proposed that the embryonic development of an individual organism (its ontogeny) followed the same path as the evolutionary history of its species (its phylogeny) (Haeckel, 1866).

4 | Back to basics: understanding[1]

In this part of the book, we have looked at the fundamentals of being present with our coachees. We have spoken about our ability to listen, to observe, and to inquire into our coachee in Chapter 2 and then our ability to engage or to relate to our coachee in Chapter 3. Chapter 4 is all about understanding our coachees, at an equally fundamental level: the ability to reflect and empathize with our coachees. The underlying idea is that coachees just want us to be present with them, listen to them, and understand them. In each of these, we can only offer so much: if we are honest, when are we really, fully present? When we think of it, how much else is going on for our coachee that we miss in our listening? And how often do we not realize the limits of our understanding, our failure to truly empathize with all kinds of biases and unhelpful assumptions creeping into our comprehension? But at least we can try. We can have the right intention to support, to be curious and to want to find out more, and to truly empathize as much as we can with our coachees. That honest intention will take us far and will be recognized at some level by our coachees.

Now for the third of these, our willingness to understand. Coachees often say that what they are looking for is new understanding, new realizations and insight (De Haan *et al.*, 2010). The emphasis on realization and insight has a very long tradition in helping conversations. At the very beginning of the history of helping conversations, Breuer and Freud (1895) emphasized understanding and insight. The founder of non-directive therapy, Carl Rogers (1961), did not fundamentally challenge Freud's hypothesis about the mutative power of understanding and insight. Rogers just insisted that such new insight should come from within ('internal locus of evaluation') and can be fostered by empathic understanding. Cognitive and behavioural psychologists also recognize the importance of insight, albeit that they aim to correct 'distortions' of reality based on 'erroneous' premises by supplanting them with more realistic cognitions and insight (Beck, 1975). All three main schools of psychotherapy (psychoanalytic, person-centred, and cognitive-behavioural) therefore agree on the importance of (mutative, realistic, actionable) *insight*. In newer approaches, such as mindfulness in coaching (Passmore and Marianetti, 2007), we see the same interest in awareness and insight as a potentially crucial ingredient.

This chapter gives an overview of the research into the 'reflective self', an idea that has the power to integrate and re-focus schools of thinking about insight and which holds the promise of:

1 offering a hypothesis regarding 'coachability';
2 providing the first empirical backing for the age-old hypothesis that 'just' understanding might be effective in helping conversations; and
3 anchoring these empirical results in well-researched attachment behaviour.

The idea of the 'reflective self' or 'psychological mindedness', 'mentalization', or 'empathy' has had immediate appeal for many coaches (see, for example, Grant, 2001; Van der Loo, 2007; Drake, 2009). This might be because it not only gives a hypothesis regarding an important 'active ingredient' in helping conversations, but at the same time proposes a new formulation of 'good' outcome. The hypothesis of reflective-self function brings together not just a vast array of theory: attachment theory, psychoanalysis, neuroscience, and cognitive psychology,[2] it also brings together the partners in coaching: coach and coachee – suggesting a single, quantifiable ingredient of coaching that is wholesome for both. Wholesome in the sense that the coachee develops his or her security in relationships or attachment styles, while at the same time the executive coach develops his or her 'reflective self' as a helpful way of holding the coachee in mind. In addition, there is the appeal of quantitative research: the fact that this notion has come out of quantitative empirical research which can be and has been replicated. The rare appeal of this function of the mind is seldom touched on in the coaching literature. Nevertheless, it is important to understand both the genesis of the concept and the claims that can be made regarding its role in the effectiveness of coaching.

4.1: A secure base for empathy: attachment

Psychology as the science of mind and behaviour is the study of the single most complex 'system' that we know – the human central nervous system – and how it interacts with its environment. We have very few definitive and demonstrated facts about the psyche. Clearly, this science is still in its infancy; and it is no surprise that most psychological texts occupy themselves with competing theories, models, and perspectives on mind and behaviour. Nowhere is this more apparent than in the field of psychotherapy, which deals with the treatment of mental disorder by psychological means and therefore mostly with higher-order functions of the mind, such as personality, mood, communication, meaning-making, adaptation, and lifestyle. This state of affairs makes it all too easy to forget that there have indeed been many valuable and universally recognized contributions in psychology, which turns some parts of psychology into a 'proper' empirical science.

Freud, as a neurologist, thought that ultimately psychology as an empirical science would base itself on our understanding of the inner workings of the central nervous system, i.e. on neuroscience or 'brain science' (Freud, 1915b). He was less interested in another nineteenth-century development, pioneered by Fechner (1860), Wundt (1862), and von Helmholtz (1867), which focused on the study of 'psychophysical' evidence, evidence from the interaction between the mind and its environment(s). These internal and external, intrapsychic and interactional perspectives are still very much alive today, and both inform the field of executive coaching (see Rock and Page, 2009, for links between brain science and coaching and De Haan, 2021, for links between quantitative experiments and coaching).

It should be noted that this distinction between the interpersonal and the intrapsychic is nowadays, to an extent, a difference in emphasis. Some modern psychophysical studies measure brain activity concurrently and modern brain research looks at the central nervous system *in vivo*, i.e. while it interacts with its environment in the shape of 'controlled stimuli'. As in any living system, internal phenomena and external interaction patterns are intimately related and mutually dependent. Findings from both fields should eventually complement and support one another.

In order to get close to the modern conception of understanding and empathy in helping conversations, it is helpful to go back to Bowlby's important work on this matter. According to Bretherton (1985, p. 14), John Bowlby made two distinct and important contributions to psychology. The first contribution is the hypothesis of *attachment* as a core, biologically based instinct, which informs behavioural and motivational drives. The second is that he theorized those individual differences in the functioning of this 'attachment system' are linked to individual *working models* of self and others (see also Bowlby, 1969, 1973). Both these ideas received much more support when they were operationalized in reliable psychophysical tests, which led to further quantitative study. Here is a brief summary of these tests.

The first hypothesis was operationalized by Mary Ainsworth in 1978 with her design of the 'Strange Situation' experiment, a 20-minute experience for caregiver and child where the caregiver and a stranger enter and leave the room, recreating the flow of familiar and unfamiliar presences in the child's life. The Strange Situation experiment has reliably demonstrated three different attachment behaviours (Ainsworth *et al.*, 1978):

1 *Secure attachment.* The behaviour of the child during separation and upon reunion is characterized by confidence that the caregiver will be comforting.
2 *Avoidant attachment.* The behaviour of the child during separation and upon reunion is characterized by lack of confidence in the caregiver's availability, and thus by attempts to control or downplay emotional arousal and to show disinterest and reduced distress.
3 *Ambivalent attachment.* The behaviour of the child during separation and upon reunion is characterized by attempts to exaggerate or up-regulate affect in order to secure the caregiver's attention.

Later, Main and Solomon (1990), upon reviewing hundreds of hours of videotape of Strange Situations, were able to add a fourth attachment style, which may accompany any of the other three attachment behaviours, i.e. an attachment behaviour which can be demonstrated in parallel with the other attachment behaviours:

4 *Disorganized attachment.* The behaviour of the child during separation and upon reunion is characterized by seeking proximity in strange and disoriented ways, such as backwards approach, freezing, staring, and moving sideways.

Bowlby's second hypothesis above was supported in the work of Mary Main and collaborators, when they created the 'Adult Attachment Interview' (AAI; George *et al.*, 1984), which provided a reliable way to assess an adult's internal representation of attachment. The interview consists of a prompted narrative about childhood, including sensitive issues such as separation and loss. The protocols are transcribed and classified according to a coding system that privileges narrative style over content. The dimension of *coherence* (comprising substantiation of evidence, succinctness yet completeness, relevance to the topic at hand, clarity and orderliness) can be associated with:

1 Attachment security (the 'Autonomous' classification): high coherence about attachment.

Protocols with low coherence can be ordered in three patterns:

2 'Dismissing': idealizing or derogatory about attachment.
3 'Preoccupied': angry or passive about attachment.
4 'Unresolved': unresolved in relation to loss and abuse.

These four classifications map both conceptually and intuitively onto the four attachment categories arising from the Strange Situation. Moreover, AAI classifications are stable over several months and independent of various IQ ratings, autobiographical memory, social desirability, interviewer effects, and general discourse styles. In fact, both instruments have high validity and high (short-term) reliability, so experiments soon began to test empirically how well they predict each other. By 1995, it was established through an 18-sample meta-analysis that the caregiver's AAI narrative coding predicts the infant's Strange Situation response to a considerable extent (Van IJzendoorn, 1995; for a more recent study covering parents and infants at different time points, see Waters *et al.*, 2018). Moreover, Van IJzendoorn *et al.* (1995) have shown that support interventions aimed at changing the mother's sensitivity or attachment representation have a significant positive effect on infant security as measured by the Strange Situation.

As Drake (2009) has pointed out, coachees' narratives in coaching can also be appreciated in terms of their internal coherence, particularly as that will give the coach a 'window' into the wider narrative patterns in their work and life. Drake continues by suggesting that 'the level of coherence in coachees' stories – about the past, present and future – often reflects leaders' own attachment experience and the way in which they lead and interact with others at work' (p. 53). It seems plausible that secure and autonomous leaders have more coherent life stories, and that insecure leaders are more at a loss for coherence in their storytelling. Part of a coach's job is to study coherence, to look out for gaps in storytelling, and to inquire thoughtfully into the relationships between aspects of coachees' narratives.

Both Ainsworth's Strange Situation and Main's Adult Attachment Interview made reliable empirical research possible in the field of attachment, which will be discussed next, including Fonagy's discovery of the importance of reflective-self function.

4.2: Empirical findings of attachment research

Here is a short summary of findings from attachment research, limited to conclusions which are well demonstrated and replicated by various studies.

The most impressive empirical contribution from attachment theory has to be confirmation that psychopathology is correlated from one generation to the next, or, in other words, that there is convincing evidence now that some psychopathology gets passed on from generation to generation. There are clear, demonstrable correlations between the attachment patterns described by the mother during the AAI and the attachment patterns that can be found in the infant with the help of the Strange Situation experiment. The correlation can be demonstrated when the AAI is taken contemporaneously with the toddler's Strange Situation experiment (Van IJzendoorn, 1995; this has a combined effect size of $d = 1.06$, a strong effect); when the AAI of each parent is collected and coded before the birth of the child and the infant's Strange-Situation classification is done at 12 and 18 months (Steele *et al.*, 1996); and also when a parent's AAI coding is correlated with the child's security of attachment measured 5 years previously (Main *et al.*, 1985). Hence, the strong concordance that is found (between 75% and 80% on each pair of attachment categories), persists in both directions and over at least a 6-year time gap. These findings lend support to Freud's hypothesis (Freud, 1940) of the intergenerational spread of psychopathology.

Another notion of Freud's that has been supported by attachment research is that of the 'repetition compulsion' (Freud, 1920), i.e. the suggestion that those who do not actively remember and come to terms with their past are destined (or more likely) to repeat it. Fonagy *et al.* (1994) demonstrated that relatively deprived mothers had a much higher chance of securely attached infants if their capacity to reflect on mental states (mentalization), operationalized by reflective-self function, was higher.

Interestingly, these findings can also be linked to other psychophysical findings, namely those coming from meta-analyses of psychotherapy outcome studies. These meta-analyses have demonstrated a surprisingly small contribution by the specific model or psychotherapeutic approach, and are much more supportive of so-called 'common factors' (factors common to all approaches, as suggested by Rosenzweig, 1936; see Wampold, 2001) as the 'active ingredients' in psychotherapeutic work. One of these common factors is the opportunity that all psychotherapy offers to reflect on and think through challenges, symptoms, and complaints. Investigators have distinguished six broad 'areas of commonality' among the various approaches to psychotherapy: relationship-related factors; coachee-related factors; therapist-related factors; change-related factors; structure-related factors; and external factors outside therapy (Grencavage and Norcross, 1990). Obviously, secure attachment, coherence, and reflectivity are common factors in the empirical sense understood by general outcome research. Fonagy and Bateman (2006) even claim that this may be *the* core active ingredient of all psychotherapy: 'It is possible that psychotherapy in general is effective because it arouses the attachment system at the same time it applies interpersonal demands which require the patient to mentalize.'

'Secure attachment' is often linked with 'successful containment' (Bion, 1963) and is then taken by many as a measure of 'psychological health'. It is important to point out, as Fonagy (2001) does, that the evidence linking early secure attachment with a healthy or balanced life is not strong. One needs to be reminded that the demonstration of the predictive power of any psychological context or relationship over the course of decades is extremely tenuous and rarely achieved.

4.3: Emergence of 'the reflective self' in attachment

Joyce McDougal (1978) has said that in early childhood the 'mother functions as the baby's thinking system'. This notion of mothering as a containing, mirroring, and reflective activity is prevalent throughout the psychoanalytical literature[3] and lies at the root of the idea of the *reflective self*.

The reflective-self function is an operationalization of the capacity to 'mentalize' (Brown, 1977) or the capacity for 'metacognition' (Main and Goldwyn, 1990) or 'psychological mindedness' (Appelbaum, 1973; Grant, 2001). The reflective-self function measures an individual's *quality of understanding of another's intentionality* and is measured on a 9-point Likert scale (Fonagy *et al.*, 1998). The measure confounds understanding of self and other, so it applies in equal measure to reflections on one's own and someone else's intentionality. The measure also confounds 'true' understanding and 'plausible' understanding, or in other words 'accurate' and 'habitual' modes of understanding, as no measure for 'objective' or 'shared' understanding is introduced (Fonagy *et al.*, 1991).

Reflective-self function is not the same as empathy, although empathetic understanding has to be based on this capacity. Reflective-self function is more fundamental and refers to the capacity to understand strivings and intentionality within oneself or within another, whereas empathy refers to the understanding from within, the capacity to feel what another person feels, i.e. to become sympathetic or 'in tune' with those feelings oneself.

Reflective-self function is also not the same as mindfulness (which we looked at in Chapter 2), although mindfulness can be seen as a capacity that reflective-self function is based on or draws from. Mindfulness is a spiritual faculty in Buddhism which amounts to an attentive awareness of the reality of things and is therefore very close to being psychologically awake ('Buddha' literally means 'he that is awake'). Mindfulness therefore extends from understanding psychological facts to natural phenomena and even spiritual experience. Nevertheless, mindfulness frequently refers to one's own bodily functions, sensations, feelings, thoughts, perceptions, and consciousness itself – in which case it would appear akin to reflective-self function.

To summarize:

1 *Mindfulness* can be seen as attentive awareness of what is going on in the present moment.
2 *Reflective-self function*, within mindfulness, can be seen as being aware of what is going on in the minds of self and others, in the present moment.
3 *Empathy*, building on reflective-self function, can be seen as being aware of and sharing in states of mind as they occur to another person, in the present moment.

Peter Fonagy went on to explore cases of apparently diminished reflective-self function and described the slow and arduous growth of reflective-self function in psychotherapy – see, for example, Fonagy and Target (1996, 2000), the first of which is a case study with a 4-year-old girl described as resistant to the development of reflective-self function, and the second of a severe borderline-personality-disorder patient in her mid-thirties.

This work led to the development of 'mentalization-based treatment' (MBT) as a treatment for borderline personality disorder. In MBT, the aim of the psychotherapy becomes the development of reflective-self function (see Fonagy and Bateman, 2006). The therapist is encouraged to focus on the patient's current mental state with the aim of building up reflective-self function. The therapist is asked to avoid situations in which the patient talks of mental states that he or she cannot link to subjectively felt reality; and the inevitable enactments over the course of the treatment are not interpreted in terms of their unconscious meaning but in terms of the situation and affects immediately before the enactment (Fonagy and Bateman, 2006). In other words, the therapist uses their own mentalization to further the patient's mentalization, and the aim is not so much deep understanding as it is the recovery of mentalization.

Another later development is the hypothesis that the biological need for secure attachment is precisely the development of reflective-self function as a 'representational system that has evolved, we may presume, to aid human survival' (Fonagy *et al.*, 2004), which therefore claims that the prediction might be both ways: reflective-self function predicts secure attachment *and* secure attachment begets mentalization.

These ideas around reflective-self function and mentalization have been taken up in adult psychotherapy, where attachment styles are considered a metaphor for working-alliance patterns and therapy is conceptualized as a 'corrective emotional experience' that may help to develop and establish attachment security and reflective-self function (Wallin, 2007).

4.4: Application in coaching practice

Attachment research seems to be particularly useful in coaching practice, as it helps us to model core relationships which are bound to enter into the coaching relationship. First, through the phenomenon of transference (Freud, 1905; and see Chapter 3), core formative relationships may enter the coaching setting. Second, the working alliance as perceived by the coachee has long been shown to be an important ingredient for effectiveness (Graßmann *et al.*, 2020). In other words, the coaching relationship has important precursors as well, which will enter the room through the phenomenon of positive transference, 'which is the true motive force of the patient's collaboration' (Freud, 1940). Third, since the 1950s comparisons have been made between the presence of the helper in helping conversations and the presence of the first caregiver. In the concepts of a 'holding environment' (Winnicott, 1965) and of a 'container' with 'reverie' (Bion, 1963), we have very similar ideas that link the maternal environment (or relationship) to the coaching environment (or relationship). In other words, the helping relationship from a 'real' (non-transferential) perspective has also been intimately linked with the earliest core caring relationship. Fourth, and not least of all, attachment relationships will invariably be the topic of coaching sessions, as coachees will bring accounts, thoughts, and concerns about both past and present intimate relationships. In summary, 'attachment' seems to figure at a multitude of levels in coaching, namely within (1) transference patterns, (2) positive transference or the working alliance, (3) the 'real' relationship, and (4) the content of the sessions.

One obvious area of application of attachment research is around what happens between coachee and coach as a result of beginnings, endings, breaks, or alterations in the setting such as rescheduling, room changes, time changes, or sponsor changes. In my experience, some of the most emotionally charged moments have occurred around breaks and interruptions. Approaching termination, the definitive 'break' in coaching, raw emotions may recur. Many examples of what happens around breaks and ruptures in coaching have already been documented (Day *et al.*, 2008), and it is clear from analysis that mentalizing in the form of shared reflection about what is going on makes a crucial difference to the outcome of those ruptures.

Drake (2009) has proposed five 'narrative strategies' for building a strong attachment relationship in coaching conversations:

1 Provide coachees with a sense that the coaching sessions are like a safe haven and a secure base from which they can explore issues which affect them.
2 Use the rapport that is gained to help coachees take a good look at how they currently relate to others and reflect on these relationships, and how they might be biased.

3   Use the coaching sessions as a laboratory for the study of coachees' attach-
    ment-related behaviour and for the experimentation with new, more secure,
    relational patterns.
4   Help coachees to reflect on how their working models and their subsequent
    interpersonal patterns are rooted in childhood experiences with primary
    attachment figures.
5   Position yourself as a coach as a 'good enough' and available caregiver to
    help coachees experience new attachment orientations and behaviours.

Here are some examples from my own practice which show attachment styles
and the reflective-self function at work. Identifying details have been disguised.

Case example 4.1

*An investment manager in a global retail and investment bank comes to coach-
ing following a number of performance conversations where it was suggested to
him that his readiness for promotion to the next level would be contingent on
improving his work relationships and that executive coaching might help to prepare him further. On the first phone call, a meeting was arranged and another
four-way meeting with his boss and the HR director followed. In the first weeks
of this coaching contract, the senior banker sent performance-related and
multi-party-feedback documentation to his executive coach, and he rang his
coach several times on his mobile phone. His motivation seemed high. Objectives were established around growing his self-confidence and his clarity as to
what type of behaviour his senior team was expecting from him. Session 5,
however, was postponed and then cancelled. Despite time spent together and
veritable openness in sharing sensitive material, the sessions still felt aloof and
as if lacking in rapport. The formal contract of six sessions was not completed.
A certain distance and formality were present in all the sessions. When the
coach raised this (perceived) aspect of the relationship, the coachee appeared
puzzled. In the notes from the fourth session the coach concludes that she only
appeared to be 'telling' the coachee about their relationship and about other
relationships, without there being much real dialogue between them.*

Reflection: It was one of those assignments with a coachee who was 'sent' by
others, doesn't really know what to expect of coaching, and finds it quickly
irrelevant as he fails to see a clear link between the 'off-line' conversations and
his personal objectives. Coachability proves low and this is partly due to a limited capacity to mentalize oneself and one's (working) relationships. Or perhaps there was a withdrawal from the reflective-self function for fear of
something painful emerging. The only strategy remaining for the coach appears
to be to focus on the coachee's reflective self directly, however hard it may be
to make a change at that level. In other words, and in retrospect, the coach
could have confronted the coachee more in terms of his limited representations
of his working relationships, including the one with his coach. In my experience,

this state of affairs occurs regularly in coaching relationships: intentions are on the whole positive, pressure and willingness to change are high, but shared moments of psychological understanding are so few and far between that the outcome is poor.

Case example 4.2

Eamonn was a dean in a university. He was very agitated during the first session. About a year ago he started working with Fiona as his faculty director. They shared the responsibility for managing the faculty between them. Their collaboration has been, in his words, non-existent. He thought he might be intimidating her, as an academic and sharp intellectual, but perhaps even more by being a conscientious planner, who turns up for meetings early and is very results-oriented. Fiona appeared to him tense most of the time. She cancelled most of their meetings or appearances together and avoided anything that had a semblance of a 'one-to-one' with him. She had other 'dotted line' responsibilities that appeared more important to her than her collaboration with Eamonn.

Now Eamonn was extremely dissatisfied with all of this, especially in view of the great changes that needed to be implemented. He talked about going back to Ireland, taking up a role in Dublin, where he thought there would be 'more respect' and a better salary. He seemed visibly agitated and eventually spoke about his profound doubts that anything could be done: 'Nobody can change the way Fiona works, nobody in our organization seems to take real responsibility for the changes that need to happen.' The coach jotted down the objectives for the work and suggested a higher frequency than he would normally do: once every three weeks.

The second session had Eamonn much more relaxed. He related successes in convincing some lead researchers and services that they would have to change their reporting structures. He reflected on his tendency to 'see the grass greener' on the other side of the road – and in grassy green Ireland – but he avoided the topic of 'Fiona' altogether. When the coach raised the topic in the second hour, he just said that nothing had changed and that Fiona had managed to completely avoid him these three weeks, and that he perhaps had been guilty of avoiding her too. He then expressed surprise that the next session would be in another three weeks' time: unlikely that he would have anything to talk about ...

During the third session Eamonn talked at length about how as a dean he tried to 'lead from the front' and how he was very good at taking on precisely those battles that he could win. Again, in the last half hour, the coach asked him about Fiona. Eamonn said Fiona and he were 'probably' working well together. They headed the faculty 'like two ships that pass each other in the night'. They turned up at different places, barely had a meeting together and if they had, Fiona was always happy that he took the lead and explained 'what had to be done'. He was better at that anyway. Then he mentioned he had always been good at this 'co-management' and that he could usually empower others, but somehow Fiona could not be reached. He felt intimidated by her behaviour: she always determined where she would be, and in what capacity. He did his best to work around that, and they never spoke about their relationship. He was very clear that she would not say anything sincere if he'd ask her about how they worked together, and that she would try to avoid the topic altogether.

The coach then asked if Eamonn had encountered any other 'Fionas' in his career – who she reminded him of? Initially he said 'nobody' and there were long silences. Suddenly, he related how recently at a party he had met an old fiancée, Cleona, Irish like himself. He was there with his wife and children. Cleona beamed into the room, looking like the successful business woman she was, full of 'executive polish'. She still had this powerful influence on him, this mixture of intimidation and attraction. She had always seemed aggrieved about something, 'hurt' by social gestures, as if someone had invaded her space – when in fact for Eamonn it was usually the other way round. She controls conversations he said, just like Fiona, who had been described to the coach in quite different terms up until now. For a good ten minutes Eamonn continued associating around his partner choices and similarities between Fiona and Cleona.

Here was a source of Eamonn's confusion, an intimidation and attraction that he couldn't escape. Eamonn started to understand the real 'infatuation' the two co-managers were having with each other, despite their coldness and distance. Another element that he discovered for the first time was the 'controlling' nature of their relationship, how he wanted Fiona to be at places where she wasn't, and how Fiona controlled him by citing stresses and other obligations.

Reflection: Here is a coachee with a well-developed reflective-self function and with high 'coachability'. In fact, he started the contract by naming two other positive experiences with a coach. He also felt quickly secure in the sessions. Nevertheless, it does take the coach and coachee some three sessions to get to the nub (or 'a' nub) of an issue and to arrive at reflections that matter to the coachee. At that point the coach enhances reflective-self function by inquiring more deeply into intimate relationships and asking for a parallel experience in the coachee's life. There appears to be a breakthrough when the coachee can begin to see this relationship in terms of others in his life, and in terms of other important relationships in his life. It then takes several sessions more to think about the consequences of this new insight and about how to improve or reflect differently on the particular working relationship. He takes up a much earlier suggestion by Fiona around 'mediation' with another consultant and this eventually proves to be very successful.

Case example 4.3

This consulting assignment began with a request to facilitate a consulting firm's away day, which would include the eight partners and the head of the secretariat, to mark the transition to a new managing partner. As so often with such events, both the wish to be entertained, to have fun, and to chill out, and the anxieties about the unspoken concerns within the firm and whether they would be addressed or even voiced, were palpable from the outset. The team of partners wished the main formal goal of the away day to be to achieve the frankness and fearlessness that they prided themselves on with their coachees, internally.

The facilitator asked the members of the group to bring something, an object, which spoke to their relationship to the company. They took their turns freely – however, in terms of group dynamics, the order turned out to be 'reverse seniority'. When finally, one before last, the old managing partner spoke, she read a poem, something like 'should I stay or should I go?' and said she wasn't clear about her next steps and might be leaving the firm. At that point, the head of the secretariat burst into tears, which prompted embarrassed looks from all present, eyes fixed to the ground. The outgoing managing partner seemed to be emboldened and she consoled her.

Their desire had been 'how to be more frank with each other internally?' In the afternoon, the facilitator felt moved to challenge the assumptions in that statement: 'Yes, frankness and fearlessness may be what clients really need from you, i.e. they want to trust you will speak out and tell them what you see, preferably in a way that they can hear it. However, internally, you are a "polis", a citizenship, a political society, however small; and it is perhaps more important to be diplomatic than to be direct.' Then he showed concern: 'Directness may become the privilege of the more powerful in the group, the "prima donnas" who can both get all the attention and give all the direct feedback, but are themselves exempt.' At that precise point, when the phrase prima donna was mentioned, a shiver seemed to go through the group. There was something electrical in the air and the facilitator knew he had said something profoundly 'wrong' – or perhaps profoundly 'right', which amounts to the same thing. There was a long silence and then people started to debate an earlier point, but just weakly and without much interest. Soon someone called 'tea break' and nobody came back to what the facilitator thought had been a major incident. In fact, he still felt utterly rejected and excluded by the group.

During the tea break the facilitator felt tense, guilty, awkward, and disconnected from the group. This in spite of the fact that one of the partners approached him briefly to say that it was good that he had 'outed' the prima donnas. Coming back into the afternoon session he realized it was difficult for him to think and to reflect, and that he must try to hold the space as this might be true for others as well. He waited and asked how people were and after a while gathered his wits together sufficiently to say, 'I have the impression you do not want to talk about this, so this is not easy to say. I noticed what happened when I mentioned the words "prima donna". There was possibly some significance in what I said and this was perhaps itself one of those frank things that you find hard to say to each other. I think this somehow links with your anxieties around the new leadership of the firm and the dilemmas of your old managing partner about where to go next.' Gradually and without exploring the concept of prima donna much further, the group now returned to thinking about the challenges ahead and people felt freer to speak about their hopes for the future and for each other.

Reflection: Here is an example of how mentalizing can come under pressure in coaching assignments. We can identify such moments almost on a daily basis, such as when we are anxious about arriving late, about meeting a new coachee, or about what is going on in the conversations at hand; when we don't know what the issues are or how to respond, when we feel we have said something wrong or too challenging, and so on. To paraphrase Allen (2003, p. 105),[4] 'Of course, we coaches must mentalize to foster mentalizing in our coachees. It is through our own mentalizing that we engage our coachees in the process of mentalizing (and, conversely, through their mentalizing that they engage us in the process). We are in the same boat with our coachees. We, too, must rely on an intact social brain, a secure attachment history, and an optimal level of arousal. We bring to the session our development competence and our current state of mind (based on our feeling of security and level of arousal at the moment) which may or may not be conducive to mentalizing performance. We, too, know the "biology of being frazzled" as our prefrontal cortical functioning goes off-line, giving way to our limbic propensities to fight, flight or freeze responses.' Often competent coaching can be regained just by re-acquiring the space to think, by stepping back for a moment, and allowing our healthier and calmer reflections to touch on the issues at hand. Paradoxically, important new reflections can arise precisely from those moments where the reflective self is incapacitated, because there would have to be something new and important for it to have the power to knock us off balance.

4.5: Reflective-self function in coaching

What these examples have in common is a sense of 'plasticity', a sense that attachment and mentalization are gradually formed during coaching, and that it is possible to build up a secure sense in coaching even if security and understanding were hard to come by in earlier attachment relationships. This must be encouraging as it shows that 'history' does not equal 'destiny'; in other words, that coachees can achieve new outcomes and can learn to build up both a more secure sense of relationship and the reflective-self function that goes along with secure attachment. In this regard, it is perhaps encouraging that the intra-subject reliability or stability over longer time periods of the AAI is rather low (see Fonagy, 2001, Chapter 2).

We have to be wary, though, of attaching too much importance to the notion of reflective-self function, and that is because of its enormous appeal. As we have seen, attachment relationships can be relevant on at least four basic levels in coaching (transference, working alliance, 'real' relationship, and content of sessions). Secure attachment can in principle be linked with the reflective self on any of these levels. This makes the reflective self a highly relevant notion for the coachee on all levels and even for the coach in his or her approach to the coachee. Moreover, as has been argued by various authors cited above, the reflective self is not just seen as a measure of good therapy, as in mentalization-based psychotherapy, it can also be regarded as a measure of good outcome of helping conversations, as in the recovery or strengthening of mentalization. This makes the reflective self into a panacea and could lead to the false impression of 'snake oil', or perhaps in modern industrial terms, of 'lactic acid' (which is increasingly used to make food ingredients, cleaning products, and plastics that do no harm to the human body): a flexible, harmless agent of questionable curative value that is natural to the mind/body and sold as a cure for many ills, to be applied in the most generous of doses. Instead, I believe the main lesson to draw from the empirical results at this stage is the importance of investigating further the properties of reflective-self function or psychological mindedness and establishing empirically what contribution they can make to coaching.

4.6: Conclusion

Mentalization, or the idea that infants become independent subjects only if they are recognized as such, as beings with minds, intentions, and feelings of their own, by their caregivers – an idea which has been operationalized by reflective-self function (Fonagy *et al.*, 1991) – is a very powerful notion precisely because it goes back to the root of helping conversations. It is first and foremost a new and empirically quantifiable way of expressing that a coachee might get better when listened to and understood by a thoughtful other who can help him or her make sense of memories, experiences, and challenges, a phenomenon which is as old as psychotherapy itself (Breuer and Freud, 1895). This new operationalization of a classic phenomenon is also distinct in that it emphasizes the understanding of another's intentionality, which by definition includes self-understanding, the understanding of one's own intentions. There is a shift in emphasis and an increase in empirically reliable data concerning the understanding of self and others. It is fair to say that this development has afforded new importance to the idea of insight (or interpretation, or realization) in psychotherapy and coaching.

The history of helping conversations started with recognition of the importance of self-understanding for healthy functioning, be it through recollection (*Erinnerung*), interpretation (*Deutung*), or insight (*Aufklärung*; Breuer and Freud, 1895). Now with the empirical research on reflective-self function providing some evidence for a link with a particular self- and other-understanding – a possible connection between mentalization and psychological health, through a demonstrated correlation with secure attachment – this journey has come full circle.

We can see reflective-self function as the first operationalization of the Freudian notion of 'insight', just like 'working alliance' (Greenson, 1965) was the first operationalization of the Freudian notion of 'positive transference'. Both operationalizations led in the next decades to corroboration of the efficacy of the original idea: working alliance correlates with coaching outcome (Graßmann *et al.*, 2020), while reflective-self function correlates with secure attachment (Fonagy *et al.*, 1991). However, as we have seen in this brief overview, the evidence for reflective-self function as an active ingredient of helping conversations is still limited. It is not at the same level as that for working alliance.

Nevertheless, the psychophysical evidence-base of these and other original hunches of Freud has now grown to an encouraging degree.

In this way, executive coaches are beginning to get an idea of the ingredients that are potentially effective in coaching conversations. Working alliance, as a predictor of coaching outcome, may come first. And reflective-self function, as a function that correlates with secure attachment, could come second. If nothing else, this evidence can help coaches to be more confident in attending as fully as they can to reflection within the coaching relationship.

Chapter summary

In this chapter, I offer a 'model' for coaching, a grounding to base your empathy on. This is the model of attachment theory and the proven links between 'secure' attachment and a coherent reflective stance, sometimes called *mentalization*. This is probably the only 'coaching model' in the book, and even this model is not a coaching model. It describes our minds and our sense of security more than our approach or interventions during sessions and has much wider applicability than just coaching alone. Coaching models are often too coach-centric, and for that reason they do not play a great role in this book. Similar to Chapter 1, where it is shown that only in recent decades have the promises of the helping professions found real validation in empirical research, this chapter shows that our hunches about the helpfulness of simple contributions – such as being present, being responsive, listening and engaging – have recently found true validation in the attachment literature, which has been able to demonstrate what the absence or a disturbance of such a simple, loving presence can mean for babies and growing infants.

Notes

1   This chapter is an expanded version of an article which first appeared in the *International Coaching Psychology Review* (vol. 7, no. 2, 2012). © The British Psychological Society.

2   It is worthwhile to compare the cognitive psychology research on 'theory of mind' with the neuroscientific findings of so-called 'mirror neurons'. The former, theory of mind, has been defined by cognitive ethologists and psychologists as the ability to attribute mental states – beliefs, intents, desires, pretending, knowledge, etc. – to oneself and others and to understand that others have beliefs, desires, and intentions that are different from one's own (Premack and Woodruff, 1978). The latter, mirror neurons, have provided support for the neural basis of theory of mind. Research by Gallese and Goldman (1998) has shown that some sensorimotor neurons, which are referred to as mirror neurons, first discovered in the premotor cortex of rhesus monkeys, can fire when a monkey performs an action but also when the monkey views another agent carrying out the same task.

3   Fonagy (2001) points to the following precursors of the notion of the reflective self: *Bindung*, the psychological capacity of linking (Freud, 1911); the *depressive position*

as the recognition of hurt and suffering in another (Klein, 1945); the caregiver's *psychological understanding* of the infant in the emergence of the true self (Winnicott, 1962); *containment* as the capacity to transform internal events into tolerable and thinkable experiences (Bion, 1963); *mirroring* or mirror transference (Winnicott, 1967; Kohut, 1977); *psychological mindedness* (Appelbaum, 1973; Grant, 2001); and the idea of *mentalization* as the function that links drive excitations with internal representations (Brown, 1977).

4 Changing only the words clinician, therapist, and patient into coaching equivalents.

Part **B**

Tune in with love

In this part of the book, I want to write about the key struggle between fear and love and how this struggle plays out for coaches, and of course ultimately also for our coachees. It is about staying calm under pressure, maintaining your calm stance and loving care for your coachee. It is about meeting fear, pressure, and anxiety with love, acceptance, and patience, hence I will speak about 'love over fear' throughout this part of the book.

We have certainly already spoken about fear and love in the first part of the book, where we looked at meeting the anxieties of an uncertain, unknown situation with listening and inquiry (Chapter 2); then looked at the longings of frustrated love relationships in the past and their relationship with transference (Chapter 3); and finally looked at how early insecurity, confusion, loss and fear could be met with secure attachment and reflective-self function (Chapter 4). We have spoken about fear meeting love and love dispelling fears in these previous chapters; now we are going to follow this phenomenon into more specific challenges of coaching.

In this Part B, we will be looking at the coach's share and what more we can do as coaches in helping our coachees along. As is hopefully clear from the first part of this book, coaching is mostly an exercise in 'self-changing', so whether you like it or not, your coachee is doing most of the work, if not all of the work, with you just present as a supportive partner, as someone who cares and listens, who inquires and thinks alongside her or him.

In the next few chapters, we look at what it means to maintain that core stance of listening, engaging, and understanding throughout the work of coaching. As you sit with your coachee and branch out into a myriad of different co-created moments, how do you make sure that the centrality of your coachee remains paramount? How do you give your own response, here-and-now experience, or even a view (an assessment, 'feedback', a suggestion) on your coachee's requests and issues? How can you make use of psychometric instruments in the interest of your coachee moving forward? How do you use the full spectrum of coaching skills in such a way that you keep supporting the coachee's self-understanding and self-changing?

Essentially, this part of the book is about maintaining your coaching stance and maintaining your quality of care (listening, engagement, empathy) as you are meeting anxiety, both within yourself and within the coachee or coachee organization. You may become anxious to offer more than just your kind presence and to start advising or instructing your coachee. Or, you might meet commissioners who are anxious for the coachee to 'improve' and may be giving you unsolicited advice on what to work on or what outcomes are 'expected' by 'the' organization. In any case, you will encounter substantial anxiety at the beginning of all coaching meetings, which is why I start with a chapter about beginnings.

Chapter 5 looks at the earliest beginning of coaching work, which is a time riddled with anxiety, and argues for maintaining a kind, welcoming stance under pressure. The first moments of a meeting are particularly rich in information, which, if received well, can shed light on the future of the session.

Chapter 6 reviews the simple practice of talking about our impressions of our current relationship, under the label of 'feedback'. Such relational conversations can help to understand what is happening in our ongoing coaching relationship, and the simple act of engaging with it transforms our coaching in a very loving way. The chapter also reviews less helpful forms of feedback in helping conversations – those that are somehow exclusively reported to a third party.

An extension of feedback is the use of diagnostic instruments. Chapter 7 addresses the question: how can we make use of such additional information in a loving way? How can diagnostics support coaching and give both coachee and coach new inspiration? More fearful applications of diagnostics, such as when we artificially reduce uncertainty by creating a small number of artificial diagnostic categories or scales, are also discussed.

A still further extension and bigger impact of feedback is when this feedback has palpable consequences, such as in assessments, either for promotion or for qualification. Chapter 8 looks at an example of assessment for qualification, and our struggles to inject love into that process, which tends to be riddled with understandable fears. How can one keep to the purpose of assessment but still organize the process in the most loving way?

Finally, another extension into our common fate: the planet on which we live. Our own ecology is now increasingly giving us alarming feedback about how it is to live with humankind. This assessment is made in the form of a crisis where living conditions and biodiversity are suffering in real terms. How can we translate our understandable concern for the planet in our helping conversations and express our love for the planet in healthy ways? Chapter 9 presents some preliminary thoughts about a possible contribution, centred around the area of toxic and hubristic leadership.

The two main questions to you of this part of the book are:

1 Do you feel ready to meet 'fear', 'rupture', and 'anxiety' with 'love'? Are you ready to 'just' care and help?
2 Can you translate your obvious care, respect, and love for your coachee into more containing interventions during coaching?

There is a theme running through this part of the book, namely that fear rears its head in many forms in coaching work, and when we give in to that fear, we harden and narrow our vision, while we aim for control and certainty, or even for defence and attack. However far we go down this path, we become less of a coach and more of an expert.

5 Love over fear at the very start of coaching conversations[1]

5.1: Introduction: first impressions in coaching

Over years of observing consulting and coaching conversations, both my own and those of my colleagues (e.g. in group supervision or in accreditation practicums), I have been amazed by the phenomena occurring just at the time when consultant and coachee commence their session. I have come to believe that there are many quick wins for coaches right at the beginning of their coaching conversations.

Once we start paying attention to those first moments, which I now believe are rather fateful, we can notice a quick succession of slightly angular movements. A sharp intake of breath, a brusque movement forward or (perhaps more often) backward, a stretching of the spine, a widening of the eyes, and so on. One can see these movements as partly in response to the presence of the other, the coach or consultant.

In those very first moments of transitioning into a personal conversation, it looks as if the coachee gathers herself, demarcates and then occupies a space (a bit like we all do when we step into a busy elevator or a tiny shop). She focuses the mind and seems to look for the right 'amount' of contact with the coach. The phenomena are as diverse as the conversations that unfold – for example, sometimes eye contact is deliberately sought and sometimes the coachee starts looking away, perhaps to find the 'right' words more easily.

Those very words, the first words, are also pregnant with meaning, in my experience. Even if they are still about the coachee's journey to the session, the weather, the news, how we all are, or what has happened recently (or whether we have eaten, in some Asian contexts), they often prefigure something of what might come later. They give us insight into forthcoming issues and 'the organization in the mind' of our coachee (see Armstrong, 1997, who includes a beautiful vignette where small talk before a session turned out to be highly relevant for the material inside the session). Then, again, when the coachee does begin talking about what is at stake in this conversation, the issue or issues she wants help with, the very first words often carry most of the meaning. I have noticed many times that they do not just convey the core problem but its potential (route towards a) solution too.

In short, I have learned over time that first moments can give me a treasure trove of impressions as a coach, a wealth of information that I can use later.

These 'first impressions' help me to understand what this conversation might be about, at a deeper level. First moments help me to come up with relevant hypotheses and challenges for later in the conversation. Here is an example from a recent group supervision session.

Case example 5.1

An experienced executive coach from Central Europe presented the case of a young entrepreneur who was looking for a new challenge. Before she launched into her narrative, she leaned back on her chair with her head bent forward as if in a plea to the group, almost seeming to placate the group in some way, before apologizing for the quality of her English. Some members of the group immediately reassured her with gestures and a soft-spoken 'no problem'; she then took a deep breath to start telling us about her coachee. She told the group about several career challenges this coachee was experiencing, the most acute of which was the tension between his new-found career interest and several very lucrative offers related to his former business which he had founded. He seemed particularly inhibited and tempted by a peer group of other more successful entrepreneurs who were making those lucrative offers, though not in line with his new-found career aspirations. After much back and forth and helpful thinking, I suddenly remembered how the executive coach had begun the session and suggested a hypothesis. Is your coachee being held back by the need to apologize (to the other entrepreneurs) for the lack of success of his former business, the way you apologized for your English in this group? And how is that apologetic stance affecting his own development now? The coach confirmed that this need to apologize, this seeking of reassurance, was one of the main features of the case and something that did hold the coachee back.

It is important to remember that the beginning of a session, and the beginning of a 'case presentation', which will usually follow slightly later on, are rather anxiety-provoking moments and that the coachee is in transition during those moments. The coachee is only beginning to settle into a session. She may therefore reveal more than intended and may later want to roll back on what has been conveyed or asserted at the very beginning. In any case, the coachee will usually feel less in 'control' at the beginning than later in the session.

However, if we accept that the beginnings of conversations are important, for us as 'helpers', they are not always so easy to attend to. That is because those first moments are equally anxiety-provoking and transitory for us. We are often still trying to settle into the session, feeling the need to 'host' our coachees or put them at ease in some way, or we may be filled with curiosity – about how they have worked with the previous session's outcomes, for instance. All of these may make us less perceptive and more self-conscious, so that we may miss some of what might be the most revealing and important material of our whole session. Marc Gaudart has undertaken some excellent research into the anxieties that coaches feel ahead of their sessions and during the first moments of meeting (Gaudart, 2021).

5.2: What we know about first impressions

It is well known that first impressions of a person are quickly formed (see Swider *et al.*, 2016). They are also long-lasting and hard to reverse. Apparently, we need up to eight 'counterexamples' to abandon a first impression of a person (although active reinterpretation of earlier impressions helps; see Mann and Ferguson, 2015). However, in the special case of helping conversations, first impressions may mask what is more relevant. What matters here is not the 'first impression of the coachee' but the 'first impression of the nature of *this* helping conversation'. A first impression of the case or co-created relationship is not the same as our first impression of the other person. I believe that as coaches we need to relearn working with our first impressions. We need to focus more on the impressions of the case coming through and to make those impressions as conscious as we can.

The coachee enters the session like a narrator, a composer, or if you wish a 'jazz' improvisor of her own 'material' to be brought to the session. No matter how much the coachee prepares for this, it is impossible to start with the eventual 'theme' or 'motive' straightaway. There will have to be some build-up towards it, and that build-up, where the coachee is often searching and gathering courage, falling over her own words, reiterating and restarting, tells you much more about what goes on under the surface, the narrative behind the coachee's story. In other words, in helping conversations the coachee comes up with a chord, a motif, a theme, or a melody, first in a slightly 'raw' form, which has many less conscious but potentially important elements. Then she re-states, repeats, finds her way deeper into it, starts playing with it, modifying it, developing it.

However, in that process coachees are also *editing* their basic theme or request, partly to fine-tune and deepen it, partly to make it more acceptable, partly adapting it to what they perceive the coach's initial (visceral) response has been. The coachee usually makes their material less risqué in the process, less revealing, and less 'shameful'. This is why first impressions are so important for coaches. The editing or censoring process tends to bury some of what is at stake, in order to make it (seem) more presentable or mature, putting away or ignoring some of the real ambiguity, ambivalence, concern, or need for help that brought the coachee to the conversation in the first place. In my experience, this happens not just once but again and again, for every new theme, and for every new thought on the current theme. The sooner we can register some of what was initially there, the more work we will be able to do with the coachee. Here is an example from a colleague.

Case example 5.2

On that day I had two coaching sessions, and I had a business meeting before and was wearing a suit and a tie. The first coachee's initial words were: 'you are very professional today'. The same coachee told me, 30 minutes into the session,

> *that his boss had told him he needed to be a 'more professional manager'. This became a key topic in the coaching session and had been present already with the first words the coachee expressed. Yet it took us a long time to remember those words and identify them as key to the issues we were exploring.*

For me, this helpful, revelatory moment at the beginning of a session is by no means the only one. There are many later moments in a session, of similar import. The coachee may move onto a new topic, or the coachee may pause, to respond to something or to provide new information about the current topic. Either way, the 'opening gambit', the first few words of the coachee, will again normally be the place where we can intuit what the coachee might be most concerned about, or where the core ambivalences lie. The feeling in the room at that first moment will provide good access to any transference feelings of the coachee at the time – to the unconscious patterns that are brought into this session from other relationships such as the one that the coachee is talking about.

Freud wrote about many ways that we can intuit what goes on under the surface, in the unconscious: slips, lapses, automatic actions, mistakes, humour, jokes, and then of course the 'royal road into the unconscious': dreams. Yet here is another one that has not been written about so much and is readily available in every conversation: those opening moments when there is no smooth back-and-forth, as yet no full conversation. This is the freshest, liveliest, truest moment of any case presentation. In my view, this beginning moment can be treated the same way as dreams, later in analysis. It is well known among analysts that dreams lose some of their freshness and openness over time, as they have now been influenced by the analysis itself and become somewhat more conscious or guarded.

I have also noted that the more creative or 'weird' statements of the problem, with quotes, slips, metaphors, and even negations ('it is *not* this ...' – in those cases when a very helpful hypothesis might be that precisely 'this' is true yet at the same time hard to accept; see Freud, 1925) occur more in the first sentences of a coachee than later on in the session.

Harold Searles (1955) also noted how revealing those first few moments can be in supervision. Eric Berne (1966) suggested that the 'first three minutes' are key, by spending a whole chapter on them in his handbook of group therapy. There are other important phenomena to do with the start of the work or a session, such as 'pre-transference'[2] and 'building a working alliance'. Even if they fall in the middle of a session, time and time again those first few moments of a new coachee presentation give me food for reflection. And there is more: the fact that I am sitting there reflecting on those initial moments also helps me not interrupt my coachee too early ... which tells me that they are a 'quick win' in helping conversations in more ways than one.

Case example 5.3

When we arrived at the consulting room, I was held back a moment by the receptionist. When I then arrived in the room itself, my coachee had already installed himself, but in my chair. He said he wanted a 'change in perspective' and see the world from my place, but also that he felt apprehensive doing that. I sat down in the chair he had left for me and we started our 2-hour session. Most of the time was taken up by a situation he found himself in on a board, where he had recently accepted the role of non-executive Chair. One month into that job he was beginning to suspect that the business was experiencing cash-flow issues. However, every time he had inquired and even offered the services of a Controller from his own company, the overworked CEO had cancelled the meetings or said he was 'too tired'. We looked at the situation from many angles, but the conversation became really animated and I believe mutative when my coachee realized he had allowed the relationship with the CEO to 'reverse'. He was trying to look after the CEO and doing his bidding, and at the same time he was not being treated as the CEO's direct line manager at all. He made an association with the very first meeting in role of Chair, where the previous Chair had been present, and the CEO had said at the opening that 'this will now have to be only half an hour, because I have other meetings coming up'. He started to wonder aloud for the first time whether that was appropriate for the CEO to do, on meeting his boss for the very first time, to curtail a meeting that had been scheduled for an hour. A little later we made the link with the concrete 'reversal of roles' (or at least seats) in which we were working. After that, we could move into a very fertile part of the session where we realized other 'role reversals' in the career and life of my coachee, the new Chair.

When I look back on the session, I realize we were both experiencing the main issue well before we got into it; well before we started to have some understanding of it, right at the moment when we were both sitting down. The actual case had only been raised after nearly half an hour.

5.3: Application in coaching practice

In the above I have mainly spoken about revealing tensions and pressures for the coachee at the beginning of sessions and meetings, and what we can do with them as coaches. I have spoken little of all the many similar tensions that coaches will feel as they approach the session. Fortunately, there is a beautiful piece written about these tensions by my colleague Marc Gaudart (2021), where he explores the highly personal manifestations and how he has learned to work with them in his practice.

How can coaches come prepared for the many anxieties at the start of coaching relationships and coaching conversations, and at the same time not come prepared but be open to whatever comes our way? That is not an easy question, more like a riddle, and can only be answered by another riddle: 'expect the unexpected'. Can we try to settle and befriend our anxieties early on, and try to understand the nature of our fears? Sometimes the fear is that we will be rejected and will not survive the chemistry call, sometimes the fear is that we are overpowered by the leadership power that will meet us, sometimes the fear is more that we will be too overpowering, too sure of ourselves. In each of these cases, the fear is trying to teach us a subtle and highly preliminary 'lesson' about the situation at hand, something about the coaching relationship that we have not understood well and that we may understand only later.

I try to calm myself down, register what it is that I am fearing, and then notice what I see coming towards me – not to confirm my fears but in a deliberate act of curiosity. What is it the coachee raises first, what is their stance and their posture, is my coachee signalling control, unease, a wish to be somewhere else? What is being expressed in their first comments, something about the weather (mood?), something about the journey (the backstory to coaching?), something about the room or the virtual environment (safety?). We know the anxieties are there, so is the coachee putting on a brave face or is the coachee visibly anxious?

At most I can register the first movements and words and store them for a later point in our session. It is virtually impossible to open up the anxieties of meeting as we meet – unless this is one of the later sessions and we already have a good mutual understanding that things that happen between us can be voiced in coaching. Usually, it is more like biding my time and waiting for an opportunity to be reminded of those very first moments. Sometimes the start of a relationship is so meaningful or difficult that we can work with it straight-away. Here is a case example from my colleague Michael Carroll.

Case example 5.4

An executive had been referred by his HR director. He seemed to be willing to be coached. But when I met him, he was quite resistant and aggressive. Almost belligerently, he asked: 'So, what are your qualifications?' I knew this would be a key moment and my response mattered. I said: 'It must be quite frightening to be here. I'm not even sure if you want to be here. Let's spend a bit of time to look at why it seems to be difficult.' He kept on repeating his challenge, until he said, 'I really don't want to be here.' I think giving those professional qualifications would have been missing the point, really. We had ten successful sessions. He was actually quite depressed. He told me later he didn't like this at all, it shocked him (the word he used was 'frightening'). It was important for me to hold my own. It was critical in terms of the way we related. Another critical moment came later in the same session, when I said: 'You find it difficult to deal with emotions.' He was shocked, but remained intellectually curious, and that was perhaps what brought him back for another session.

Chapter summary

This chapter studies the anxieties and doubts that are present before and at the beginning of coaching relationships. These are argued to be also present at the beginning of every conversation and even at the start of a new topic within the coaching conversation. The meeting of these anxieties with a loving, containing relationship is part of the power of helping conversations. I give several examples of the phenomena that one might encounter at the beginning of coaching. I try to show how, if we can rise above our own similar anxieties and doubts, we can glean very helpful information from our first impressions or from the opening gestures of the coachee. Several examples of this valuable information, through either gestures or words, are explored. For this reason, I recommend in this chapter not to actively open the conversation but instead to be as passive as we can, provided we can do this in such a way that our passivity or silence does not become overly noticeable and thereby itself anxiety-provoking or figural in the encounter.

Notes

1   This chapter is an expanded version of an article which first appeared in the January 2020 issue of *Coaching Today*. © The British Association for Counselling and Psychotherapy.
2   First written about by Sechehaye (1956), who makes a comment on page 271 that is, in my view, relevant for the topic of this chapter: 'Whatever be the level at which we undertake to establish relationships with patients, we can be quite sure that they perceive our work long before any sign indicates that they are conscious of it', i.e. well before they even arrive at a session.

6 Love over fear in feedback: fearless directness[1]

2020 marked the one-hundredth anniversary of the word 'feedback' (Patent GB130432, 1919). During the hundred years of its existence, 'feedback' has delivered momentous gifts in terms of self-regulating systems, and it has arguably benefited human relations in the workplace. Healthy, direct, and sensitive feedback has led to many a 'role negotiation' (Harrison, 1976), which has strengthened leadership and collaboration. Nevertheless, I see important risks in some of the latest guises of feedback, partly driven by social media, which may turn out to be anything but healthy and generative.

A supportive relationship is one where a variety of issues can be raised, and where the relationship itself is open for reflection as well. As soon as we reflect openly on a relationship that we are in, we are practising 'feedback', we are 'feeding back' experiences of the relationship into the relationship. Through such reflections the relationship can learn and evolve, and genuinely become more supportive. We express love for the relationship by being open to notice and reflect on happenings in the relationship. In contrast, the more fearful thing to do is to 'report on' the relationship, reflecting on the relationship with others, in the hope, for example, of changing something without having to face it with the person in the relationship.

For me, love and fear in helping relationships are clearly distinct. Love resides *within* the relationship: noticing, speaking its truth, reaching out to the other person; fear, on the other hand, is *outside*, i.e. about the relationship: taking our experience elsewhere, reporting on it, offering feedback on the relationship to other parties such as the consulting organization or the commissioner. We can grow fear by continuing to 'triangulate' in this way, involving third parties, nudging them to help out in this relationship. And we can grow love by speaking our minds to one another and by finding new ways of sharing what matters to us in this relationship. As simple as that.

This chapter attempts to show how coaching relationships are changing in the modern world and how the potential for more fear in helping relationships has grown. It speaks out against the checks, balances, and controls that are placed on coaching even during the assignment itself, and it tries to show that however fancy the feedback technology is, it is not always an improvement on older, more direct ways of doing things.

6.1: What is feedback in human relations and how does it work?

The word 'feedback' is exactly a century old, but it is constantly developing and acquiring new meanings. Its origins are in the earliest discoveries of electrical engineering. It appeared first on the patent of a transformer that consisted of a 'feed back circuit' (Bennett, 1979). Non-electrical applications are centuries older: think of the float valve we still use in toilets or the 'fly-ball governor' that ensures a constant amount of steam in the cylinders of a steam engine. Later applications include thermostats, amplifiers, oscillators, and logical circuits. The sound distortions that are created by feeding loudspeaker sounds back into amplifiers were used by electric guitarists, Jimi Hendrix among them. Spectacularly creative results can be achieved by returning the output of a system back into its input signals – and this is also true in coaching.

The human mind itself is full of feedback loops. For example, we use gravitational and optical feedback to stay upright and to keep our eyes fixated on a moving object. When you know that there will be a feedback loop in the future, you will adapt and mitigate your behaviour in anticipation. At work this is a very helpful property of feedback: you anticipate that the quality of your product or service will be checked and therefore you make a greater effort to stay within specifications and to delight your customers. However, when part of your service offer is to 'challenge' or 'confront' existing thinking in some way, your service may initially be less welcome to your coachee, which means that feedback loops could actually impoverish and reduce your service level, as I aim to show here.

6.2: The best use of feedback in coaching relationships

Directness and openness are obviously important in the coaching relationship. One could argue that a coaching session is suffused with feedback from beginning to end. The coach comes alongside you and reflects on what you offer to the session, openly sharing with you how this comes across. Similar to other helping, teaching, and consulting professions, coaching works in large part through 'feedback' from the coach, and the days when coaches or therapists were advised to be a 'blank screen', neutrally absorbing but rarely responding to what they receive, are long gone.

The strongest forms of feedback for me are those inescapable moments that Daniel Stern has called 'now-moments' or 'moments of meeting' (Stern, 2004): episodes where both coach and coachee are aware of their responses at the same time as they are meeting, which includes an awareness of each being aware. These have also been called moments of 'reflexivity' or of 'relational' coaching (De Haan, 2008a), where coach and coachee are explicitly looking at their own interaction and making sense of that interaction, exploring what is happening right now, between them, while they are engaged in their encounter. These 'relational' moments provide the essence of good feedback: coach and coachee together form a living collaboration that is being reviewed by each of them independently and together. This review is made explicit and thus forms a starting point for further, emergent conversation, which completes the feedback loop.[2]

Relational feedback is open and explicit, and it critically, consciously reviews the conversation or meeting, up to that point, so there is a degree of challenge as well as of mutual recognition and reinforcement. The 'relational' feedback loop is only sustained when both coach and coachee can allow and bear a rupture, i.e. the emergence of a fresh insight into their relationship. In my experience, this kind of in-the-moment feedback only occurs in the presence of high trust, psychological safety, and openness to learning.

Case example 6.1

A coachee began speaking about a colleague who had recently joined his team, and whom he found extremely unreliable and somewhat manipulative at work, e.g. he avoided many tasks and meetings. My coachee reported a kind of fascination with this person and described him as a 'train wreck waiting to happen'. As we spoke about this for almost an hour, I began to realize that his issue was well outside the bounds of our contract and that I kept on asking questions because I too felt a fascination hearing about someone who pushes work boundaries to such an extreme. When I shared my 'parallel' feelings with my coachee, there was a real 'touché' moment where we both felt caught at prying into this 'train wreck' of a person and his machinations. This then helped my coachee to see for the first time that he might have a responsibility for raising the disloyalty with his colleague and possibly also with their mutual line manager.

6.3: The worst use of feedback in coaching relationships

The single worst use of feedback is also very clear to me: when feedback is undertaken in a roundabout way, delivered from outside the relationship it refers to. Unfortunately, this roundabout way of delivering feedback is increasingly common today, exemplified by the encroachment of the NPS ('net promoter scores') on all service relationships. NPS are the old way of collecting feedback after a session, through 'happy sheets', becoming sublimely automated: compared and collated with other data about the helping relationship.

Case example 6.2

In modern business schools, NPS ratings are ubiquitous, sometimes occurring every hour of a programme, i.e. fully automated: using the mobile phones and

laptops of participants.[3] The attained sum revenue of various (e.g. MBA) pro-
grammes and services bear a direct relationship to the ratings. More generally,
published ratings and rankings of business schools, which are just one form of
'offline' or roundabout feedback, are directly proportional to the profitability of
those institutions. As a result, it has become evident that participants are now
very much more pampered and pleased, and only rarely challenged. I am aware
of several major postgraduate masters programmes from top-ranked institutions
where Fail marks have been weeded out, so that participants can literally never
do anything wrong and, according to their marks, do not have much left to
learn. In return, the institutions hope that participants will not fail faculty either
and that they rate faculty highly throughout. However, it is no coincidence that
in those same programmes which shall remain unnamed, participants also regu-
larly appeal or request more evidence if they have 'only' received a Low Pass
mark. They know that is the lowest mark possible and are as upset as if it had
been a Fail. In such institutions, faculty members are increasingly being trained
by their institution on how to best request the in-class NPS so that it has the best
possible outcome for their school. Instructions in class are as follows: 'Listen
everyone, results are aggregated and compared in a highly competitive busi-
ness-school world, so nowadays scores from one to six are basically giving a
"negative", while sevens, eights, and beyond are considered "neutral" scores, so
if you are satisfied and you would like to recommend us to others, please mark
a nine or even better, a ten, on your surveys. Please make sure you use those
high marks throughout on the questions. And please don't rate us but speak
with us if your rating is anything lower than an 8.' At that point feedback is
requested live in class (after all, class ratings produce a better score than the
more truthful measurement a week or so after class).

The first and biggest problem with NPS is that it opens up backchannels. Feedback and evaluation instruments take the feedback outside of the relationship that matters, i.e. outside the relationship between learner and coach/teacher. This triangulates the relationship and offers the coachee (and in some cases, the coach) a pathway to a third party (O'Neill, 2000): the institution or line manager of the coach. Coachees can then safely review their service outside of the relationship that the review is about, and they will celebrate, gossip, and complain to the institution rather than the coach. Of course, such a third party should always be available, but in my view only as a last resort, such as when the coachee feels in some way oppressed or ill-treated within the coaching relationship. Usually, this is not the case at all, and then it remains much better for the coachee to raise issues directly with the coach.

In many of our own development programmes at Ashridge, we offer participants ample time for review in the teaching space itself, at least half an hour in the mornings and another reflective session in the late afternoon. This is a 'live review' with the group, which we hope gives valuable insights to everyone about how the learning community is doing, offering a challenging but relational way of reviewing the live relationships in the room. This may require some new learning in itself: the challenging nature of open and direct feedback means it is unusual in many workplaces.

Another problem with NPS is that it introduces the premise that good learning relationships should always be 'positive' and score highly on the instrument. In other words, it introduces an expectation that learning is fun and should 'feel good'. Coachees with this mindset may be adversely affected by a rupture in the coaching process or in critical evaluations as part of a 360-degree process, as if there is something 'wrong' with the process itself, or with them. Following from this difficulty of experiencing a rupture, coachees often respond as if something needs 'fixing'. In fact, we should *expect* important learning to be painful, something Edgar Schein captures in his idea of personal learning as a heroic battle between two existential and co-existing fears: the 'learning anxiety' and the 'survival anxiety' (Schein, 1993). From this perspective, automated systems of feedback will only create more defensiveness against learning, and a culture of 'likes' imported from social media, which strengthens the pretence (and fallacy) that life – and learning – *should* be fun and eminently like-able. Personally, I want the best feedback scores but only from those I rate, those who actively and vulnerably participate. At the same time, I prefer the worst feedback scores from those who haven't taken responsibility, and I expect bland feedback to come from those who just consume my coaching or teaching. So, I choose to digress from the universal idea that feedback scores need to be optimized in helping relationships. In some cases, the desire for high polling numbers leads to an inversion of core values and is therefore particularly unhealthy.

Case example 6.3

Jennifer worked as a senior accountant and advisor in a global accountancy firm and had moved (part-time) into internal leadership development and leadership coaching within the firm. The firm's philosophy being what it was, closely aligned with Enlightenment ideas and rationalist, autonomy thinking, she found herself regularly using quantitative questionnaires to review her coaching practice. One day in supervision she expressed some concerns about one coachee's ratings, which seemed a little lower than those of her other coachees. At that point, her supervisor challenged her. 'These are the marks of your coachees. How are they relevant to you? What marks would you give yourself in your work with them?' Jennifer was initially baffled and took some time thinking about what to say ... 'Well, they are my clients so my marks would be the same as theirs. These marks tell me how much they, as the key beneficiary of coaching, have taken from our sessions.' After this, the supervisor spoke about her own practice: how on several occasions she would give herself excellent ratings although her clients' feedback had been poor; and vice versa, how on some occasions she received high praise but would rate herself much lower. The latter were occasions where she thought she had been 'coasting', or in other cases 'struggling' to come to a deeper understanding of the client's issues.

Jennifer remained quite shaken in her beliefs and returned to this conversation several times over the next years. She said it had opened her eyes both to think about who decides about the quality of her work, and about the limited availability or relevance of quantitative, hard feedback data in helping conversations. On a personal level, the conversation had liberated her to be more 'herself' in helping conversations: more authentic and freer in her interventions, worrying less about her client ratings.

A third problem with NPS is its potential for 'sales': business developers often pounce on high scores to sell more work to the same coachee or to others in the same organization. This may lead to mixed messages from the coach organization, a breaking of confidentiality boundaries, and a general impression of neediness on the side of the coach.

It is important to realize that, despite all helpful intentions, feedback systems can actually make learning *less* likely to occur, as it becomes more problematic and riskier to do, both for the coach and for the learner. To see how offline feedback is not only inhibiting for the coachee, bear in mind that feedback scores from coachees using NPS become public and part of the discourse at the coach's work, where back-office staff will administer the NPS and therefore see the scores. Next, client directors may take up any indication of below-perfect scores with the commissioning client. Working in such a context, coaches are bound to become less daring or experimental in their interventions. They will want to avoid rocking the boat and so engage more in flattery and other niceties. On the other hand, low performance ratings, open criticisms, and ruptures within the coaching relationship could be starting points for important learning, if the coaching itself is not foreclosed by third parties' scrutiny of ratings or diffused by the naïve expectation that learning should be fun and pleasant. The following case study demonstrates how an emphasis on feedback and evaluation can make the work unsafe for coaches and coachees alike.

Case example 6.4

As part of a leadership development programme for a large bank, participants could select a coach from a number of profiles. They were offered six sessions in total but the first three were taken up by various forms of programme-related exercises, written feedback, and psychometric reports. When by the fourth session the work could finally get started, it did not come as a surprise when one of my coachees asked me: 'So, tell me, what should I be working on today?' By then, expectations were that I would lead sessions and the coachee would be a kind of 'consumer' of my interventions. After the final session, the human resources department gave every coachee a call to report on the quality of the coaching. Again, no surprise that given this opportunity, coachees tried to find something critical to say about their coaching experience. Several of the coachees reported observations of the coaching as 'ineffectual' or 'meandering', that it did not seem the best use of their time, or that they did not really know what it was about. Many coaches did not feel safe to take on new coachees, in case their wider reputation might take a hit. Pressure on results, measurements of opinions, and roundabout feedback were emphasized to coachees and coaches from the very start, and the whole undertaking did not achieve much more than mirror the rather unsafe culture of the larger organization, without an opportunity for challenge or reflection.

More recently, some wider issues have emerged which are also linked to the rapidly increasing connectivity on our planet and the opportunities to provide personal feedback at lightning speed. The very serious nature of current 'online hate crime' is just one example. My concern though is not just the minor 'hate-crime' that one might facilitate by moving feedback online and making it anonymous and indirect, it is also the 'Tinder effect' of expressing your coach preference just by clicking a few buttons. Coaches are increasingly forced to have an online presence for which they have to pay an emotional as well as a financial toll. They need to align themselves with messaging boards and brokers such as CoachHub.com or BetterUp.com (or whoever will be the eventual 'market taker' in this crowded field!). The psychological damage that these practices can do is underrated and underappreciated because of the innovations that they offer. Nevertheless, it is extremely traumatic to see your highly personal and critical feedback (which you would love to receive in a safe relationship) being shared with all in your LinkedIn or Twitter feed. Equally painful to be rejected by a simple click on connective software as you cannot talk it through and benefit from whatever the underlying message is.

In the process of going along with the most modern platforms, coaches now have to expose themselves in text, photos, and even video, just to stay connected with hidden but potential clients, and they even have to pay a brokerage fee to do this. I have already encountered such cases where coaches did not choose to sell their pound of flesh as 'adult work', but their university or consulting firm, or even their professional network, still went along and signed them up anyway, so that they have no other option than to start engaging with the rather shallow and meaningless online video-conferencing beauty parades that emerge from the subscription.

Often, the brokers or management of coaching outfits have not really thought through what such online representation actually means, both psychologically and relationally. It just seems to them a good 'tool' to organize their services and 'grow' their market. Repercussions are immediate though, and very severe. Coachees can click on a single session without having met the coach and without any responsibilities or obligations on their side, after which they can shop around for their next coach. Such a light and fleeting commitment will not be without serious consequences for the results of their coaching. Not only will it have a real (denigratory) effect on both coaches and coachees, but more importantly, it will make it much harder for both parties to strengthen the coaching relationship and build reflective-self function (see Chapter 4), which we have seen are core to the helpfulness of coaching. Not to speak of the risks to confidentiality when third parties can access information about any coaching relationship, however short. Indeed, we increasingly see evaluations and 'Tripadvisor'-style feedback published online. Available with immediacy, at a click of a button, and impossible for the partners in the helping relationship to erase or amend online. I would predict that this will be the first time in the history of mankind where the professional implementation of helping relationships will itself lead to fear, trauma, and the need for after-care and help.

I do not want to come across as a rabid conservative, a Luddite, or a pessimist, but I do believe there is a real risk here of the ingredient of 'love' being confectioned out of the helping relationship. Let us all watch this space very closely and make sure that we uphold our profession and professional boundaries, so we can continue to serve our coachees in the twenty-first century.

6.4: Application in coaching practice: a way forward?

Is the coachee really the best person to say coaching is going well? Would that not be the coachee's line manager, direct colleagues; or rather the coachee's direct reports and customers, who all hope to see a more effective, perhaps more receptive leader? Modern technology may help to include these other stakeholders in the review, but that is not the same as when all interested parties come together *in person* to discuss the developmental effort. The latter is a much richer and fertile approach to sharing feedback, on account of the directness of the review and the opportunity to make links and reflect on the merits of findings and the impact of the sharing. A coach or other independent moderator can help to facilitate such a direct and open conversation.

I often feel we have not done so well in a session even though the coachee appears very satisfied. And vice versa: with a dissatisfied coachee I still see worthy moments in the session, and even in some of the dissatisfaction itself. There can be interesting echoes in not being satisfied, e.g. when the coachee is also less satisfied in other relationships. We have to allow for the possibility – not a rare possibility in my experience – that even a coachee who is not happy about the coach may still be benefiting from the coaching. Negative net promoter scores in cases of 'remedial coaching' may actually indicate that the process is working, not that it needs 'fixing'.

Other than simply no longer requesting written feedback, as I do after most of my own assignments, I have experimented with two other ways of making more satisfying use of feedback systems:

1 Undertake the 'objective' feedback process *ahead of* the intervention. Start your development programme by handing out the feedback forms. This inspires your coachees to consider that they themselves can really influence

the outcome and NPS feedback scores, more than anyone in the programme, including their coach or teacher. In my experience, coachees will become more responsible for the outcome if they can give the feedback in advance (this is sometimes called 'feedforward'; Block, 2008).

2 If you must, then only ask for NPS when service provider and coachee are becoming less dependent on one another, i.e. towards the end of their collaboration. Then take it away from the direct relationship with the coach and make it clear that the feedback is being requested in order to promote the service to others. This seems a much more ethical way of collecting feedback and will lead to the greatest number of 'likes', serving the underlying but usually hidden 'sales' purpose.

True, in-the-moment feedback is a relational phenomenon and a here-and-now intervention, something that has been shown to be a powerful and helpful phenomenon in the helping professions. Authentic, honest feedback facilitates coachees and coaches to do a live review of their work, which deepens their relational awareness and helps them to optimize the work they are doing together.

Case example 6.5

Simon had recently been promoted to a role just below the board of a large multinational company. He was recommended executive coaching, as were many others in his position. Perhaps he knew it would be difficult, because he postponed the coaching for nearly a year, and then he found it hard to choose the right coach and had to see many profiles. A 360-degree feedback process was recommended. I interviewed many of Simon's colleagues and stakeholders, asking their permission to share any comments and wishes for the coaching process directly with Simon (with attribution as I did not want to create a 'roundabout' feedback process). Although there were a lot of positives, there was also consistent feedback about his 'board presence': he was experienced as nervous, shy, and somewhat withdrawn in large meetings. This feedback, although recognized, did somewhat crush him initially and he became similarly agitated and tense at the coaching meetings. His behaviour at high-level meetings and conversations did not initially improve. We had to sustain a few difficult sessions, where I felt guilty for bringing the critical feedback and Simon could not see a path to change. How to rise to these expectations? During coaching, I gave Simon space to think through his anxiety, the roots of which were found in bullying experiences at school, among others. New coaching themes appeared, related to the ruthless politics and attempts at exclusion near the top of his organization. Finally, after some six sessions, another word that was regularly used for Simon in the initial feedback process – 'thoughtfulness' – helped Simon to integrate his feedback and become more forthright in meetings and presentations. After eight sessions we extended by another five and spoke again to Simon's manager, who was full of praise for him and the work.

It is important that coaching remains safe for coaches and coachees, even when third parties are invited to give their feedback and suggestions. Together they have to maintain a 'castle and battlefield' situation (Harrison, 1963), where profound support and profound challenge can be sustained at the same time. I would argue that all coachees can choose their coach with intent but also vote with their feet if their expectations are not being met, so it seems to me that the request for written evaluations of coaches has more cons than pros.

Chapter summary

This chapter is a celebration of the helpful phenomenon of 'feedback' in bio-logical systems, in coaching conversations, and in organizational collaboration. Feedback helps us in our understanding of how we are experienced by others around us, and it pushes us to adapt even better to their needs. In coaching, we use relational interventions to let our coachees know our current experience of them or of our being with them. These are very impactful, inescapable, and transformative interventions, which have the additional advantage of increasing liveliness within our sessions. The chapter gives some examples of such best uses of feedback as I have known them. Furthermore, I warn against taking the directness and immediacy out of feedback. In complex systems and technical applications, it is often straightforward and entirely unproblematic to relay the feedback via other nodes or subsystems. However, in human applications, i.e. for coaching and most other organizational applications, this can be distinctly bruising. Indirect feedback stokes fear and breeds unhelpful power relationships. This phenomenon is called 'triangulation' and psychologists have long established how fearful and harmful triangulation can be in interpersonal relationships. The chapter therefore ends with a plea to bring feedback back to the immediacy and contact of the relationship to which it pertains.

Notes

1. This chapter is an expanded version of an article which first appeared in the July 2020 issue of *Coaching Today*. © The British Association for Counselling and Psychotherapy.
2. There is a subtle difference in feedback between review and evaluation, which is not always appreciated: review is undertaken in a spirit of inquiry and curiosity, while evaluation is based on a desire to measure, value, and judge. Judging (evaluation, assessment) often forecloses learning or triggers automatic defences and is therefore less helpful in coaching.
3. The fact that participants are increasingly using screens in class is already a triangulation which takes focus and energy away from the helping relationship itself, weakening its impact. When those screens are used for setting up a feedback loop, the distraction becomes a lot worse.

7 Love over fear with diagnostic instruments: the temptation to guide rather than coach[1]

with Carine Metselaar

"O, wad some Power the giftie gie us
To see oursels as others see us!
It wad frae monie a blunder free us,
An' foolish notion."

Robert Burns, To a louse, 1786

7.1: Introduction

For more than 20 years, we have been working with diagnostic instruments in organizational assessments, development, and coaching, mostly with questionnaire-
based instruments. I wrote the original study for this chapter with Carine
Metselaar. We are certified users of more than ten widely applied instruments,
most of which are directly based on a psychological theory or at least related
to one. Carine was involved in a research project that included assessment tool
construction and validation in the early years of her career, and I have launched
two instruments with good reliability and construct validity through the
Ashridge psychometrics department (the Consulting Roles Inventory and the
Coaching Behaviours Questionnaire – see Chapter 11 for the latter). Carine has
also been an associate of one of the largest publishers of psychometric tools,
facilitating workshops based on their diagnostic assessment reports.

All this work should have made us strong advocates of psychometric instruments, with our likely main concerns being in the area of statistics as well as the
proper construction, validation, and certification of such instruments. To our
surprise and, on the contrary, we have increasingly found ourselves becoming
less and less comfortable with the widespread use of psychometric instruments
that are meant to provide something that comes close to a diagnostic value, for
the benefit of consulting or coaching work. We therefore find ourselves increasingly reluctant to suggest diagnostic tools early on in our coaching practice.

Lately, with new developments in user-friendliness and scalability of diagnostic tools, as with the general use of feedback (see Chapter 6), we have seen

an increase in the use of diagnostics behind the employee's back (i.e. where diagnostics are only reported to management) as well as uses in recruitment and even restructuring decisions which are not warranted by the tool or scientifically appropriate. This makes the whole field understandably more controversial (Harrell, 2017) and has heightened our caution in using psychometrics. One can see from where the increases in popularity are (recruitment, restructuring, leadership development), that psychometrics are experienced as a means to reduce uncertainty: they deliver numbers and facts about executives. Even if these facts do not relate to any reality outside the instrument, which, as we will see, is the case for all of them, at least to a considerable degree, they do provide reassurance and guidance where difficult and consequential decisions have to be taken – which, unfortunately, arguably reduces the quality of those decisions.

With this chapter we hope to contribute to a professional debate among coaches about the use of psychometric instruments in our profession.

7.2: Coaching and the use of psychometric instruments or other diagnostic tools

For us, coaching and diagnostics are like oil and water – they do not want to mix in the same relationship and when you do try to mix them, there is a good chance that one will repel the other.

On the one hand, diagnostics will put us in the role of expert authority. For the coachee, we become a figure with authority, knowing, for example, which diagnostic to use, how to interpret the diagnostic's findings, and what recommendations to make on those findings. On the other hand, coaching will make us enter a relationship fresh and free, unhindered by what we know and can do, in order that we can connect on a personal level with our coachees' own doubts and vulnerabilities.

Diagnostics are used 'on' the coachee, while coaching is the coachee using us, or at least coachee and coach wondering together what might be going on. Diagnostics impose a language on the coachee, while coaching inquires into the coachee's language when the coachee is really free to talk. Diagnostics use the relationship for something else while coaching explores the relationship for what it is.

Diagnostic tools in the widest sense

By diagnostic tools, we refer to all instruments and interventions that claim to give insight into a person's personal preferences, interpersonal needs, values, motivations, attitudes, behaviours, or other less commonly used concepts related to human characteristics. We obviously *do not* refer to the clinical use of the term, because clinical diagnostics include fuller anamnesis and a tailored clinical formulation which is intended for a clinical context that is different from coaching assignments. However, even in clinical assessments, diagnostic instruments have met with substantial criticism (see, for example, the chapter on 'Dethroning the medical model' in Duncan *et al.*, 2004).

Diagnostic coaching instruments can be divided into three categories:

1 *Psychometric self-assessment instruments,* which are aimed at producing objective measurements of a candidate's psychological attributes and usually come in the form of a questionnaire. The output is a report with numbers and graphs. Examples are the California Psychological Inventory (CPI), the Myers-Briggs Type Indicator (MBTI), the Occupational Personality Questionnaire (OPQ), the Hogan Development Survey (HDS), and the Baron Emotional Intelligence Quotient Inventory (EQ).

2 *Psychometric feedback instruments,* which are aimed at aggregating feedback from those who work with the candidate or know the candidate from a close personal relationship. Examples are feedback tools based on the above instruments, 360-degree multi-party feedback instruments, and tailor-made surveys.

3 *Observational instruments,* which do not claim to be objective measurements of a generally accepted concept. Their claim is that the observations, facilitated by the instruments, reveal a certain hidden truth about the individual or group taking part in the observation. Examples of these instruments are equine-assisted coaching and organizational constellations.

Observational instruments

Often, psychometric instruments refer to theories and models developed by established scholars, some, but not all, of them psychologists, which have been accepted for many years. The observational instruments are a more recent phenomenon in coaching. The conceptual models and related assumptions underpinning these interventions are not thoroughly researched and sometimes questionable. For instance, the site of the only EMCC accredited equine-assisted coach training mentions that research related to this methodology is still scarce, though there are some positive therapeutic effects found in clinical contexts (Gilling, 2013). Another example is the Family Constellations methodology, used as the basis of constellation work in coaching, which refers to 'natural orders' or 'laws of nature' that should not be violated in order to achieve balance in a system (Manné, 2009; Whittington, 2012). Not surprisingly, most constellation books can be found in the spiritual/religious/esoteric sections of academic bookstores.

7.3: How valid are diagnostic coaching tools?

Using questionnaires to get insight into characteristics of human beings is common practice yet debatable from an epistemological perspective. We never really know what we know. At best, we have a certain chance that what is 'measured' represents a psychological concept that has consensus within the professional community and relates to a set of behaviours that the majority would also acknowledge as representative of that concept. We are never sure whether the respondent interpreted the questions in the way we think, but if the statistics point out that the results of these questionnaires relate consistently to what we expect, such as to answer-patterns, sets of observable behaviours, or descriptions by others, the instrument passes our validity thresholds. Psychologists have agreed upon the different types of validity standards that need to be met in order for an instrument to be considered robust (Passmore, 2012).

With regard to the majority of the instruments used by executive coaches, no verifiable psychometric data have been published. When psychometric data are made available, this is often only done by the publisher and not verified by independent researchers. Yet some of these instruments, which refer to psychological theories but have no independent evidence behind them, come with certification training and user protocols, and are frequently used in the corporate world. Examples of such instruments are Management Drives, Enneagram, LIFO, TKI, and HBDI. Other instruments are thoroughly researched and tested and show satisfactory reliability and construct validity, which can be verified through publications, but still have a questionable reputation in the domain of social sciences related to their validity and consistency as predictors of other variables such as human behaviour and performance. Examples are the MBTI and Firo-B (Hurley, 1990; Furnham, 1996; Gardner and Martinko, 1996).

Surprisingly, given the ubiquity of psychometric assessments in organizations, there has been almost no rigorous research into the *effectiveness* of personality assessment and feedback. Some systematic review studies have been undertaken and have indicated that 'there is little evidence on how psychometrics can support individual development' (Batey *et al.*, 2012; see also Jelley, 2021), which is quite a damning statement. In other words, no clear indications have been found that the feedback based on personality inventories improves workplace behaviour, performance, or indeed results. The scant and inconclusive evidence to date does not mean that psychometrics do not (or cannot) work. However, what is clear is that there is a mismatch between the decades-long popularity of these interventions driving a billion-dollar industry and the potential for these interventions to have negative side-effects such as stigmatization, pigeonholing, negative rumination after surprising (negative) feedback, the statement of problems that are really non-existent, and so on. It is important that we remain sceptical of anyone who claims or suggests that research 'supports' a given psychometric instrument for development or performance improvement.

Case example 7.1

Glenn had been providing team coaching for the top team of a large public-sector organization over a period of about a year and was now asked to help another team in the second tier. They wanted to be introduced to a diagnostical instrument that had helped the top team a good while back. In his first call about this work with the HR director Frank, Frank told Glenn that meetings were not going well and that there were regular clashes between personalities, in particular between the leader of the team and one of the members, a logistical manager who was described by Frank as being reluctant to 'move to the new way of working' and to 'implement the changes'. If this member were to gain insight into his own personality as part of the team feedback, then the difficulties could finally be spoken about and hopefully be resolved. Glenn felt that this sounded more like a case for team coaching than for using a diagnostical instrument, but the HR director insisted. Glenn felt loyal to the organization and wanted to be of help, so he overcame his initial doubt and sense of confusion around the contract. He thought to himself that this work could still be helpful as and when he could speak with the whole team.

During the following months, the team member who was seen as the 'stumbling block for change', was slowly prepared by HR for the session and it was a great relief to Frank that he consented. Then the psychometric questionnaires were sent out to all, and data collection took another two months as no date had been put in by Frank, at least not as far as Glenn could see. At that point and only after a few reminders, Glenn was asked to first analyse and report Frank's results on the instrument to Frank himself as the HR director. This was in line with agreed process: individual feedback would come first before meeting together as a team, and as a matter of good contracting for the team session Glenn would ask everyone if they would be willing to share the feedback with the others. Glenn prepared for a routine conversation but when he said that the feedback results for Frank showed a lower-than-average 'Ambition' (a dimension on this questionnaire), and that it also appeared to show some irritability under pressure, coupled with a risk of lack of assertiveness or indecisiveness under pressure, their conversation became very stilted and uncomfortable. Glenn was suddenly wading through treacle. Frank wanted more explanation, he said he did not recognize some of the scores, and he became visibly agitated. By this stage Glenn was completely wrongfooted, somehow he had expected the conversation with the other team member, the logistical director, to be difficult and not this one – but he patiently listened to Frank's queries and responses and upon being questioned, explained the instrument further, taking great care to state time and again that a low or high score on any of the dimensions did not say anything about performance or about the calibre of the person, only about apparent personality differences compared with the norm group.

The assignment had been moving slowly already, but after this feedback session all sense of direction was lost. Glenn was not contacted at all for a full four months. He did not get to discuss other profiles, let alone work with the team, until five months later, when Frank admitted that he had found the confrontation with his profile excruciating. Glenn offered another conversation to Frank to help process the initial feelings and to help again to understand what to take from the profile. The assignment was then completed as an individual one for the members of the team. The other team members found the personal feedback based on the instrument helpful and interesting. There was no hint of difficulty around the one team member who had been singled out at the beginning, possibly because by this time the team leader had moved on and had been replaced by a very different personality. In fact, the individual conversations were so productive that Glenn did eventually work with the whole team to look at their 'team profile', but without Frank: under the new leadership, HR was no longer considered part of the top team.

What does validity really tell us?

On an epistemological level, the question 'what does validation really tell us?' remains. We must remind ourselves that validity expresses the amount of agreement between social scientists, based on language. There is no such thing as objectivity in relation to psychometrics, even if this is often claimed by their advocates. Data related to external criteria that could support these claims are scarce and, if presented, part of definitions that are continuously changing, and in fields where experts disagree significantly. Examples are the criteria and definitions informing leadership effectiveness or career success. In other situations, objective research data that are relevant to the field of psychometrics have become available and do not support the existing theories. An example is that today's neuroscience research findings do not support the existence of overall left brain or right brain dominance, which is used as the theoretical basis for some instruments such as the HBDI (Nielsen *et al.*, 2013).

In summary, it is often unclear what the language produced by a diagnostic report actually means and whether the feedback it offers is really related to improvement in the chosen field. This does not, however, imply this kind of description and feedback cannot be helpful at all in a coaching process, as we will see later in this chapter.

7.4: Dangers of 'instrument attachment'

Research into the effects of coaching is still in its infancy and the outcomes of diagnostic instruments in coaching have not yet been studied quantitatively (De Haan, 2021). One could hypothesize that using properly developed instruments, such as the Hogan tools, would be better and maybe more effective than, for example, using 'parlour games'. However, there is as yet no scientific evidence to support this. With the lack of objective data supporting a clear preference for one instrument over another, criteria to suggest the use of an instrument become subject to different factors, such as commercial considerations, practical considerations, or personal experience and preference. It is not hard to imagine that coaches will suggest the use of a particular instrument more often if they are familiar with it, and still more if they are an accredited user of the instrument. One of the obvious reasons is that coaches usually have to pay a significant amount of money to acquire the training and certification needed to be able to use an instrument. Therefore, most coaches would make a deliberate choice for no more than a few instruments and try to stick to these. Our own quick scan of a (Dutch) national database of coaches confirms this: most coaches use fewer than five instruments. Another reason could be that being familiar with an instrument enhances the chances of being comfortable using it. The assumed correlation between a coach's familiarity with an instrument and the suggestion to use it is a phenomenon regularly found with clinicians as well. For instance, Van Minnen *et al.* (2010) found a clear link between therapists trained in the use of a certain therapy and their preference to indicate this therapy for their clients instead of another therapy that was also highly recommended by the formal treatment guidelines. Of course, indicating a clinical approach is not the same as proposing a psychometric instrument, but there are certainly similarities. In 2017, a survey among qualified test users showed that 80.5% said their decision for a specific psychometric was guided by their own experience and familiarity. Factors like test reviews or academic literature played a significant minor role in this decision (McDowall and Redman, 2017).

The potential harm we are concerned about is that coaches would become 'attached' to the concepts produced by the instruments they use, to the extent that these concepts become a reality to them. We have heard coaches talking almost religiously about 'the richness of information the instrument *produces*', saying things like, 'the more I work with it, the more interpretive value it has'. If the attachment goes unchecked, it grows and coaches say things like, 'I used MBTI to determine his type', language which suggests that they find it hard to resist the temptation to believe that their instrument is truly superior to any other instrument or to their own intuitions. In our experience, seasoned coaches who are overly familiar with a certain instrument tend to become more convinced of the added value of it, which is expressed by a tendency to use the instrument persuasively with their coachees. In the area of what we labelled observational instruments, it is often hard for coachees to argue with the 'wisdom and honesty' of the feedback produced by a horse (equine-assisted coaching), or with the 'truth revealed by the system' (as in coaching constellations), especially if they feel they benefit from the increasing sense of certainty.

The more a coach starts to think there is an absolute 'truth' in the language produced by the instrument, the less room will be left for the coachee to produce and own their own language and understanding. We have seen this happening on many occasions. A recent example was when a leader, who scored dramatically different on a coaching instrument after having experienced some significant life changes, was told by his coach that 'this could not be true' because 'what the instrument measured was a stable trait, not subject to life changes'. Here the model was prioritized over the experience of the coachee. This also regularly happens with ipsative instruments such as MBTI or OPQ, where the model forces the coachee into one of two poles despite coachees often feeling that they do not have a real preference for either one of the two poles. Here coachees are usually advised to just make a quick decision that fits best. The model does not allow the coachee to *not* have a preference.

When coaches take their instruments too seriously, some basic coaching principles might be violated. This goes in particular for the following principles, part of The Ashridge Code of Conduct for Executive Coaches (De Haan, 2008a):

- *Coach and coachee enter into an equal relationship (which is used intentionally for the benefit of the coachee)*. This is at risk when the coach presents the coachee with a 'truth' the coachee does not fully understand.
- *During coaching the goals, resources, and choices of the coachee have priority over those of the coach*. Related to the use of resources, the coachee

usually does not know what the other options are, beyond the limited offer of the coach.

- *Coaches are responsible for ensuring that they are not dependent upon relationships with their coachees for satisfying their own emotional and other needs.* Coaches may benefit from using an instrument in several ways, not in the least just to gain provider privileges or to get more experience.
- *Coaches recognize the power inherent in their position: they realize that they exert considerable influence, both consciously and unconsciously, on their coachees and possibly also on third parties.* Coaches can get away with low-quality instruments if presented persuasively and coachees hardly feel in a position to question the choice of instrument.

7.5: The positive impact of using diagnostic instruments in coaching

Let's turn the argument around for a moment and look at the advantages of working with diagnostic instruments in coaching. Although there is little scientific evidence of the efficacy of psychometrics, in our experience, it appears that many coachees are satisfied with the reports they receive and the help of their interpreter. Coachees generally report that the results give them new or additional insights and help them to clarify their thinking. Using a model as a framework in a coaching process can be supportive in different ways. One is that it can give words to something that was felt but only vaguely intuited. Another is that it can normalize behaviour or feelings that were first thought of as problematic or unusual and may have been rejected by the coachee. If we take into account coachees' thirst for sense-making and new realizations (De Haan *et al.*, 2010), providing models and data that 'explain' our feelings or doubts can be helpful. For instance, we recall coachees expressing relief because the instrument indicated that their preferences or values might not match well with their jobs or core activities. As if they needed to hear they were perhaps somehow 'wired' that way, which made it easier for them to make a different choice in their careers. Thus, using a model can be supportive in a cathartic process.

7.6: Ethical considerations and a plea for more transparency

As we have seen, positive effects of using diagnostic coaching tools may co-exist with some of the drawbacks. These drawbacks may be limited particularly if we can be sure that 'instrument attachment' has been contained. However, several factors may be behind the overuse of some instruments. One is that the financial investments made to develop a robust instrument lead to the production of verbose, glossy reports to confirm its value. These reports often include different representations of the same data, tips on how to deal with our profiles, and areas to which we can apply our data (leadership, working in teams, risks of derailment, work/life balance, career choices, etc.). The reports conspire to exaggerate the importance of the data and, as with some dubious contracts or pharmaceutical products, all the unknowns, side-effects, and biases either disappear entirely or are consigned to the 'small print'. Another factor is that coaches also invest in their certification training and may be motivated to get returns on that investment.

A third consideration is that coachees are rarely interested in the validity or reliability of an instrument. In our coaching practice, no-one ever questioned the validity or quality of the models used. The trust in us as coaches can be overwhelming. Whereas the organizations which use our services judge us by our credentials, most coachees judge us by the rapport they have with us and the tangible outcomes of the coaching process (De Haan, 2008a). This may preclude us from being fully transparent about the values and limitations of an instrument.

For all of these reasons, we would be strong advocates of regulation of the use of diagnostic instruments by executive coaches. As the coaching profession is becoming more professional thanks to certified training, accreditations, and formal supervision requirements, it does make sense to introduce at least health warnings regarding the use of instruments. We believe no diagnostic instruments should be introduced and administered without basic psychometric training (such as Levels A and B of the British Psychological Society in the UK). Such training covers guidelines and regulations around instrument use. Furthermore, coachees should receive clear information on the limitations of testing, including:

- Instruments only compare their scores reliably to a model of reality (not to reality itself) and to other people using the same instrument, who may have interpreted aspects of the instrument differently.
- Findings are based only on their questionnaire scores which may change over time.
- Findings may not be reliably related to other measurements of similar properties, so they may not reliably relate to any of the coachee's behaviour, feeling, or thinking; moreover, coachees may not recognize or accept the findings based on their own scores and should exercise their own judgement.
- Findings will be shared only with the coachee himself or herself and will be kept securely and deleted after a specified period.

Related to observational instruments, similar guidelines could be developed and applied in order to enhance transparency. For instance, it could be made clear to coachees which general assumptions underpin the theories and models used and that (as in most cases) there is no scientific data supporting the efficacy of the instrument.

7.7: Application: recommendations when it comes to diagnostic tools and coaching

Executive coaching differs from other forms of coaching and counselling in several respects. One is that performance improvement is usually part of the objectives, leading to a goal-focused, results-oriented, and rather practical approach. Executive coaching is usually involved with personal development and the unlocking of leadership potential (Hawkins and Smith, 2006). It therefore makes sense to include diagnostics that help to understand, for instance, why leadership potential might be blocked, or what makes someone behave in a certain way. However, as in every personal or organizational transformation process, such diagnosis is only valuable if it is fully owned by the person, group, or organization involved. As facilitators of this transformational process, executive coaches serve their coachees best by 'helping them to find and activate their natural, inherent abilities' (De Haan, 2008a). In the context of the lack of evidence, using a tool to identify these natural abilities may be pretentious, may miss the most relevant ones, and may even distract us from what should be the focus of our work: our relationship with our coachees and what is going on for them.

This does not apply to observational instruments, where data-gathering and sense-making happen within the process so that they can be a more integral part of the coaching. However, even with observational data, leaders are offered 'instant' (external) insights into what might be blocking them or serving them in using their potential. We believe that as coaches we should focus instead on helping the coachee find their own truths, while staying away as much as possible from offering them our perspectives and data.

Personally, we attach great value to allowing our own intuition to work on all aspects of the meeting, the coachee, and the issues (see also Chapter 2), allowing new observations and experiences to emerge within the encounter. In such a setting of meeting and inquiry, diagnostics are like a stone thrown into a calm pond or a sudden transistor being switched on at high volume in nature: they disrupt and loudly claim attention. Whether we find the diagnostic data inspirational and truthful, and we embrace the new picture, or we want to resist and rebel against the new picture that is held out in front of us, diagnostic instruments have thrown us off course and have nipped any fresh and tentative intuitions of our own in the bud. For this reason, we increasingly prefer to employ a diagnostic instrument later on in the coaching, not in the beginning. At such a later, perhaps even final stage of the work, diagnostics can help to check and enrich what coachee and coach have already found, e.g. regarding aspects of the coachee's leadership shadow (De Haan and Kasozi, 2014).

In our view, the coachee's centrality to coaching will be most at risk during remedial work, where diagnostics feel more like an assessment. Diagnostic instruments may still play a helpful part, in communicating more of the organization's critical feedback directly to the coachee. However, these diagnostics need to be handled with care and they can stigmatize or confirm prejudice. As noted in Chapter 6, it is usually more helpful and sensitive to forego the diagnostic instrument and allow the coach to do interviews with key stakeholders, or even ask the coachee herself to undertake a round of interviews. In this way, potentially stigmatizing views can be placed in a wider context, including more charitable interpretations for the coachee herself.

7.8: Conclusion

All in all, the old Hippocratic saying *primum non nocere* ('first, do no harm'; also mentioned in Chapter 1) applies: given the existing problems with diagnostic tools, it may be best not to use them at all; better to leave out some potentially useful information than risk doing more harm than good. Certainly, in our own work as executive coaches, where psychometric data have often been generated recently or happen to be part of a pre-designed intervention, we leave it to other professionals to guide our coachees. As mentioned earlier, we feel rather strongly that administering and feeding back on such instruments take us away from the role and relationship we (aspire to) have as a coach. It may even take coachee and coach considerable time and effort to 'recover' from such diagnostics. In such cases of usually programme-related coaching work when diagnostic instruments are somehow an agreed part of the assignment, we prefer to leave the administration, scoring, and interpretation of diagnostic instruments to someone else, if possible, in order not to confuse or confound roles and relationships.

Chapter summary

Reflecting on our experience using diagnostic instruments in executive coaching, we have found a number of problems and drawbacks. As a result, we have developed our own preferred ways of combining such instruments with coaching contracts. Drawbacks include: (1) the lack of validity of many instruments, (2) poor prediction of measurable behaviour or improvement for coachees, and (3) 'instrument attachment', which can cause the coach to reify and trust the outcomes of psychometrics more than their own eyes and ears. Suggestions made in this chapter are first and foremost to use the instruments late in the assignment if at all, instead of early on and as an initial orientation as happens too often at present. This helps to enhance the valuable impressions from first meetings and allows the coachee to introduce herself and her objectives in the way she wants. Second, we try to implement all diagnostics in such a way that we have no 'informational advantage' over our coachees. In other words, any impressions from 360-degree interviews and other instruments are shared fully and with reference to our sources, which is again something that is (unfortunately, and to our surprise) unusual in our field.

Note

1   This chapter is an expanded version of an article which first appeared in the July 2015 issue of *Coaching Today*. © The British Association for Counselling and Psychotherapy. The article was initiated and first-authored by my colleague Carine Metselaar.

8 Love over fear in assessment: searching for a secure base for evaluation[1]

with Robin Shohet

Assessments are opportunities for learning through direct feedback and for promotion and betterment, but they often do not feel that way. In reality, assessments are often riddled with fear, engendering an unhealthy kind of competition and envy: even though they are never intended as a competitive game and are designed for strengthening and development, candidates often cannot help but compare marks, smirk, and begrudge. What can be done about this?

At Ashridge we have always felt that our mission with assessment needed to be that we would try to 'overcome fear by developing love'. Although assessments need to be rigorous and equitable tests of the achievement of a narrowly defined competence, we also want our assessments to be important learning opportunities. The latter means that our assessments need to provide safety and security so that candidates feel they can be vulnerable and can experiment, while at the same time those assessments must remain rigorous and open-ended. Some of our qualifications are passed by less than two-thirds of candidates at the first attempt, although we always offer candidates the possibility to retake a 'licence to practise' if not successful the first time around or after resubmission.

8.1: Our experiment with assessment

This chapter reports on an experiment which we have undertaken several times and here captured in reflective notes, where we tried to marry rigour with authenticity, and to allow the love of learning to overcome the burning desire to succeed. In moderating the final accreditation for our Supervision Postgraduate Diploma at Ashridge, we have experimented with radical ideas to challenge conventional ways of assessing, to preserve the learning from the process, while keeping the assessment process meaningful and distinctive.

Regrettably, assessments are often unconsciously designed to keep the assessors in a position of power under the guise of maintaining standards.

What that teaches students is how to second-guess the examiners, to divine their 'currency' and to give them what they want in order to get through; a legacy from our school examination system, which we believe there is no need to perpetuate.

Here is the story of one such assessment including the experiences of all the candidates, in their own words. Two moderators for the Ashridge Supervision Postgraduate Diploma were asked to read written work by five students and grade them along with three other tutors, before the live practice assessment day. On the day in question, we met with the five applicants in the morning. Each was to make a 20-minute recording of a supervision session in another room which was live-streamed to the two assessors and the four other students. All seven of us were there for the whole day, watching and giving feedback. Volunteer supervisees were sourced by Ashridge.

Based on the quality of the earlier submissions and after a careful check between the two moderators, we agreed to introduce the day by telling the candidates that they had all passed. There was an element of laughter and a sense of relief, a moment of catharsis. As accreditors we noticed that we felt a little uneasy – as if the words had not really fully sunk in, so one of us fed that back and added that there were no tricks but the mind can do funny things, such as 'This diploma can't mean anything if everyone passes'; or 'I am better than x, so if they pass, that means that I have not been recognized'; or worst of all, 'He is just saying that. I don't really believe him.' This was particularly true of one student who had had negative experiences of assessment. It seemed to us that she was not willing to move into a new possibility, so we suggested she might be willing to forgive those previous experiences. This she later shared had a big impact and enabled her to let go for the day.

We provided our rationale for this way of working. Part of the day would involve students giving feedback to one another, so there would be a fear of giving and receiving robust feedback in case it contributed to a fail. We thus proceeded by having the students give their feedback on a particular recording, and then the two moderators added their own views and made the final decision in terms of the precise grading. This way of working meant that we could all participate, as there was no final pass/fail decision to make. The power balance, an unfortunate concomitant of most assessments, was altered, and we could get on with the task of learning together.

As well as reducing the fear of giving robust feedback and reducing fear generally, the impact of passing everyone from the beginning meant the students could enjoy their sessions and therefore were more likely to do good work. They would be free to take risks, rather than play safe. This seemed to us a good justification for this way of working, being as it is based on the tenets of *appreciative inquiry* – that we are more likely to both find, and create, good practice if we actively look for it and encourage it, which is what this method of assessment aimed to do.

We won't go into detail about the day, except to say that one person who shared that she had been dreading the assessment stated that it had been the best day of her year. We were all moved.

It was relatively easy to put this into practice as it came at the end of the course, and even though one of the assessors (Robin) had not met the students, he had read enough of their written work, which included very frank self-assessments, to determine they were good enough to pass. To use a footballing analogy, the course and the main tutor (Erik) had done all the work in midfield and Robin was there to stick the ball in the back of the net at the end of the move. Would he have been able to play with such ease if he had been a main tutor from the beginning and there had been someone whose work he did not think was good enough? There are many questions such as these, but what we set out to do was to find ways of making assessment as fear-free and creative as possible. This remains an ongoing inquiry.

The second assessor, a module tutor on the course, felt a rush of anxiety when Robin suggested we tell the candidates that they'd all passed at the start of the accreditation. The more cautious and compliant part of him was concerned that we'd be subverting our carefully designed assessment process, making decisions before we'd had a chance to review the entirety of the candidates' performance on the day.

Although he knew the candidates through his teaching and tutorial work with them, his role thus far had been almost entirely developmental rather than evaluative. Despite his habitual ambivalence about the evaluative role, it seemed that we might be losing something important. If we were to automatically pass them all, what value would we be adding to the process? Might the candidates feel short-changed when they learned that they no longer needed to prove themselves under exam conditions? Might their qualification be undervalued as a result? What if we ended up having serious misgivings about a candidate's fitness to practise?

The experiment nevertheless appealed to that more playful part of the second assessor that loves to improvise and experiment. As he reflected on the likely (as opposed to imagined) risks, he realized that this was something that he wanted to try. These were senior, seasoned practitioners whom he knew were competent. If we allowed ourselves to 'break the rules', rules that were largely self-imposed in any case, we would be opening ourselves to new learning and growth.

Our experience of the accreditation day was unlike any previous assessment process that he had been part of. He indeed felt more alert and alive in his body, rather than busy in his head, as would have been the case had we been judging and evaluating. He felt more relaxed and attuned to the candidates and to one another. Although this was our first time as co-accreditors, it felt natural and easy working with one another. We were able to be ourselves, mostly aligned but able to accommodate our differences when not so. This became a defining quality of the day overall. Freed from our roles as evaluators, we were able to relate to the candidates as peers, collaboratively inquiring into the dynamics and sensitivities of the supervisory relationship. We did not detect any of the suppressed competitiveness that so often characterizes these kinds of processes, or the awkwardness of an imposed power differential between accreditor and accredited. Instead, we were able to create a safe-enough space where people could take risks, be vulnerable, and hold one another to account in a spirit of respect and goodwill. The fifth and final candidate gave the strongest performance of the day, which was not only a testament to her own skills but to the quality of the group's work as a whole. It was a very moving end to their process. To borrow a phrase from the world of improv, they had truly 'made one another happen' (Barrett, 2011).

8.2: Reflection on the process with further suggestions

At Ashridge we have always felt that our assessment needed to be based on us trying to 'overcome fear by developing love'. Our accreditors are usually most anxious to pass a candidate, and we dread the moment when we find that more learning is required in order to meet the standards. At that point we would still draw on our love for the participant and the profession to speak our truth fearlessly and mitigate the shock of the unwelcome news. However, in the field of love, even too much is often not enough, as Figaro famously ponders during the intrigues leading up to his wedding, his own celebration of personal love.

I believe the assessment for a qualification is very much like the preparation of a wedding, a full and consummate union with a new profession, culminating in a sense of obligation and a freedom to act, as well as other festivities and love-making.

In a wider sense, we want to help reduce the abuse of power in the helping professions by growing the ability to 'contain' fear, anxiety, and self-doubt. We have not always been as successful as on this particular day. Oftentimes we have oscillated in the swirling turmoil between Scylla and Charybdis (the mythical sea monsters in Homer's *Odyssey*, where if you manage to avoid one, you will have to confront the other):

- On the one hand, the punitive and rigid nature of the assessments, as exemplified by many of our professional institutions, where you 'upload' your best and most personal work only to receive a dismissive half-page of impersonal feedback, or worse still, where assessment is done in secret and you only hear from your supervisor that you are 'unfortunately not ready yet' without receiving any reasons for this ominous judgement at all.

- On the other hand, the Rogerian idea of asking all candidates to give themselves the final mark (Rogers, 1957). Rogers asks us in this provocative article to do away with *all* top-down teaching, with examinations and assessment, and even with 'degrees' as externally driven testaments of learning (i.e. driven by the repudiated 'external locus of evaluation'). When we follow Rogers' attractive ideas, as Erik has done on several occasions, we end up celebrating all learning and achievement, and naturally everyone passes. However, a lingering doubt remains in each person's mind, as they have truly only been passed by themselves.

8.3: The participants' voices

Here are the reflections of the five candidates on their own experiences:

The assessment was an incredibly rich learning experience, although we as students had almost completed the journey already by attending the workshops and submitting our required pieces of work. The only gate we had left to pass was the assessment. By acknowledging the work we had done at the beginning of the day, the assessors enabled a deepening of the process and the exchange of our experiences and viewpoints with almost a free mind. Of course, it had not felt right if we were given a pass when it was not well considered. But I assume, as we can see in the above deliberations, we had shown enough of our capacities already. It was relational supervision in the real sense of the word. (Candidate 1)

My initial response when Robin made clear we all started the day with a pass, was first a moment of huge catharsis, as expressed by all in the group. Amazingly how soon my doubting mind overruled that catharsis by disbelief, due to negative assessment experiences in the past. This was noticed and followed with an invitation to consider the past as – indeed, the past – and enter the day from a generous attitude of forgiveness. This was a helpful and liberating perspective with the impact that I was able to make that shift, so I could really contribute in reflections and feedback conversations in the spirit of a deep joyful learning time and space with all involved, assessors, candidates, and volunteers. (Candidate 2)

As I believe that the quality of my interventions as coach and supervisor depends on the quality of my presence, this approach allowed me to connect more deeply with myself. This was both beneficial to the coachee and me as we could enter a supervision dance together, without being triggered in survival behaviours caused by earlier traumatic examination experiences. I felt carried by the energy of the group, stimulated by the learnings from other candidates. I could access love and joy instead of competition with my 'perfect self'. (Candidate 3)

I experienced the assessment day as being full of support and love. The decision to announce that, providing we didn't do anything extremely wrong, on the basis of our written submissions that we had all passed, was liberating. The work of the day was therefore going to be about 'the mark' and giving and receiving constructive feedback. I felt a sense of relief and slight excitement. The metaphorical distance between the assessors and us seemed to close and in that moment, it felt like all of us were in essence, 'one team'. The day was an absolute pleasure. Whilst I was still slightly apprehensive before my live supervision session, I felt that wherever it landed, it would be OK. As I write, I recall that despite this I was still 'holding' back a little, trying to be the 'professional' supervisor, which led to me adopting certain 'formal' behaviours, which actually I don't do in 'real life' with my supervisees. I realize now, that if I attended another supervision accreditation day that was set up in the same way, I would take more risks. (Candidate 4)

Based on earlier experiences I am not comfortable in situations where I feel looked at and judged by an authority, especially when the situation or outcome is precious to me. For me, it has to do with power and being dependent. Understandably, the days preceding accreditation day I felt disturbingly tense. So, when Robin told us straight at the start that we all passed and their intention was the day to be a learning experience, I felt like a balloon suddenly losing all air. I felt relieved, happy, and a bit suspicious all at once. The earlier experiences warned me from a distance. But after Robin conscientiously explained their choice, I was able to believe it and to step into this new reality: a collective learning experience, which I sensed as warm, caring, and stimulating. (Candidate 5)

8.4: Conclusion

We are aware we need to hold the power entrusted to us in this role of assessor with the utmost care and humility. We need to be firm and containing, but we also need to be open to scrutiny such as through an Appeals or Complaints process. Such a process was in place here through standard QAA practices: the Ashridge Postgraduate Diploma in Organisational Supervision is a higher education degree.

This is a report of one successful experiment benefiting from the high performance that all these five candidates had shown in earlier modules of the programme. Our nagging question remains, what if that performance had been more equivocal, what if we did question in advance the maturity or competence of even one of these candidates to become a qualified supervisor? We have always made sure that as part of the supervision accreditation we also ask the candidates to assess the accreditors, but of course this is a less fateful assessment than that of the candidates themselves. We also try to make sure that if we are lacking confidence in a particular candidate, for whatever reason, that we let them know well in advance of the final accreditation process and advise her or him to think about our views and consider delaying their final accreditation.

We believe our next experiment, perhaps with a group where we are not so sure if they are all ready to become qualified supervisors, could be to try to make it a truly collegiate day, and invite all candidates to contribute to the assessment of each colleague. This will be difficult for us to hold together and contain, and it will be difficult to help all present to take part in such challenging and responsible assessments, but it would certainly be worth the effort, in our view.

Chapter summary

In this chapter, we muse on the impact of assessment processes on both the coach and the coachee, which can be so strong that assessments defeat their own purpose: instead of measuring any qualities or performance as set out to measure, we will only measure the individual-under-exam-conditions which is a very different animal. To varying degrees personal assessments make us fearful, anxious, or excited, which affects our personality, mood, and balance. The chapter describes an experiment where we tried to take the stress out of the exam situation, so as to allow a more mature and balanced performance to emerge. Yet, strictly speaking, the experiment was no longer an (open-ended) assessment. By taking the stress out, the assessment itself also disappeared to a degree. Alternative approaches are discussed. It appears that fear can be measured and fragmented into 'good' and 'bad' constituting elements, while love is intrinsically immeasurable. Fear constructs boundaries, criteria, grades, and assessments, while love has no boundaries, suffuses, and makes whole. We look into what this experiment means for coaching and coaching qualifications.

Note

1 This chapter is an expanded version of an article which first appeared in the July 2018 issue of *Coaching Today*. © The British Association for Counselling and Psychotherapy. The article was initiated and first-authored by Robin Shohet.

9 Love over fear for the planet: our contract with the wider crises in the world

In this final chapter of Part B of the book, the series around 'love over fear' in our practice, I try to take a good many steps backwards from our intimate one-to-one conversations, to take an overview of the field and our connection with what is happening with our planet. Does 'coaching' have anything to say about the current crises affecting our planet, any relevance at all for politics and society? Certainly, I can see the concern and motivation among individual coaches to contribute something of value, sustainably. I see coaches speaking out about climate change and diversity, urging us to take global issues into account and make a positive difference. I believe we can indeed fulfil a small role in society, even if it is not an easy or straightforward one, namely to provide space for reflection about what 'crisis' is and what we might do in response. I describe this presumptive role for coaches over the following pages.

9.1: Coaches' understandable concern for the planet

All of us have experienced in 2020 what a truly global crisis looks and feels like and how such a crisis poses severe challenges. The 'corona crisis' reminded us how fragile and how connected we are, both in terms of our biology and increasingly our global connectivity. The crisis focused our minds on stopping the spread of the virus, on providing what is necessary in a short amount of time, even if humanity's collective response still left a lot to be desired.

During the corona crisis, there was an explosion in the use of video-platforms, and we were grateful that in this way we could keep in touch with one another during lockdown, keep holding meetings, even engage in consulting and coaching conversations, virtually. However, our rather discursive and fragmented screens, which often looked like a randomly arrayed series of rather bland postcards, also underlined the kind of crisis that we were dealing with, a crisis which drove us apart, stoked fear and death, blocked intimacy and many a meaningful, intimate connection.

It is clear to most of us that we will tumble from a grave health crisis into a graver financial crisis, splits and wars undermining our global security, and then into the gravest of all, our self-made climate crisis. Crises are becoming ever more jarring, haunting, and disruptive to us all.

It is understandable and ethical to want to do something about this and become an activist. Crisis invites us all to take a stance.[1] This pull is particularly strong on us coaches, who are, after all, professional *helpers*. We feel the urge to 'stand up and be counted', to use the considerable personal and professional power that we have, to use it for what is clearly a 'good' cause.

But is this actually, truly helpful? As consultants and coaches, at some point in our lives we have chosen to become professional helpers and to put ourselves in the service of the fortunes and objectives of others. But this pull can overstep a boundary if we run the risk of trying to do our coachee's work for them or otherwise get overinvolved. Naturally there is a big pull in most of us to help others and in some cases a real preference to attend to the needs of others over and above our own. This is sometimes called our helper's syndrome (Miller, 1979). The best coaches have learned how to step back from becoming too helpful and to address our visceral needs to help in other ways, such as by allowing ourselves to be helped as well as helping others, or just by spending reflective time by ourselves for ourselves.

Case example 9.1

Claudia is the eldest daughter of three. When she was two years old her brothers were born: identical twins, and the family was thrown into some disarray. Her parents were still in their mid-twenties and only establishing themselves as secondary school teachers. At an early age she learned to look after her brothers and help out around mealtimes. When the time arrived to study, she initially chose Geography but felt that she was not really motivated. Only when she switched to Psychology, after her Bachelors, did she find new motivation, after which she managed to qualify as a clinical psychologist. Three years into her first job she suffered a burnout after which she took some time to reorient herself. She found that she had taken on a lot of administration and managerial work, plus a considerable caseload. She realized after some therapy and reorientation that she was better off becoming self-employed, and in some years she had become a successful coach, who was often asked back by her coachees, in addition to having a strong pipeline through word-of-mouth. Now she had more control over her working hours, but again she managed to overbook herself and it was only through regular individual supervision that she managed not to succumb to the pressures a second time. Gradually she learned that she had been extremely generous with her time with a natural tendency to overlook her own needs. Working with coachees made her feel useful whereas if she was not busy, she often felt helpless – but by attending to this feeling and talking about it regularly, she was able to find a better balance and started to make better choices in her practice.

I think it is important to remember what we can and cannot do as a professional helper. There are clear boundaries to our effectiveness. If we become too expert – and that includes advocacy – or too much of a 'pair of hands', we run the risk of becoming less effective as coaches and consultants.

Important, too, is the fact that these crises are (mostly) man-made, that they are crises of our consciousness, including the hold of our own leadership shadows on us: our greed, our corruption, our narcissism. So, I would argue if we as coaches take a stance, by turning to leadership and advocacy, we will grow our leadership shadows at the same time, predictably only aggravating the crises, however well-meaning our initial intentions.

We need to be doing what we do so well with our individual coachees: taking a step back and not getting involved with their decisions or actions, simply coaching them through their choices. Can we lovingly observe and make sense of these crises that we are ourselves a part of, and can we nurture reflection where reflecting has become so difficult all around us?

I think that in order to do so, we need to reflect on the roots of the crises and think deeply, alongside the organizations we work with, about the mentality underpinning the problems and see if we can hold this mentality in mind, lovingly, safely, so that other values and a healthier side may emerge from within. This is not so much activism and advocacy – it has more to do with observation and sense-making.

I know we need to 'fight' the crises we face, in fact, we should have begun doing so some time ago. My question is, nevertheless, even at this late stage: how do we fight? And: what happens to us when we fight? As we fight, we will be in advocacy mode, our lecturing no doubt putting a lot of good people off. And what about ourselves, will we not switch parts of ourselves off by calling for action (e.g. climate action), by suppressing those other more thoughtful parts? If we fight other nations, institutions, or individuals, we won't achieve our ends because ours is a global crisis that encompasses all of mankind including ourselves, however 'green' our own agenda.

In Greece there were two gods of warfare – masculine, violent, offensive Ares; and the protectress Athena, who held a secondary interest as the goddess of wisdom. I would argue that in this fight wisdom is to take Athena's stance and to strive for protection and reflection in the interest of defence not attack. And I firmly believe our predominantly feminine, protective coaching profession can play a role but only under the banner of Athens, and not Ares.

9.2: Coaches are familiar with crises of leadership

Let us think a bit more about the kind of crises that we are facing. I think, first and foremost, they are crises of leadership, in manifold forms. We know that on the whole mankind has the resources to feed – and vaccinate – the world, to celebrate our human diversity, and to reverse climate change – but this requires joint strategies, joint implementation, and joint action. Yet these are plainly hard to achieve, especially when we consider the many forces that exist to drive us apart and have us compete with one another for ever-scarcer resources.

Green activists, researchers, and politicians often focus on the biological, technological, social, and political. With something as mind-bogglingly complex as climate change, it is easy to overlook the psychological. Nevertheless, there is a strong argument that psychological and leadership factors underpin our man-made crises. Experts, activists, and politicians may underestimate the power of the human mind both to create the issues in the first place and to resist their solutions. If we take our own minds more seriously, including our unconscious drivers and unresolved issues around self-esteem, then we may begin to admit that self-regulation of consumption is a tall order. Indeed, my prediction is that as soon as 'green energy' takes hold, instead of waiting for the planet to cool down, energy consumption will only rise.

We have never been able to establish full global leadership even though clearly global leadership was called for during the corona crisis and was to an extent provided by the WHO, global pharma companies, and careful communication between governments and institutions.

Leadership is a very basic process, to do with the effectiveness of a team or an organization of which we may be a part – sometimes from a very early age. Leadership was only very recently conceptualized: the word only emerged in 1821, and 'leadership studies' only in the late twentieth century. Over time, technological advances have seen the role and influence of leaders change out of all recognition, impacting many people's daily lives and creating the need to respond to frequent change, especially as the world is becoming increasingly volatile, uncertain, complex and ambiguous ('VUCA'; Barber, 1992).

Psychopathology and leadership are highly correlated: leadership corrupts and therefore creates pathology over time (De Haan and Kasozi, 2014), while psychopathology produces leadership. In other words, free-flowing leadership processes do not automatically converge on the best possible solution or decision for all or to resolve crises – and, conversely, many individuals who are not the best leaders, unfortunately, end up in leadership roles.

I think crises in our leadership, which date back further than the current health, financial, and ecological crises, lie at the root of our problems, and our common leadership crisis, at least in the Western world, needs to be addressed as much, if not more than, those other crises we face. This means addressing the manifestations of selfishness, greed, fear, stubbornness, and prejudice among our leaders, so that they can begin to make better decisions for everyone.

In *The Mask of Sanity*, Cleckley (1941) was the first to describe the specific configuration of traits that capture the essence of the psychopathic personality. Psychopaths were described as superficially charming, self-centred, fearless, impulsive, articulate, callous, and guiltless. Out of this thinking, the triarchic model of psychopathy evolved (e.g. Patrick *et al.*, 2009), where the most common psychopathic traits are clustered around boldness (e.g. grandiosity, interpersonal dominance), meanness (e.g. lack of empathy, callousness), and disinhibition (e.g. impulsivity, irresponsibility).

Although boldness may add to positive task performance and charismatic leadership, and disinhibition may add to positive adaptive leadership, an overall negative contribution of meanness and a partially negative contribution of disinhibition to leadership have been reported (Vergauwe *et al.*, 2021). In

Vergauwe and colleagues' research, the effectiveness of leaders was rated by subordinates, which we argue in *The Leadership Shadow* (De Haan and Kasozi, 2014) is a helpful perspective for measuring leadership effectiveness. However, if one measures the impact of psychopathy from the perspective of quality of life on our planet or for future generations, these negative, demonstrated links between psychopathy and leadership effectiveness are expected to become even stronger and to also include boldness.

Unfortunately, leadership appears to be a key example of 'successful psychopathy': it attracts individuals who are interested in power and self-promotion, and/or the pressures and projections on top leadership have a pathology-enhancing effect, especially over time (Owen, 2008). This means that either through self-selection or through experience on the job, such as inescapable projections onto leaders, the number of triarchic traits is expected to be greater than in the general population (Patrick *et al.*, 2009).

These crises of leadership, and the dark leadership shadows that they have occasioned (De Haan and Kasozi, 2014), are responsible for all of the world's current major challenges, involving exploitation, inequality, threats to biodiversity and to the climate globally. Greed, narcissism, and fear lie at the root of these issues. So, we need to find better ways to counter greed, selfishness, and fear.

9.3: A vision is needed for a loving way to confront this unprecedented global crisis

Science and technology can help address the complex crises that we are facing, as we have seen to a remarkable extent with the corona crisis. However, many experts are pessimistic about the ability of new technology to be brought on board fast enough and to be clean enough to stop the accelerating climate crisis.

Without a different form of leadership, and an understanding that we have to change our priorities collectively and make them more sustainable collectively, rapid technological change will not be enough and will itself not be sustainable. We will have to engage in many more conversations about ecotaxes, rewarding lower climate footprints, accepting healthier and more vegetarian food, etc. These will be very tough conversations that need to have real consequences both for politics and large organizations. Difficult choices will not be made without strong collective leadership.

The recent UN report on climate change with its alarming warnings (IPCC, 2021), has convincingly shown that this is a crisis that is growing exponentially and can only be addressed by similarly exponential changes in our approach to the planet. This means we are dealing with a second-order challenge (Bateson, 1972), both in terms of the need to change the mindset that has created the problem and in terms of the observer and change agent being herself also part of the problem. Fortunately, this is something that organizational-development professionals and coaches know about and can facilitate, however difficult it is in practice. This is another reason for us to be involved in addressing the leadership challenges as well as the mindset that has created the crisis.

9.4: Application: recommendations for coaches

Bad leadership is not something that can be 'fixed' in the way that processes and machines can be fixed. It cannot be 'located' in a single person or group of people, as we know it is often co-created or enabled by other teams around and by determining factors such as power, discretion, time of service, industry norms, and so on. Nevertheless, as coaches we can work with leaders in transformative ways. I believe we can provide a relationship where bad leadership can be observed and allowed to become more healthy and sustainable.

If a leader is challenged head-on and without offering support, the only response will be defence and counter-attack, as we have seen with all whistleblowers and even journalists who try to address issues associated with global leadership.

Case example 9.2*

Kevin is a leadership coach who works with fast-growing founder firms, supporting them through stages of growth which often involve doubling or tripling their turnover or staff from year to year. He works both with the individuals and with the top teams, taking time with them to redesign their teams, departments, and organizational structures – and most of all, working through what the new structures and teams mean for their work together and their relationships. There is usually a two-day retreat every two months where the top team works through the changes, and individual sessions in between both for themselves to understand the changes and their own stance within change, and for others in the organization where they try to translate the views of the top team. Founders have had a creative contribution and they have found vast markets for their ideas, but they often have no experience with or understanding of leadership, despite a rapid growth in their leadership responsibility.

Kevin has found the participation in fast-growing, meaningful businesses very rewarding. However, he has also noticed that despite his experience as an executive coach, the 'founder teams' have a particular way of making him co-responsible for their leadership struggles. He notices that oftentimes he finds himself filling a void of leadership, such as at the two-day sessions or during the coaching conversations with the founders) themselves. This usually has adverse results: as soon as Kevin starts explaining or organizing the way forward, the leaders in the team lean back and give him the space, without successively implementing any of the great ideas that Kevin has proposed during the meeting. He is beginning to notice that his high levels of engagement and involvement with these coachees do not always yield the objectives he and his coachees are aiming for. This leads to assignments getting turned over, Kevin being retained much longer term and wondering to himself what value he is adding to the founder team and the company. Currently, Kevin is considering the formulation of a 'policy' of what to do after a number of trials with certain teams and organizations.

---

*The team coach 'Kevin' is Dr Katrin Hinzdorf who has submitted a paper on founders' team coaching to the Consulting Psychology Journal, which will appear in 2023.

I think there are two prongs of attack (or actually, protection!) that have made a difference in coaching conversations, when it comes to leadership and the leadership shadow, which can in principle be provided at scale:

- Understanding more about leadership and links between power, hubris, and psychopathology. From the study of leadership, we may formulate better checks and balances on leadership, such as are in place with political power (two independent chambers, voting rules, democratic control).
- Challenge and support provided in a safe setting, so that leaders can truly reflect on what they are doing and reappraise their priorities and values. With appropriate challenge, leaders can step back from their shadow, put their contribution onto a more positive and balanced footing, and integrate their more primitive urges as expressed by their shadow sides (Nelson and Hogan, 2009; De Haan and Kasozi, 2014).

But we can only do this by staying independent, by just observing and reflecting on the mindset, not by taking a stance and advocating for particular ways forward.

This is where coaches can play a unique and, in my view, important role: *witnessing* the mindset that underpins the crisis, being sensitive to the greed and hubris that are at stake – and calling it out. Naming the unwholesome (greedy, lazy, selfish …) processes that are compounding the issues but not taking a side against them – just lovingly opening them up to reflection.

For this it is important that we learn to reflect on our own minds first. Our minds can be seen as polluters emitting toxic substances, when they are fuelled by irrational fears, usually in response to feeling unsafe or unloved (Shohet, 1995). When in such a state we feel we need to consume more or lead more in order to feel safer, and our irrational greed remains unrecognized. This irrational fear can just as easily be expressed by coaching, by advocacy, or by altruism, i.e. by aligning ourselves to a 'worthy' cause and a 'worthy' profession. We therefore need a lot of self-reflection to determine whether a piece of work (e.g. helping others) is truly worthy or only an expression of fear. The value of our coaching – or advocacy – is not an empty question with an obvious answer, but rather something that we will have to study regularly and at length to become gradually more sure of ourselves.

Chapter summary

Where Chapter 8 highlighted the contrasts between assessment and love, this chapter does the same for advocacy and love. Increasingly, I see coaches turning to advocacy for highly ethical and wholesome causes, such as the survival of our planet and its ecological diversity, or the rejection of racism, slavery, and inequality in corporate organizations. I try to show here how these same ethical coaches may be pulled out of their roles. Advocacy takes us away from coaching and makes our own agenda important to us, to such an extent that we might miss aspects of the coachee's agenda, to the detriment of coaching. Conversely, if we use all we can muster in terms of curiosity, courage, and warmth, we might just help a coachee to look at their leadership shadow, where a lot of the problems for the planet and for human society lurk anyway. Internal and everyday racism, bigotry, greed, hubris, and more generally fear, are what we are bound to find in an executive's shadow. All these tendencies can be reintegrated, they can actually be helpful and strengthening, e.g. a leader's fear senses danger, highlights risks, and spurs to action. However, taking on board our shadows is very hard work and requires large helpings of love and forgiveness. So, a coach distracted by her love for the planet is of little use. I explore how our unflinching love for the coachee may be a wholesome manifestation of our love for the planet.

Note

1   It is worth looking at the ancient Greek meaning of crisis (κρισις), which is 'judgement' and 'decision', so it is very much 'taking a stance' and having a new 'determination' – and therefore, perhaps, it is time to respond to crisis with crisis, i.e. a clear judgement on what we want to be a personal commitment for, how we are prepared to play a constructive role in crisis.

Part **C**

Stay humble longer term

There is plenty of evidence, some reviewed in this part of the book, that over time successful coaches, just like successful leaders, start to think the change they are witnessing is really very much to do with themselves. They increasingly believe it is their own work and that they are deeply wise, helpful, and guru-like leaders or coaches. Indeed, we can spot and measure very gradual cognitive biases that slowly increase over our lifetime and as we gain more experience, all towards experiencing ourselves as more coach-like and more helpful. These biases make us more confident and generally more satisfied and even happy (Tierney and Baumeister, 2019). At the same time, there is no evidence that these biases are reflected in practice. No evidence that we indeed become more effective or helpful for others (clients, observers, commissioners) as we mature and stay in the profession for longer – if anything, the opposite is more likely to be true.

It is as if our doubts and fears, which were such an important source of understanding our emotions and vulnerability, have over time ossified into a hard layer of self-confidence, which we can call a mask (of 'professionalism') or a protection (against feeling our underlying decline and demise).

I have felt this within myself, that as I stay in this profession over time, I start to believe I am jolly good at it. Moreover, I am treated with more deference and my words of advice are heeded with growing respect and as if dutifully, something I might have wished for when I was only a novice or a trainee. Nevertheless, these are not healthy developments, in my view. Practising humility and stepping back from leading witnesses in conversations (rather than treating them as adult coachees) become a real concern for senior coaches, which is why I want to devote this final part of the book to 'staying humble'.

Chapter 10 looks at humility in the context of listening. It advocates the assumption of modesty in terms of what we are picking up, what we understand, and what we know about the coachee. Staying humble might help us to just be present a little longer or attend a little deeper and to park all those things we think we know, remember, and desire for our coachee.

Chapter 11 focuses on the self-images we have as coaches and the extent to which our coachees recognize them. Again, this research seems to tell us that

Figure C1: Based on 948 coach profiles using the Coaching Behaviours Questionnaire, we can see that *self-reported* coaching behaviours change smoothly with age, towards a more non-directive, 'coach-like' profile with older age. The same picture emerges when we plot 'years of experience' rather than 'age' as the independent variable. When compared with the profiles of the clients of these coaches, we do not see those coachees recognizing these trends (De Haan and Nilsson, 2017).

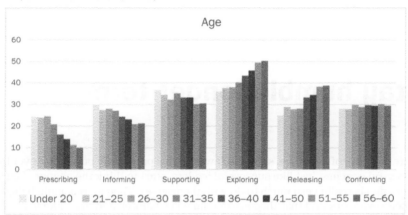

we need to be humble and not assume that we are as good as coaches as we think we are.

Chapter 12 reviews the field of coaching ethics, an important field as we witness our coachees' confessions and vulnerabilities in our practice. We have all learned about confidentiality, indemnity insurance, and putting transparent procedures in place such as contracting. But does that 'make' us ethical? And will we stay ethical when under pressure? Again, it appears the most experienced group of coaches is most at risk of becoming less ethical or overly cavalier with certain helpful precautions and protections.

Chapter 13, finally, briefly looks at the new, emerging field of team coaching. Here, it is often easier to practise humility, simply because as coaches, we are outnumbered. Nevertheless, it is very easy for a team coach to be pulled in and become rather central for the team during the limited time that we spend together. We are surreptitiously, or sometimes quite openly, invited to chair, to teach, or to show the way. One can even argue that in team coaching there is no way that we can avoid becoming part of the coachee, part of the team, during our engagement. As a result, we struggle to hold our stance of just 'witnessing' and 'nurturing' change. The chapter looks at my own experiences with this tension and how love may dissipate even this daunting, unavoidable fear of losing our role or wherewithal to coach.

The two main questions to you in this part of the book are:

1   What is your 'seniority' shaping up like? Where lies your arrogance, your irritability, your rigidity, your conceit, or what form does your increasing self-confidence take for you?

2 Can you face the fact that the ethics of coaching are likely to become more important to you rather than less; how can you approach the boundaries in your practice, your ethical decision-making, with increasing freshness despite ethical questions becoming more and more familiar, even potentially 'boring', for you?

There is a theme running through this part of the book, namely that love is not a given or a stayer, that love needs to be earned with hard work. If we do not do this work, we first let go of our freshness and curiosity, then we become somewhat set in our ways, and finally unbeknownst to us we abandon the field and become overly confident, pompous teachers rather than learners.

10 Practise humility in noticing: enhancing our sensitivity as coaches

I dwelled on the topic of listening in Chapter 2 … and yet, listening remains such a fascinating process even for experienced coaches. In this chapter, I would like to highlight my more recent learnings about listening and how they help me slowly to improve my listening even though at the same time I am gradually losing my sight and my hearing, through the natural ageing process.

10.1: The deceptively simple art of listening: always something to improve

The simple yet mysterious art of listening is something that we can all improve on throughout our lifetime. This contrasts with many other skills which we can bring to a certain level, to our own 'personal best', after which they consolidate. Think about sport, leadership, and communication skills. With expert input we can work to improve them and then most of us arrive at a 'satisfactory' level where we remain or descend, no matter what new teaching we obtain.

Listening is quite different from other skills, if only because nobody is truly ever very good at it: so much of what is highly relevant to the speaker's experience remains hidden from the listener and even from the speaker herself. This is nicely illustrated by the Johari Window (Luft, 1969), where everyone is represented with large hidden, blind-spot, and unknown areas.

All speaking is based on listening. So, I would heartily agree with Plutarch, who observed, some two thousand years ago, that even though most ambitious professionals spend a lot of time and effort on learning to speak better, it is the faculty of listening that really deserves their investment.

What makes listening so difficult is not just that a lot of relevant 'material' is not being communicated, but also that we ourselves habitually distort and limit our own powers of listening. We arrive in a certain state of mind which comes with natural biases. Moreover, we cannot switch off our sense-making apparatus during listening, thus we recognize, retrofit, and remain on the lookout for patterns and conclusions. These early hypotheses or conclusions can have a limiting impact on what we can actually hear freshly, and what we can hear next. Such is the problem with 'active' listening that we actively search in directions which deceptively take us away from listening despite our best intentions – active listening takes us away from being here, now. This led Freud and Bion to remark that rather than a laser-like beam of bright light to spot more information, we need a 'beam of intense darkness' instead.

Case example 10.1: 'Listen well, consult less'

If coaches are able to detect the irony in a presenting problem, they may often save themselves a lot of work. We discovered this a little late, some twenty years ago, when we were asked to facilitate a programme on project management for Nike Europe in Belgium. Over the previous years, the Nike managers concerned had made a considerable effort towards becoming professional project leaders. They had read books, attended courses, and implemented their learning, but for some reason this had never brought them the hoped-for improvement in their work. After some preliminary conversation and agreement on the programme design, we started to facilitate the first module on 'advanced' project management. The managers responded enthusiastically, asking about ways to complete projects more successfully. When it came to the writing of a project plan and the need to map project goals, results, and milestones, someone responded unexpectedly: 'This won't work over here. We always follow our company motto "Just do it!", which inspires us to believe that nothing is impossible so long as we dedicate ourselves to it one hundred per cent. So, it won't suit us to create a lot of paperwork first and only then to begin to actually do things.' This was such a compelling remark that we decided to use the remainder of the module to listen to the participants and the circumstances under which they might be prepared to commit to any planning ahead and thereby to complement their motto. Together with them we then cancelled the rest of the programme because we all became convinced that there was no lack of knowledge or training in the field of project management. The strong company culture and motto of Nike had led to repeated requests for training in the field of project management. As far as I know, this might very well still be the case all these years later.

10.2: Our own fears of listening are our biggest obstacle

Listening often seems the easiest thing for a coach: the interest is there, the motivation is there, the empathy is there, listening skills have been developed to a sufficient level, and so on. For the coach herself, the mere choice for this profession indicates that she cares, places the coachee central, is sincerely interested, and listens well. In this way, coaches often assume they are good listeners (see also Chapter 11).

They may also assume tacitly that their session has not really begun when they are 'only' listening. We often overlook how risky and fearsome 'just' listening is, and many of us overestimate our own listening skills. To quote Plutarch (first century AD) again: 'Some people think the speaker has a function, while the listener does nothing.'

In fact, listening is the only communicative skill that we need to be truly skilful in of all other communication, and often the only skill that even experienced practitioners must admit that they have a lot to learn about. This is partly because accomplished listeners can notice all the better that they still have sub-optimal skills. They notice they are missing cues or that they are not certain about what they pick up, as there may be very few signals and it remains a struggle to read those signals well. Our fears often decrease our faculty of listening, even if we are not conscious of them or do not attach a lot of weight to them.

Reviewing my own difficulties with listening, I have come to conclude that there are four basic fears that block my listening at different times. These are only *my* fears; the reader may have others not mentioned here.

1 The fear of not contributing enough or not being useful enough. This is a central theme for many coaches (see my research on critical moments for coaches – De Haan, 2008b and 2008c), and has to do with the fact that the coach is not in charge, and not herself responsible for results that ultimately belong to the coachee. Naturally, a coach will be keen and therefore anxious to prove her worth and make a difference. When the coach is 'only' listening, this fear is heightened and may develop into a distraction which itself undermines listening.

2 The fear of not understanding enough. The struggle for understanding is always part of the work of the listener. Being keen to understand more seems of benefit to a listener, but it can also stand in our way. We become conscious of how much we are missing, which can make us too focused and too alert for free listening. The listener may become less open, for example, to what they are not picking up just yet, or to what the speaker has (surprisingly) *not* said. After all, what a coachee does not bring to a session can be as important as what they do bring.

3 The fear of exposure of self. When we are listening carefully, we are offering our full attention and we are trying to 'let in' as much information as we can. This means we suspend our judgements of what we see and hear, and we develop empathy for our coachees. We also let go as much as possible of our own interpretative processes and our own agendas. We find ourselves listening 'without memory and desire', as Bion wrote (1970). This can leave us feeling awkwardly exposed, lost, or vulnerable as we are giving up any sense of control or direction in our work.

4 The fear of loss of self. Another fear when we are listening carefully, offering our full attention and being as open as we can, is that we almost dissolve into the coachee's frame of mind. I have often experienced a trance-like state when I was listening with all my heart and mind, becoming myself almost an extension of the thoughts and feelings of my coachees. This risk of losing oneself in trance is heightened when we are listening to emotional accounts, or to ambivalence and ambiguity, so that neither we nor our coachees know what will come next.

Interestingly, the four basic fears above seem to complement each other as they are oppositions. The first two are about (1) underplaying the task that is involved in 'just' listening versus (2) being overly daunted by the task of the listener. The second two are about (3) becoming self-conscious about the vulnerability of being there for someone else versus (4) becoming self-effacing in the process of listening. The art of listening for me seems to be to keep Aristotle's golden mean between them.

10.3: Listening without fear: negative capability and embracing the negative

The experience of listening when we do not feel fearful is rather exquisite. We feel a great freedom and no obligation. We can immerse ourselves and let go of our self-consciousness, just to be there and listen. I rarely achieve this state of listening where my sense of duty, obligation, uncertainty, risk, and fear disappears. It occasionally happens after what I feel has been a very satisfactory session, namely at the beginning of the following session. Or after something has been achieved in this session, so that I can finally let go of that anxiety to achieve or to deliver, albeit usually only for a fleeting moment.

Those situations of listening without fear are worth observing closely, as they remind us of what good coaching is and what listening can be. They have been studied by many good listeners. Well known are Bion's ideas about good listening – he described it as a 'negative capability', the inverse of a competence or capability, or as those moments when we can work 'without memory or desire, or understanding'. With his aim for 'negative capability' Bion drew on Keats' learning for poets, which Keats describes as 'being in uncertainties, mysteries, doubts, without any irritable reaching after fact and reason' (Keats, 1817). An ability to perceive and recognize fresh truths beyond the strain and reach of so-called active listening and beyond the fears of losing out, not knowing or knowing too much.

I have often noted that beginning coaches struggle to listen to anything until and unless they can recognize it as their own experience (rather concretely). Later they say the coachee or the story reminds them so much of themselves, or that 'this particular coachee is like myself' (usually an earlier version of themselves). It seems that we begin to learn about listening through projecting our own life and experience onto our coachees. One might call this a narcissistic stage of empathy, where a degree of empathy is achieved by claiming the coachee as our own. It is often difficult to move away from this perspective and to begin seeing coachees as they are or might be, rather than as we can recognize them.[1] At the other end of the spectrum, mature listeners learn to welcome projections from the coachee and begin to feel things about them that coachees are not (consciously) aware of themselves.

Case example 10.2

An experienced coach has been asked to work with the top 50 of a logistical organization after a new strategy has been decided upon. 'Digitalization' is set to become even more at the core of the business and a new Chief Digital Officer has been added to the board. The coach feels insecure even before meeting his first group of leaders, and the probing questions they ask him at the start of the session cause him to feel even more insecure, and powerless. He frets and he manoeuvres, tries to infuse the session with meaning and moves along with the strongest voices in the room, leaders who request changes to the seating and the scope of the session. After this initial debate, he is finally able to organize some useful work with one of them, as the group works with this leader's doubts and questions. But even after the session he feels small and uncertain, and he dreads the five further sessions that he has been contracted for. It is only when he realizes that his uncertainty is what they must be feeling after the imposed changes, and the belittling effects of the new Chief being landed on them, that he regains his composure and trusts that his feelings are perhaps co-created (and not just his own), after which he realizes, he need not worry so much about the next session.

In order to nurture that process of receiving projections, I have learned to ask myself, time and time again, what is *not* there – what is being left out of this conversation, what is not being mentioned even though one would expect it to be. For example, when there is a complaint, why do we not see an angry or frustrated face? Or, if there is a goal, why don't we sense the motivation to achieve it? If there is a loss, why do we see a smile at the same time, and why do we not sense the experience of a loss? Similarly with a success or an achievement, where is the pride, where is the 'owning' of that achievement?

I know my listening is partial and flawed, so what I do is ask myself questions. I do not ask my coachees any questions as questions will distract from the presentation and from using the time in the way my coachees want to use it. But I will ask questions of myself, questions which may reveal some of the things that are being expressed, but less openly. Here are some examples of those questions:

What is my coachee not saying? (…) How is my coachee making me feel right now? (…) How is the boss of the coachee, or the organization of my coachee, making me feel right now? And as a corollary: how might the organization of my coachee make my coachee feel? Is there any overlap between my feelings about this organization (or team) and how my coachee might be feeling? Or is my coachee feeling something entirely different, perhaps even the opposite of what I am feeling?

Any use of negatives by the coachee should also make our ears prick up. In my view, they are always revealing. Negatives are often used at the beginning of sessions, as we saw in Chapter 5. The coachee says, 'it is not this ...', e.g. 'I have not been naïve ...' or 'It is not that they are taking advantage ...'. This is usually a strong indication that at least an important part of the coachee thinks that indeed they themselves have been naïve or have been taken advantage of (see also Freud, 1925).

It is almost as with a politician who says that they are not aware or they cannot remember: in those cases most interested observers are near 100% certain that in fact the politician does know and does remember, but that it is just too uncomfortable and risky to say that. In the same way, when a coachee uses a negative, she is usually pointing to something that she is fearful of admitting. Love needs to come to the table to make the fear disappear, after which the coachee can be more fully understood and feel safer, hopefully safe enough.

10.4: Application: recommendations for coaches

I have been writing about the same theme once more and all over again, the eternal themes of love seeing through fear, understanding fear, making fear disappear. This time love appeared as that capability that can sustain us when we are not doing anything or reaching out towards something, when we are just being fully present. This loving glance is almost the inversion of who we are normally at work and in our everyday business: in control, in command, capable, immersed in activities such as sending, delivering, speaking, active listening. The mature listener is 'in' negative capability, or one might say 'in love' if that does not conjure up too many images of butterflies, desire, or adulation.

What do my hunches about listening mean for how I might listen in the future? First, I can let go of a lot of things – the need to prepare, the wish to be 'in the zone', meditation, and actively emptying my head – all of those just make me more active again and would prepare me for hyperfocus or a sporting competition but not very well for coaching. I can let go of any preparation, except for two glances. One, my customary glance or a walk into nature which helps me to realize where I am. And two, a curious glance at my notes from the previous session to help bring the client back to mind. I can do this within a minute and so I do not mind back-to-back coaching conversations. As soon as my coachee enters the room, she takes over my world anyway.

Second, I can keep an eye out for what is not there, what surprises me by its absence, and what is explicitly denied. What distinguishes itself by its absence takes more awareness to become present. I remember that every gesture, every word, and every feeling I receive are relevant, and reveal something about what wants to be known. Even the gestures, words, and feelings I am not receiving are relevant. There is simply too much that sheds a light on our work, which again spurs me on to let go, to let go again even just after receiving new data, and not to try to capture all of what comes across.

In conclusion, I believe letting go and embracing the richness and diversity of a session are two sides of the same coin, and both illustrate listening at its best.

Chapter summary

This is the second chapter about listening, after Chapter 2 which was mostly about the spirit of inquiry, the need to get over prejudice and previous knowledge, in order to open ourselves up for new information. This chapter adds to that idea some views about the listening process, from my own experience. Fears are shown to impede our ability to listen, which strengthens the (Rogerian) idea that listening has to be done with love, empathy and understanding. After highlighting the importance of listening and the curious fact that listening can truly improve over our lifetime (even despite our declining senses), the importance of the 'absent' and the 'negative' are emphasized. What is absent is often as important as what is being presented, as it constitutes what is being left out or what is being forgotten. What is brought as negative may re-emerge as a positive, upon deeper understanding. Conversely, our greatest strengths are often our greatest weaknesses. A denial or negative hunch ('it is not this ...') is often a give-away for something being positively important, instead.

Note

1 To be precise, what happens here is not just 'identification': these listeners are also projecting – usually less esteemed – parts of the self onto their clients. In other words, some coaches first project and then also identify with that part or narrative of the client that they recognize (Melanie Klein, 1946, wrote about this and gave us the term *projective identification* to describe it). It is interesting that this kind of identification can also be an important hindrance for clients in understanding their own world. In a general sense, founders and owners of businesses are often leaders who strongly self-identify with their organization and the people in it. They may see certain roles (unconsciously) as an extension or a part of themselves, and they often go around passionately nurturing cum admonishing 'their' people as if they were properties or extensions of themselves. When this kind of identification is rife in the client or client system, we may become still more tempted during a coaching session to identify with our client or our client's issues (as a so-called parallel process – see Chapter 3).

11 Practise humility: you are not the coach you think you are[1]

Any coaching relationship can be looked at from different perspectives. It is possible to check what other partners in the relationship have seen and experienced. When we do this, we often find surprising results, such as around the quality of the relationship and the results of sessions. They are not really the same as seen through different eyes, and those participating in coaching may disagree widely and still find something of their own value in the sessions (De Haan, 2019c).

One such area where perceptions may differ is around what we do in the sessions, what 'interventions' we use. Coaches often – naively – think that how they act is how they come across, and that their interventions are understood the way that they were intended. When we actually research these matters, we coaches are in for a surprise, and a humbling one at that: we are not as 'coach-like' as we would like to believe!

At Ashridge, we recently studied coaching behaviours both as reported by executive coaches, consultants, and managers, and by these coaches' coachees. The latest version of the Coaching Behaviours Questionnaire (CBQ) was used in a large-scale study of coaching behaviours, involving 537 coaches, 196 consultants, and 559 manager-coaches from 54 countries, and also 221 coachees. The study demonstrated significant differences in perceived behaviour by age, gender, and nationality. Significant differences were also observed between those who identify themselves as managers, consultants, or coaches, and the recipients of coaching – the coachees. Some differences can be attributed to more experienced coaches perceiving themselves as developing different coaching behaviours. Below is a summary of our findings; a more extensive report can be found in De Haan and Nilsson (2017).

11.1: Coaches' skills and what we think we are doing

Executive coaches have a wide array of behavioural responses at their disposal during coaching sessions. The vast amount of possibilities can be dizzying and a real source of doubt and anxiety for coaches. As I argue in other chapters, the amount of choice, the fact that we can only choose one option at a time, the uncertainty as to which response will be most helpful at any given moment, plus the many unknowns generally in each and every coaching conversation, result in a considerable amount of fear on the part of the coach, let alone the coachee for whom a lot more is at stake in the session. How to confront this fear and how to grow helpfulness and love out of such turmoil and anxiety, are one of the greatest challenges for all coaches.

I think some coaches ignore the question of options and choice and 'just' do what comes to mind, naturally, with a degree of confidence and wishful thinking. I think this indeed solves the dilemma and is quite soothing for the coach. However, it may not be the best response to the anxiety and fear of not knowing what to do and having too many options: the anxiety just goes underground while the coach acts on her sublime but naïve self-confidence. I think it is always better to consider those options, not run away from them, especially not the more scary ones, such as support and closeness versus challenge and boldness. We should welcome them, embrace them, and be open to the full range of interventions, just like we try to be open to the full range of coachee concerns and queries.

As you mature as a coach, you will learn how to 'expect the unexpected'. And you will undoubtedly continue to spend time reflecting on which 'intervention' to use and when. At the same time, your coachee will be wondering what to say and when to say it, and how to invite you as the coach to respond. Meanwhile, both parties will be forming views of one another's behaviours; in other words, you and your coachee will be making inferences about what those behaviours tell you and how to respond.

In the coaching literature there's been much discussion and a proliferation of models of what I'd call 'the coach's best behaviours', i.e. which interventions to use and when. Thus far, most of this debate has been without much evidential support: without much knowledge of which behaviours coaches think they use and which behaviours coachees think they receive (and vice versa!). Measurements of coach behaviours or coaches' and coachees' own views on coaching behaviours are scarce (exceptions include Ianiro et al., 2013, and De Haan et al., 2011).

To start investigating coaching skills, a basic tool is needed to measure the full range of interventions, one which is general and broad enough, not too detailed and complicated, and with a limited number of classes of interventions, so that reliable measurements can be made. The model should have high validity as well: both coachees and coaches need to be able to recognize each of the classes of intervention from a short description, and their ratings should conform to their intuitive appreciation of the interventions. Here at Ashridge, we believe such a model is the 72-item Coaching Behaviours Questionnaire (CBQ),[2] an adaptation of the Heron (1975) model of counselling interventions.

11.2: The coaching behaviours model and questionnaire

The CBQ has three 'push', coach-centred (directive) sets of behaviours: *Prescribing*, *Informing*, and *Confronting*, and three 'pull', coachee-centred (non-directive) sets of behaviours: *Exploring*, *Supporting*, and *Releasing* (see Figure 11.1).

Figure 11.1 The so-called 'Heron Model' of counselling and coaching behaviours (after Heron, 1975), stretching from highly directive to highly facilitative interventions, and from challenging to supporting options.

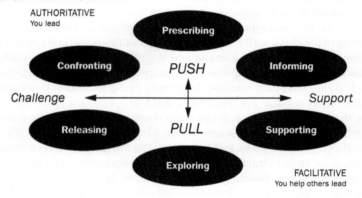

The six classes of intervention illustrate that as a coach you have a broad range of interventions at your disposal. At any point of time in a coaching conversation, you will have the options of:

- not doing anything, devoting your energy to following the coachee and to listening;
- offering a piece of direction, either through advice or suggestion (*Prescribing*) or by means of information that might help the coachee (*Informing*);
- offering a challenge to the coachee, consisting of a different way to look at their issues (*Confronting*); or
- offering facilitative interventions, by offering warmth and support (*Supporting*), a chance to summarize and inquire more deeply into the issues at stake (*Exploring*), or an invitation to open up emotional undercurrents to the issues and the conversation itself (*Releasing*).

With the CBQ, coaching and consulting professionals have a reliable and intuitive tool to hand to measure coaching behaviours through the eyes of coaches, consultants, manager-coaches, coachees, and even observers. The statistical properties of this tool show that it can be used to make measurements that result in highly personal feedback to coaches, either given by themselves or by others. In the current version of the CBQ, this feedback is related to a large norm group of managers, consultants, and coaches. Thus, participants are automatically compared with the norm-group results of the group that they belong to. Moreover, all participants receive percentile scores that indicate what proportion of the norm group with their particular job description (manager, consultant, coach) score lower than they do on each of the six dimensions.

11.3: Findings from systematically comparing different coach profiles

In our research, we were able to show that the CBQ is reliable and valid, and that self-reported coach profiles change significantly with coach demographics such as age, gender, job description, and nationality. Finally, we found that coachee-reported behavioural profiles are different from self-reported profiles of the same coach. Below we report the systematic differences that we found in our sample between various groups of coaches and also between coaches and their coachees. In practice we run up against all the issues with diagnostical instruments discussed in Chapter 7 – however, here I am reporting only on correlations between the profiles, not on how relevant or true the findings of the profiles are for the professional coaches who take the instrument.

Gender differences

Female coaches score themselves higher on the non-directive interventions and lower on the directive interventions than their male counterparts, whereas they do not differ significantly in the amount of 'challenge' and 'support' they think they give their coachees. There is also some evidence that female coaches are slightly more effective in the eyes of coachees than their male counterparts (De Haan *et al.*, 2016). It is important to remember that in research with the CBQ, we are not measuring effectiveness.

Age

Older coaches/consultants/managers scored significantly lower on directive interventions than their younger colleagues. They also reported giving less active support, while their emotionally *Releasing* interventions were more prevalent in their self-scores.

Job role

Job role also has an influence on CBQ scores, with manager-coaches, consultant-coaches, and 'professional' coaches self-scoring progressively lower on directive and supportive interventions but progressively higher on non-directive (*Exploring* and *Releasing*) interventions. In other words, participants who describe their primary role as 'coach' report a more 'coaching' (non-directive) profile in their scores. This may be the influence of progressive 'acculturation' in the coaching profession, where coaches learn to think about their interventions progressively in terms of more 'typical' coaching interventions, i.e. the 'pull' behaviours within *Exploring* and *Releasing*. In fact, we find that if coachee scores are compared to all three categories, the discrepancies are largest for professional coaches, which indicates that coaches may be changing their self-perceptions more than their actual coaching behaviours.

Country of origin

There were some significant differences in scores when measured against country of origin. We found substantial differences in terms of how many *Confronting* interventions were reported: highest in the Netherlands, intermediate in Belgium, and lowest in the UK. Similar contrasts of 'directness' and 'non-avoidance' were reported by Van Meurs (2003) in her PhD thesis on negotiations between Dutch and UK managers. From personal experience and studying cultural assessments of national cultures (e.g. the dimension of internal vs. external control in Trompenaars' Cultural Dimensions Model), we recognize the progressive increase in *Confronting* from the UK, to Belgium, and then to the Netherlands. Coach profiles from North America and the Middle East were also significantly different (De Haan and Nilsson, 2017).

Coachee profiles compared to coach profiles

Coachees of workplace coaches scored the coaches significantly higher on directive interventions and significantly lower on some non-directive interventions. Three effects were significant, in that the coachees believed their coaches did more *Prescribing* and *Informing* and less *Releasing* than the coaches themselves did. This appears to show that coaches may be more central in their interventions than they themselves realize: they may be giving more advice (*Prescribing*) and information (*Informing*) than they think. Moreover, coaches appear not to go as deeply into the coachee's inner world and emotions (*Releasing*) as they perceive themselves to do. We don't know if any of this 'general feedback for coaches' is related to skill; however, it's tempting to think that these coaches are sometimes so busy with their own ideas and suggestions that they attend less to their coachees' emotional process and are less effective as a consequence. Certainly, their coachees are saying to some significant extent that the coaches are engaged in more coach-centric interventions than they think. It would be worth testing if coachees also *wish* their coaches to be less advisory and informing, as well as more in tune with their own highly personal emotional experience. We know from other studies that coachees may perceive the empathic behaviour of coaches differently from the coaches themselves (Will *et al.*, 2016) and that they perceive effectiveness of coaching quite differently from their coaches (De Haan *et al.*, 2016). Given that the coachee sample was small and the effects nonetheless large, we believe more research needs to be done and are looking forward to replicating this analysis with larger samples.

Self-perception

We found evidence that the differences in self-perceptions of coaches are not replicated by their coachees, namely for the 'gender' and 'job description' dimensions where this could be tested. As the sample was relatively small, we need to be cautious in drawing conclusions, however, it does seem that self-identification of female and professional coaches is more non-directive, while this is not reflected in different behaviour towards their coachees. It's always possible that such perhaps more sophisticated coaches change something about their behaviour that the coachee does not even notice while still being impacted; however, there is no evidence of a differential impact on coachees. To restate, the coachees reported exactly the same behavioural profiles for the professional coaches as for the managers they work with, and also similar profiles for their female and male coaches.

This study shows that we can now reliably measure a wide range of coaching interventions and make powerful comparisons between samples of coaches and between the coachee and coach perspective on those same interventions. There seem to be systematic scoring patterns in terms of directive and non-directive coaching styles; and also in terms of the amount of support or challenge provided by the coach/consultant/manager. The patterns we found are indicative of development and adaptation, with older and more professional coaches displaying more 'typical' non-directive and coachee-centred coaching behaviours over time and as they specialize more as coaches. There is some indication that these are mainly self-perceptions on the part of professional coaches, not shared by their coachees. We found some support for viewing coaching as more a 'female' profession with females displaying more 'typical' coaching skills in their own work. Finally, we found some evidence of coaches adapting to their national cultures and becoming more confrontational, direct, or explorational, especially in those cultures where this is considered the norm. However, the systematic patterns we found still need to be linked back to measurable behaviours and skills – as this is not yet the case, we only found evidence for patterns in the *perceptions* of coaching skills.

11.4: Application: recommendations for coaches

It would be interesting to bring in the observer's perspective (both during live sessions and based on recordings), and to compare more of the scores directly on the same coaching relationship and even session by session. The CBQ could be further modified to rate observed behaviour both in terms of frequency of occurrence and impact/effectiveness. Ultimately, a tool like this can be used to assess the *efficacy* or *skill* of a coach to produce desired outcomes, namely when scores on this instrument are correlated with reliable outcome measures, such as in randomized controlled trials. Only then will we be able to establish beyond doubt whether the significant differences we observed between different coaching professionals are indicative of a different approach in their conversations, whether they correlate with differences in competence, and ultimately, in their effectiveness as coaches.

Chapter summary

This chapter invites coaches to think again about their coaching. Too often we are too proud of being coaches, and too convinced that we are in the service of our coachees. Our intentions may very well be coach-like, and they usually are. But that does not mean that our stance and the way we come across are very coach-like, and often they aren't. If we compare how coaches see themselves with how their coachees see them, then we find some striking differences, especially for more experienced and external coaches. I believe this should make us all think again about how we may be perceived by coachees, and, as a consequence, more humble regarding how we come across. Even though our motivation is laudable, our devotion sincere, and our competences well honed, we may still come across more as consultants or mentors or managers than, actually, as coaches. Bottom line is that it seems important to stay humble and embrace our not-knowing, especially the more experienced we become.

Notes

1 This chapter is an expanded version of an article which first appeared in the January 2018 issue of *Coaching Today*. © The British Association for Counselling and Psychotherapy.
2 The first version of the questionnaire was created and used by Richard Phillips in 1994, and subsequent versions were developed with help from Alex Davda, Helen Lockett, Judy Curd, and Viktor Nilsson at Ashridge. The CBQ questionnaire and coachee feedback version can be taken by writing to psychometrics@ashridge.hult.edu.

12 Practise humility in ethics: coaching power corrupts like any other power[1]

with Annette Bienfait

We are both long-standing members of the European Mentoring and Coaching Council (EMCC) and of other coaching bodies. Annette has been a member of the ethical complaints committee of EMCC The Netherlands for more than ten years. Erik has been involved in postgraduate training and formal accreditation of coaches for more than twenty years. Besides being formally accredited by Ashridge, EMCC, and the ICF, Erik is a qualified psychotherapist.

Throughout all those twenty years, there has been no let-up in the squabbling about the 'Wild West' conditions of our profession ... the 'cowboys' and 'snake oil salesmen' who seem to prevail in our cherished coaching field. Most of the attacks on the seriousness of our profession appear to be based on the fact that anyone can call themselves a coach, as well as on the risks that commissioners run by exposing vulnerable coachees to unqualified coaches. If anything, these criticisms have only grown louder.

This chapter is intended to reflect on this criticism from a professional-ethics perspective. Should we as coaches be worried about our profession? Should we set our own house in order first and only then, when we are above reproach, dare to contribute something and earn the right to speak about ethics? It shows that we were indeed quite keen to lay down some of our credentials at the start of this chapter, fearing that we might get dragged into polemics and would then need some kind of protective device. Like many other coaches (see Berglas, 2002, p. 88, where he similarly emphasizes his qualifications), we find ourselves using our credentials as a protective cover, ready to be employed when someone brands us with the terrifying epithet, 'unethical'.

We have noticed over the years how much of our ethics and accreditations in coaching are essentially fear-based and mainly serve to protect against possible criticism from within or without. They claim to be strengthening the protection of the coachee and the duty of the coach. But do we really need that sort of body armour? Do we need to go along with the assumption that executive coaches, especially less experienced ones or non-psychologists, are not very professional, not very thorough in their approach and interventions, not to be trusted unless they fulfil all their duties and can demonstrate strong credentials and proof of competence?

We think not.

We think that a trust-based ethics can indeed *assume* that all coaches, including new coaches, will have the right motivation and plenty to offer to our profession. In this chapter, we want to assume that every coach is of good will and bona fide, from the moment she or he enters the profession. With this assumption in place, professional organizations will offer new coaches experiences in the profession where their trust grows rather than diminishes, alongside our own trust in them. We believe they should be offered good education, many hours of supervision, and an opportunity to show what they are worth as they get validated through accreditation. Even such an accreditation process should be enhancing and built around the understanding that, provided you can demonstrate basic aspects of coaching, accreditors will be there for you to help you through. Such basic aspects that need to be demonstrated may include contracting, placing the coachee central ('non-directiveness'), and an ability to reflect on your own coaching and work with unexpected feedback, such as the viewpoints of peers and accreditors.

The only executive coaches who do need to worry and be fearful about their ethics are, in our view paradoxically, the ones who are 'beyond fear' and consider themselves standard-bearers, champions or guardians of the profession. They may think of themselves as beyond fear, but ultimately, they *instil* fear with their standard-bearing behaviours. Therefore, we believe in reducing the power of all 'seniors' in the profession, including the 'professional associations' themselves, so as to help put trust-based work more central in our practices.

Tim Bond (2006) defines an ethics of trust as one that supports the development of reciprocal relationships of sufficient strength to withstand the relational challenges of difference and inequality and the existential challenges of risk and uncertainty. He argues that in the presence of ethical challenges, trust can build bridges by focusing on the embodied, helping relationship itself and the varying needs of all parties within that relationship. Such an ethics of trust could be invoked to *assume* rather than police many important tenets of our profession, such as:

- New coaches have the right motivation and are therefore worthy to practise in the coaching profession.
- With time they will need a fair amount of education and supervision, and a chance to demonstrate the basic ingredients of good coaching, i.e. become validated and qualified.
- Validation and accreditation can be based on the trusting recognition of competences and are therefore best held in person, not at a distance. In this way, the developmental opportunity will be more central than the assessment tasks.
- Any conflicts between coach and coachee (or coachee organization) are best dealt with by dialogue and mediation, which include all parties.
- The profession is best regulated from the outside, e.g. through national credentialing.

In this chapter, we want to take the opportunity to explore what a trust-based ethics would look like. We will illustrate our argument with real examples from the Dutch EMCC complaints procedure over the last decade, which have been ruled on, anonymized, and published in the records of that committee. We have disguised these cases still further from the published record, so that the original case bringers won't recognize themselves in the cases.

12.1: Strengthening the trust of beginning coaches

By the time a coach becomes qualified, they are tempted to add to the chorus of voices against those who are still unqualified, even if just to legitimize and capitalize on their investment in a formal qualification. Increasingly, our own thinking goes the other way, wanting to include *all* coaches, also the beginning coaches, i.e. the unqualified. How else can the unqualified gain realistic experiences on their way to qualification? We believe we can be inclusive and even a little bit proud of our largely unregulated profession. At the same time, we are strong advocates of engaging in more research and reflection about truly effective and loving forms of regulation, and – on a more personal level – of subjecting our own quality to close inspection, scrutinizing our coach quality keenly and developing it further where possible.

The best way to strengthen our own self-critical capacity and to monitor the quality of our work as executive coaches on an ongoing basis is, in our view, by discussing issues from practice regularly with an independent, professional supervisor. Accreditation can be a very good guarantor of quality as well, particularly if it encompasses a live session and/or recorded vignettes from the coach's practice, but it is only a momentary assessment with most of the measurements not purely of coaching prowess but just as much of the coach's ability to deal with exam conditions and anxiety (see also Chapter 8).

Here is an example of how fear and anxiety may lead coaches to act unethically with their coachees.

Case example 12.1

A coach specializing in first-one-hundred-day coaching for newly appointed leaders obtained a new request through her website. After a short phone call with the potential coachee, the coach suggested a face-to-face 'introduction' session. This session took place in the coachee's offices, and lasted more than two hours. However, after a few days of deliberations the coachee decided not to make use of the overall, six-session, coaching offer. When the coachee's PA rang to inform the coach that they would not be making use of her services, the coach let it be known that an invoice would have to be sent for the first, introductory session, which the PA confirmed as she didn't know the ins and outs. Some two weeks after this phone conversation with the PA, the prospective coachee received an invoice for an introduction session. Then, a month later, when the invoice was not paid, the coach escalated and subsequently, after a few reminders, included admin and collection costs. More escalation followed including some threatening emails, and eventually the prospective coachee responded with a formal complaint to the professional association of the coach. After hearing from both parties, the adjudication panel decided against the coach as it had not been made sufficiently clear in advance that there might be costs associated with the introduction session.

We think new coaches who do not have the opportunity to talk such escalations through with their supervisors, are exposed to these and similar mistakes. In their anxiety about incoming work, coupled with their keenness to please the coachee, they can easily be drawn into 'overdoing' their helping and subsequently getting onto their high horses in terms of a reasonable reward for their troubles. New coaches need to be supported in these decisions, either by the larger firm they work for or by their supervisor, so that they do not expose themselves to escalations. Being dragged in front of an ethics panel can be an immensely painful and traumatic experience.

Coaching conversations are an important opportunity for often vulnerable coachees to reflect openly on their current issues, sensitivities, and aspirations. These conversations and the two participants therefore deserve protection. How can we make sure there is sufficient protection in our profession? Where can coaches go who are getting anxious about work challenges or how to respond to their coachees? And where can potential coachees go to make an independent choice within the profession, and to receive a guarantee of quality that is meaningful and non-commercial?

One meaningful criterion is entry from a psychology degree such as is the case for coaching psychologists. Similarly, one can qualify formally as a practising coach with a dedicated degree in executive coaching. However, more secure entry points do not take away the fact that anyone can call themselves a coach and the coaching profession admits large numbers of newcomers every year, from management ranks or organizational-consultancy practices, including experienced consultants and leaders who are turning their backs on working within organizations after a demanding career. This latter group often shows a degree of bitterness about corporate life or some prejudice regarding working within organizations, and so they may struggle with the open, unbiased, and independent view that is so important when considering coachees' questions and goals.

Becoming a 'coach', however – that is, someone who helps a learner think for themselves and produce their own insight and decisions – is a lot harder and more exposing than leading the witness. If coaching were another form of mentoring, then there would hardly be a need for training or professional ethics, because we can all talk about our own experiences and solutions, usually all too gladly. On the other hand, the two years of study it takes to obtain a masters degree is generally not enough and at the end of training most coaches realize that there is so much more to learn; for example, the ability to offer true 'containment' and safety, to contract carefully for outcomes from the coachee's perspective, to listen between the lines under difficult circumstances, or to use the developing here-and-now relationship to gain new insights – to name just a few of the more difficult coaching competencies.

An ethics of trust is what we believe we need within our profession. To make coaching as safe and trusted as possible, firm outside boundaries are necessary. In this regard, we are fervent advocates of *external* regulation or registration, i.e. regulation not (or not solely) by professional organizations but by an independent body or a national charter, because only this type of regulation is truly trustworthy. Self-regulation has major drawbacks, such as creating a false 'exclusivity' in the profession, favouring experienced and powerful members of the professional bodies, and too readily over-reacting when incidents occur.[2] Unfortunately, though, we are still a long way off from truly independent regulation: in both psychotherapy and coaching, we currently have various degrees of self-regulation, i.e. regulation by colleagues.[3] In this connection, we believe it is important for coaches to take out professional liability insurance so that, in the event of conflict, they can rely on representation and mediation by independent external bodies.

Ethical codes are no great help either and possibly even a hindrance in steering away from the serious risks in our profession. Diochon and Nizet (2015) analysed 27 'moments of ethical challenge' from the practice of an equal number of French accredited coaches. They concluded that codes of conduct have very limited use during and after such challenges: ethical codes are experienced by coaches to be irrelevant, insufficient, or even at times an obstacle when it comes to resolving immediate challenges. What is needed, they say, is careful and shared dialogue about the issues at stake and about the boundaries which the code seems to be indicating. They recommend talking things through with supervisors or peers to make better use of the codes and to avoid ethical compromises.

12.2: The power of experienced coaches and how to balance this power

In our view, the most widespread risks of coaches and coaching are linked to experience and standing in the profession. Based on published case studies and complaint procedure evidence, we think the biggest problems occur when the power of the coach becomes too great or when routine sets in, in some form or other. With coaching experience comes power and standing, inevitably, and with power comes overreach and even, in the worst cases, corruptibility. Some relevant risks have been described well by Steven Berglas (2002) in his article on the dangers of executive coaching. He talks mainly about the coach's misunderstanding (due to incompetence) of the psychology of the situation, about self-overestimation on the part of coaches, and about abuse related to power and influence. All three of these can be traced back to unwarranted overreach and limited checks and balances on the overreach. Let us look more closely at the three areas of concern that Berglas raises.

Incompetence

Incompetence is the risk of making an interpretation or drawing a conclusion when the facts of the matter do not bear out the approach, such as when another explanation – for example, based on personal history, transference, or personality derailment patterns – would have been a better hypothesis. Berglas offers the example of an executive who had been flattered and strengthened in his grandiosity by the coach, rather than being challenged on the damage he was causing to others.

Like Berglas, we believe this risk confirms the importance of psychological preparation, i.e. coaching psychology and ongoing supervision. If coaches can be open about their assumptions and willing to explore them with their coachees and their supervisors, we believe this problem becomes relatively harmless. Whether we have studied psychology or not, we will only understand certain situations in part, until we gradually come to understand them better and from different perspectives. As long as we remain open and modest in our hypothesizing, we show ourselves willing to learn.

Self-overestimation, or 'the lure of the easy answers'

A further escalation of the problem of incompetence is self-overestimation by coaches. Berglas (2002) gives two similar examples, the first of a coach who 'toughens up' a client with speeches and exercises whilst underneath the executive was really rather anxious and frustrated. The underlying feelings being missed by the coach lead the coachee towards more anxiety and even depression. The other example is of a coachee who has 'workaholic' features and receives training in delegation, when again there are underlying issues stemming from her family background that also need to be processed.

We see this pattern of simple solutions for complex challenges more with experienced coaches than those lacking experience. Long organizational or 'life' experience with limited psychological understanding can lead to overvaluation of one's own views and solutions. Senior managers who re-train as 'coaches' may initially operate mostly as mentors, passing on their own answers and approaches to their coachees. They retire or semi-retire and then, without much training, go on to work as coaches, armed with all the opinions and impressions they have formed about what constitutes good leadership. Such coaches place themselves somewhat outside the reporting lines of the organization, but nevertheless retain a great deal of influence. There is no corrective mechanism for their prejudice and opinions, and they can harm their coachees through unconscious projection of their own unprocessed organizational experiences.

Case example 12.2

An experienced executive coach who often mediates in crisis situations has got herself involved in the arrangements for a funeral in her private network. She has offered to help with funeral arrangements when a student, who is a long-standing friend of her son, suddenly passes away. The family of the student has gone through a difficult divorce, so it appears to be best if mother, father, and the friends of the student, each have their own distinct 45-minute period in which to commune with the coffin and say goodbye. The coach has stated her field of work ('crisis coaching') as a motivation to be of help. No payment is involved, just an offer to help the group of friends and family. On the day of the funeral, however, the first family grouping to say goodbye is a small group around the mother of the student. They remain huddled around the coffin after their allotted time in a very emotional state. The coach, aware that two further groupings are waiting their turn, and the funeral service itself is naturally limited in time, takes the matter into her own hands when more than an hour has passed. She insists on a change-over and after a short scuffle manages to make sure that the original plan for the arrangements is preserved. The mother of the student, now much aggrieved, decides to bring a case against the coach. The case is heard by the professional coaching body of the coach, letters are written from both sides, and arguments are heard, after which the ethical committee decides to uphold the coach's integrity because of her careful, contracted, and ethical approach during the funeral proceedings. The case serves as a reminder that coaches can even be held to their own ethics outside of working hours, particularly if they boast of their own 'crisis coaching' in their private lives.

The trap of power and influence

The third risk – abuse of power – is less common but more damaging. Berglas offers the example of an executive coach who over time acquires more and more power within an organization, to such an extent that he advises management about strategy and appointments, but without sitting on the management committee.

Other examples here involve coaches who, after successfully completing a single assignment or based on a strong reputation within the field, are asked to do more and more work for the same organization, and at ever higher levels, so they become increasingly embedded. This can grow into unrestricted access to top management, with a corresponding, Rasputin- or Svengali-like influence, an unavoidably toxic power-without-accountability. One of us remembers one such colleague who would invite himself to coach middle managers he regarded as 'dysfunctional', while repeatedly prescribing his own book as 'homework' in between their coaching sessions. Here is a similar case that came before the EMCC ethics committee.

> ### Case example 12.3
>
> *A middle manager in a large organization is approached by an established coach in the same organization for some coaching sessions. The manager states later that he felt very uneasy about the approach, but felt he had no choice but to consent. A first meeting is then put into the diary, which lists also the manager's boss and a board member who is the coach's commissioner in the organization. In that conversation, the coach again confirms that the manager needs coaching, without seeming to check the felt needs of the manager. They arrange a further two coaching sessions, which the manager describes afterwards as very one-sided and coach-led. The manager states that as his director seems to know and value this coach, he seems to have no alternative but to take on the coaching. The coach, on the other hand, believed that they had agreed goals for the coaching, but has foregone a written contract. The coachee cancels the third coaching session stating that he has just started therapy and would prefer to complete the therapy before continuing the coaching. This was the only way the manager felt he could get out of the coaching. Some four months later the coach turns up unexpectedly at the manager's desk, suggesting that they have a conversation and pick up the coaching from there. When the manager is reluctant to do so without speaking with his psychologist first, the coach offers to speak with the psychologist as well. The coach also suggests she informs the same board member as before. Two weeks later the manager launches a formal complaint with the professional body of the coach, which is eventually sustained, after which the coach is asked to apologize and take more supervision, among other things.*

Looking again at the three dangers Berglas describes, we believe the least damage is done by novice coaches except where they continue to 'coach' as ex-managers in the same organization where they themselves worked for many years. After all, in the same organization they are not novices and may be too powerful for their coaching boots.

In most other situations, where novice coaches are coupled with 'novice' (i.e. fresh) settings, they run much less of a risk of transgression. In fact, they usually are highly motivated, well-intentioned, and not overreaching, even beset by doubts, including self-doubts (De Haan, 2008b), and do their utmost to really help their coachees.

We know from Berglas (2002) and Day *et al.* (2008) that it is often the established, powerful (and male) coaches who receive the most complaints. The same is confirmed in psychotherapy, such as around sexual abuse of patients (see, for example, Eichenberg *et al.*, 2010). Surveying the literature and executing a comprehensive study surveying 342 qualified counsellors, Marmaros (2019) found that male professionals, those with more years of clinical experience, and those providers working in private practice, themselves reported engaging in more boundary behaviours and were therefore deemed most at risk of transgressions. These experienced, mostly male and independent ('maverick'?)

professionals may need to have a good 'showdown' from their supervisors at regular intervals.

Ultimately, we stand the best chance of minimizing the above risks if we ask coaches to expose themselves regularly to supervision, especially *after* qualification, because supervision significantly increases the chances of picking up some of the problems outlined above.[4] We also think it important that qualification should include a form of accreditation, a test of the quality of the coach's practice which involves a form of live assessment in which the coach can be observed and interviewed. We are somewhat critical of the many coaching associations that believe accreditation can be done remotely, by sending in a written practice overview or a tape recording. As we have experienced ourselves, in the latter case it is both much easier and less instructive to pre-select the vignette that an examiner will assess remotely.

12.3: Towards an ethics of trust

As argued before, it is not always wise to trust mainly the coach's qualifications and years of experience. Much wiser to trust the coach's humanity, frailty, and good intentions. Other than just good faith in the motivation and trustworthiness of coaches, it is wise to trust the practice of regular supervision. Safety, trust, and high quality are ultimately best guaranteed by regularly opening up one's own practice to the benign yet critical eye of another professional, and then sitting together at the feet of our experience in difficult moments from practice. More generally, knowing that less experienced coaches have excellent results and are less exposed to righteousness and harm (see, for example, George *et al.*, 2020), should also help to lower the premium we tend to place on 'experience' in our field.

Maintaining trust means we assume good faith and good intentions within those we work with, and that we respond in kind, by offering our own openness and sincerity. As many treatments of the ethics of helping conversations will confirm (see, for example, Carroll and Shaw, 2013), the professional helping relationship presupposes good faith on both sides, offered with respect for differences and diversity, and normally this good faith and trust are only strengthened by the ongoing collaboration.

If there are doubts and tensions in the relationship, good coaches will go towards them and towards the other person, to clarify and reach renewed understanding and trust. After all, the helping relationship needs to be built on good faith and joint understanding, as well as on common interests. In this process, it is important to pick up any doubts and tensions as early as possible and to offer calmness and containment in exploring them.

Supervision is often one of the first places where small niggles and doubts can come to the fore and be explored by coaches in a safe way, namely offline from the coachee. An ethics of trust teaches that supervision should be regular and coaches should try to practise maximum openness in supervision, however difficult that sometimes may feel. When coaches (Day *et al.*, 2008) and therapists

(Lawton, 2000; Gray *et al.*, 2001) were asked how open they are in supervision, they consistently reported that there are areas of concern or shame which they do not bring to their supervisor, although coaches' trust in their supervisors is high (De Haan, 2017b).

Supervision may be the first place where we find out that there are tensions or mistakes, although this can also emerge within the coaching relationship itself. When there are indications of possible mistakes or escalating tensions, then it becomes important as coaches that we maintain our duty of candour[5] in addressing these. It is hugely important to recognize and communicate about such mistakes and tensions, to try to explicitly address any possible differences of perspective or perceived mistakes, and to seek mutual understanding of what may have gone wrong (at the earliest possible stage). As the following case will show, opportunities to seek better understanding in cases that have escalated, for coaches to apologize and find a mediated solution are often missed. When this happens, cases will continue to escalate with ultimately the need for written statements from both sides, the involvement of lawyers, insurers, and professional bodies, followed by an independent assessment of who is the most 'guilty' party. However, there are generally no less than two losing parties at this stage: for having invested in the coaching and never to have attained full satisfaction nor a full redress. Such redress tends to remain mostly elusive and in any case rarely satisfies the aggrieved party, let alone the other side.

We believe it is important that we as coaches come off our high horses well before we are accused. Supervision and reflection may help to calm our beliefs in our own righteousness, which are so often strengthened by our professional identity and training, but not always that helpful to us.

Case example 12.4

In a merged care organization, one of the merged teams of professional clinicians has never gelled well and seems to be nostalgic for their earlier independence, leading to unclear mutual expectations, conflict, and disgruntlement with management. A new director decides to bring in a recommended team coach who, in view of the size of the team, decides to work with a trusted colleague. The two coaches propose a series of team coaching days for the whole team: 16 professionals, their line manager, and the director. Everyone stresses commitment to this important work to develop the team.

After the first team coaching day, the second coach suggests a different approach in the interest of safety within the team, where the director would not be part of the team coaching days. After the second team coaching day, the second coach also engages in a number of calls with individual team members. In a subsequent meeting with the director, the two coaches state that they had underestimated the assignment and that some in the team are not feeling safe. From her side, the director objects to the individual conversations undertaken by the second coach. Neither the first coach nor the director was informed in advance about these conversations with team members, which, according to the second coach, were on the initiative of those team members. The two coaches proceed by offering the director suggestions about her leadership contribution, suggestions that are experienced as intrusive and demanding by the director.

The next team coaching day takes place without the director and a lot of grievances are aired about management, including the director's leadership style. After this day, the second coach argues with the first coach that they should engage in a meeting with the board to inform them about the difficulties of this team. The first coach consents but argues that the director needs to be informed in advance. Both coaches then speak again with the director but fail to mention their plan to escalate and instead are even more critical of the director's style and contributions. The director finds herself defending her approach. After this conversation, the two coaches arrange a meeting with the board, where they communicate their own lack of trust in the director as the commissioner of this team coaching work.

At the next team coaching day, still without the director, the coaches inform the team of their conversation with the board, where they have tried to help the team by openly addressing the shortcomings of the director. On the same day, however, the director also speaks with the board, after which it is decided to discontinue working with the two team coaches. The director then convenes the team, and they reflect together about the escalated situation, where both the director and several members of the team find themselves very critical of the coaching days, which some experienced as bruising and unhelpful.

After this exploration with the team, the director writes to the professional body of the coaches to fault them for undermining trust by speaking with the board, for undermining her authority, and for acting unprofessionally and unethically towards all parties, e.g. by not informing her as the commissioner in advance about the meeting with board members. A large part of the defence of the first, lead coach is that she did not always agree with the more radical and critical position of the second coach and was not always informed of his actions in advance. The ethical complaints committee rules that the first coach, who was in charge of the work and had drawn up the contract, is still liable for the mistakes that had been made by both coaches. Moreover, the coaches should not have spoken with the board without not only informing the director but rather having substantive conversations with her so as to take her guidance and opinions on board before contemplating an escalation beyond the contractual terms. As to the other formal accusation by the director of causing damage to the team and the organization, the panel ruled that it did not have sufficient information to establish the facts in sufficient detail.

In this case, the outcomes are dire for all involved and the initial splitting within one department spreads to the coach-commissioner relationship and further to the two coaches and the minds of each of these coaches and leaders, where we can only begin to imagine the extent of regret, shame, and grievance.

12.4: Application: recommendations for coaches

Just like feedback (Chapter 6), psychometrics (Chapter 7), and assessment (Chapter 8), ethical boundaries, and where we stand within them, are an awe-inspiring phenomenon. We all want to do right and are understandably fearful of doing wrong. As Socrates said, no one willingly does wrong. Fear causes splitting and polarization, first in our own minds and then often in the coaching relationship, so that eventually coach and coachee may end up on opposite sides in a judicial trial, which is the worst outcome for all and antithetic to coaching (see Bernier and Kearns, 2018, for a gripping account of what happens when difficulties in a helping relationship were escalated to a formal complaint). We know intimately about the cold sweat and shivers that we felt when accused of having wronged someone or of defaulting on a coaching contract. We know the extent to which fear can take over in such cases, how panic can break out, isolation can escalate to what has been called 'othering', and still further to what feels a hopeless yet existential fight for our survival, a nightmare scenario in our waking life. It is essential that we try our utmost not to fall into this escalating spiral of fear. To do our utmost to keep exploring ways to honour the other as part of us, and to improve our ethics, working through dialogue, bringing coach and coachee together precisely when there are misunderstandings, ruptures, or disappointments. A mediated solution is always better than a litigated one, even if a third party is needed to be able to gain an independent perspective and to feel ready to apologize or atone.

We would recommend implementing an ethics of trust and a duty of candour in all codes of ethics for coaches, so that trust and openness are maintained to the highest degree and in the presence of mistakes and other difficulties. In 2021, we incorporated a duty of candour, including the commitment to admit all forms of mistakes without delay, in our own (coaching and supervision) ethical codes at Hult Ashridge.

An ethics of trust is all the more important in very sensitive cases. Referrals often include executives on the verge of burnout when under high stress and duress, or in the early stages of 'derailment', a leadership dynamic that is veering off track (for case histories, see De Haan and Kasozi, 2014). Coaching as a tailored intervention seems to be an effective approach for these types of highly personal tensions (Nelson and Hogan, 2009), but there is a risk of harm precisely when in these cases coaches need to be not only supportive but often challenging as well.

Chapter summary

This chapter is a continuation of the argument for a humble stance among professional coaches in the face of our own cognitive biases and narcissism. We look at the impact of love and fear on trying to practise ethically. Making use of real-life cases that have come before an ethics board, we study the differences between an ethics of trust and an ethics of fear. We explore what an ethics of trust means in practice and argue why it is worth implementing. Such an ethics of trust starts from the premise that no practitioner willingly does wrong, i.e. our intentions as helpers tend to be very well-meaning and ethical. However, coaching psychology tells us that our intentions do not always match how we come across, such as retrospectively, when ethical committees scrutinize our work. Despite being fearful of not practising ethically, we may still fall short of actually doing so. One reason is that fear is not always a good guide and can make us cautious, protective, and withholding, so not necessarily a better coach. Another reason is that with practice we grow our self-confidence and seniority, which may delude us into thinking that we are more ethical than how others experience us. We believe that it is good to be warned that coaches are much more vulnerable to unethical behaviour than they believe they are. We argue how an ethics of trust can nevertheless be built on our humility, our coaching qualifications, and our ongoing supervision.

Notes

1   This chapter was co-written with Annette Bienfait who has been a member of the ethical complaints committee at EMCC The Netherlands over the past ten years.
2   We recently came across an example of a one-year expulsion handed down to someone who had self-reported a minor overstepping of boundaries to his professional association.
3   In the UK, psychotherapy and counselling are unregulated but in several other countries including the USA there is governmental registration. It is relevant in this regard to note that most of the coaches who were reprimanded by the professional organization in the case examples in this chapter (and others), reacted by immediately leaving that professional organization rather than following up on the outcome, the stipulated conditions for further practice. With governmental registration this would not be possible.
4   A recent example from Erik's own supervision: he contracted with a new coachee who was married to someone he had worked with several years earlier. His supervisor asked some very hard questions about this which he had not considered and made him change his mind and offer a referral instead.
5   The professional Duty of Candour arose in the UK from the recommendations by the Mid-Staffordshire NHS Foundation Trust Public Inquiry into poor patient care.

13 Practise humility in team coaching: a fleeting balance[1]

Nowadays, the field of executive coaching also encompasses team coaching, as the same 'coaching' stance seems to benefit teams as well. Nevertheless, the setting of team coaching is very different, and one feels much more immersed with the coachees as they are literally all around us. The challenges are no longer just conversational, they are also much more to do with the group dynamics in the room. It is as if all those hidden dynamics and meanings in individual coaching are now, to an extent, laid out in front of us and are pulling us in different directions. One wonders how the theme of 'love over fear' plays out in a setting where anxieties appear *between* our coachees as well as between us and the coachees, and where team members are continuously seeking proximity and psychological safety as well as fleeing closeness and seeking autonomy, cuddling up against one another (agreeing and forming bonds and coalitions), as well as asserting their individuality and difference for fear of losing themselves. There is usually a certain ambivalence between two fearful poles: losing oneself in others or remaining isolated and out on a limb. The well-known hedgehog dilemma described by Schopenhauer (1851), and taken up by Freud, seems apt. Here is Schopenhauer's original formulation:

> One cold winter's day, a number of porcupines huddled together quite closely in order through their mutual warmth to prevent themselves from being frozen. But they soon felt the effect of their quills on one another, which made them again move apart. Now when the need for warmth once more brought them together, the drawback of the quills was repeated so that they were tossed between two evils, until they had discovered the proper distance from which they could best tolerate one another. (Schopenhauer, 1851, vol. 2, chapter 31, section 396)

With this dilemma one can well understand why work in teams and meetings often feels so lifeless, aimless, and detached, so cognitive and suppressed, and so lacking of love: two fears have accommodated to, whilst the original impulse, one of love, has not been addressed or realized!

Team coaching with its strong pull on the coach to become another semi-detached hedgehog, is indeed a relatively new field. If we take the publication of Hackman and Wageman's (2005) article as marking the launch of this profession, then team coaching is only just over a decade old. Most practitioners would argue that although the name 'team coaching' may be new, the contribution of team coaches is not; for example, Lawrence and Whyte (2017) trace a history in this field going back to Edgar Schein and his 'process consultation' in the 1990s.

I believe it helps greatly to use the term 'team coaching', if only to indicate a contribution that is distinct from team chairing, facilitating, building, or training. Team coaching provides a simple name for an important practice where we try to *lovingly nurture more or deeper reflection in a team*. In other words, I believe that the core of the team coach's role is simply to be fully present and focus on making the team *feel or think better*; on creating wholesome space for common reflections, and on providing protection and inspiration for fresh reflection on team goals, decisions, ways of working, strategy, etc. Ultimately, shared reflection is key for developing a team that will be both more effective and united.

It often seems to me that, somewhat similar to the hedgehogs' predicament, team coaching is in 'unstable equilibrium'. If not maintained carefully, team coaching can relax into either 'abstinence', where coaches remain too far outside of the team, or 'team leadership', where coaches are tempted to facilitate, cajole, chair, give feedback, or educate. Team coaching sits just in the middle of these polarities and needs to be protected as an intermediate position (neither inside nor outside the team, or perhaps better, both inside and outside of the team) from moment to moment. The best team coaches try to make reflective, provocative contributions that are at the same time powerful and thought-provoking, as well as offering invitations for further exploration, without making their own presence too central to the team.

Only in this way are there clear parallels between team coaching and individual coaching, both being essentially *vehicles for development* and *containers for growth*, very much in line with the original meaning of the word *coach*; a horse-drawn carriage from the Hungarian village of Kocs (pronounced 'coach'). Coaches provide the means for a reflective journey through a safe, nurturing, and thoughtful presence, but they do not take charge.

13.1: Why is team coaching important?

Helping the team to think better is no easy task but some of the best research into teams (as cited below) shows that high-quality team reflection results in:

- Understanding and insight – both key motivators for positive change.
- The combining of more diverse opinions and views – leading to improved levels of performance.
- Contributions from team members at all levels – a kind of 'upwards feedback' which is known to improve leadership decisions.

A study of 100 work teams in China found that those teams that reflected on their tasks were more innovative (Tjosvold *et al.*, 2004), while another study found that such reflection also resulted in higher performance (Schippers *et al.*, 2008). Further research in 2015 with nearly 100 work teams from within the NHS found that reflection helped particularly with innovation under conditions of heavy workload and high psychological strain (Schippers *et al.*, 2015).

In order to promote reflection, team coaches can help create new opportunities for the team to reflect on what is working well for them already, and where biases and obstacles to reflection may present themselves. Coaches should be good observers, relationally aware, containing, and self-effacing – but at the same time bold and challenging in offering new areas for reflection and hypotheses. This paradox of both sitting back with observation and leaning in with hypotheses creates the dynamic instability around presence that many individual coaches will recognize, and which is so much more pronounced when working with teams.

13.2: Presence: the greatest challenge for team coaches

Essentially, as a team coach you want to help the team – and each individual member of the team – to reflect more deeply, innovate, and become stronger at addressing and resolving issues. Team coaching differs from team building, facilitating, or chairing; in that, as a coach, you cannot just claim your presence and 'lead' the team. Indeed, presence with the team is delicate and tricky. You are aiming for 'not too much' but also for 'not too little', and you are working in a context where it is very hard to predict how all the people in the room are experiencing your presence from moment to moment. As you attempt to make an impact on reflection for the team, you also want to leave the team in charge so that as a team they themselves can attain higher levels of reflection and reflexivity.

Team coaching interventions involve the art of claiming *and* letting go of your presence with a live team. In team coaching, as in individual coaching, I experience every intervention as an experiment.

13.3: Team coaching in action

Here are some vignettes from my own practice as a team coach. A team is leading a large organization through a number of challenges, particularly in terms of the need to modernize their products, which in their case includes modernization of their leadership structure, in the sense that responsibilities will need to be handled much lower down in the organizational 'hierarchy'. I offer a series of stand-alone reflective team coaching sessions and I am also invited to join their regular managerial team meetings. The case examples below demonstrate how as a team coach, we can be surprised by our own perceived presence within a team.

Case example 13.1: Too much presence?

At the beginning of the board coaching session, I notice that one person is making notes on his laptop. I decide to make a gentle intervention around how taking away barriers might make us all more open and reflective, and I suggest an experiment: how might he turn up without the laptop? The impact is immediate and very strong. He looks furious and obviously feels ticked off. I sense other members of the team looking on with slight glee, and one or two nod as I am speaking. For a few seconds, there is an awkward silence as he looks deeply into my eyes – then he says, 'Fine. I accept the challenge.' Later in the coffee break, he seeks me out, apologizes, and explains how note taking on his laptop sometimes helps him to reflect better, but that he now realizes it was not really appropriate for this session. The day otherwise passes without incident, and team members speak openly about their doubts and resistances about the new strategic direction that they have only ambivalently agreed with recently, and about their scepticism regarding plans for a new, more distributed, leadership. By the end of the day, people are thanking me and the team member for the decision to leave out laptops and for being so open and vulnerable. A very good day for the team, they all agree, but I am left with strong doubts, as I feel I intervened too brusquely. I suspect that from beneath the surface, I had emerged as a powerful informal leader for the day, one who had in that moment stifled rather than opened up genuine, deeper reflection.

Case example 13.2: Too little presence?

I am attending another one of the top team's regular meetings at the organization's head office, which I observe from a slight distance. The team are preparing to make some important decisions, and guests from both within and outside the organization have been invited to join the meeting for particular agenda items. In the intervals between longer agenda items, I join the team throughout the meeting to comment on their seating, their turn-taking, the repetitions in their 'rounds' of deliberations, and the impression that they are largely ignoring the needs of the visitors, as well as how I perceive the dynamics of their collaboration here and now. They listen as always with heightened attention, as if they do not want to miss a word, then thank me and turn to each other to address the next agenda item. There is barely time for any processing as other than conveying my impressions in a few words, I am only observing the meeting. As I leave, I believe I raised a few important areas of conflict and ambivalence, but that nobody had responded to me. Now I have to sit on the feeling of having very limited impact on 'my' team, until the next team-coaching day in a month's time.

My presence as a team coach is a very tricky one for me, and one that leads to substantial doubts every time. Coachees are often unaware of the amount of internal processing that goes on for the coach. Similarly, coaches may miss important information regarding how the team experiences them from moment to moment. Often you do not know if an intervention 'works' until well after you have tried it out.

Having given examples of how a coach might emerge from sessions feeling they have made an impact that is either 'excessive' or 'lacking', let me also give an example of where the amount of presence the coach maintains appears to be 'just right' for the team. In this case, I found the team can work with a large amount of new and relevant information, themes, and observations that emerge during the session, without needing me to lean in too much as their team coach.

Case example 13.3: The right amount of presence?

The same top team has recently been able to fill the vacancy of an important role. At the beginning of our team coaching session, we agree it would be helpful to make some introductions to acknowledge the changed composition of the team. I begin by asking everyone to name one 'value' that is important to them, a value that they bring with them from childhood, and then to name one 'moment' from their life that they believe has shaped them as a person. We hear moving accounts of determining influences and deep losses and how much each single team member has taken from their significant others and major life events. It is an open and intimate start to the day, with very careful listening. As their team coach, I hypothesize a few patterns emerging in the team: I notice and name some common values held by team members and some contributions that team members are making that sound beautifully complementary. The team are so focused on meeting each other in this new way that my hypotheses are welcomed but do not become overly dominant. We look at a recent 'case'; an important decision that has not yet been made, despite promises made to those directors in the organization who had prepared the decision-making process. I merely reflect on the here and now of this meeting, and on the patterns that I see emerging. Again, I feel that my observations and hypotheses are welcomed and used, without becoming the centre of attention.

We finish the session with a period of reflection, gauging where people are now and with what feelings they are preparing to leave the meeting. There is a strong sense of togetherness, a newfound determination in terms of how their case for a decision might be resolved, and a much deeper understanding of others within the team. People stay behind chatting with one another in the meeting room, which I believe is often a very good sign of a successful team day. I leave in a positive mood, believing that there had not been a moment in that meeting where I felt I took over the proceedings or that I was struggling to be heard or understood.

In the case of larger and more pressurized teams, I find that the only way to keep this precious but intrinsically unstable equilibrium that sits in the middle between too much presence and near-abstinence is to work with a team-coaching colleague with a similar background. One of us can then go slightly closer to the team and facilitate, while the other deliberately holds back and observes.

We work together like the abdominal and dorsal muscles keeping the 'spine' of our presence – our 'backbone' of coaching – strong and yet flexible. The dynamic instability becomes more stable due to the presence of the second coach. During intervals and breaks we can then share our observations, and the observing colleague can help the 'lead' team coach to see how he or she is being pulled in by the dynamics of the team. Only in this way can a team coach gently 'notice' while at the same time be exposed to the full force of the anxious, conflictual, splitting, or otherwise pressurized dynamics.

Case example 13.4: Team coaches working as a pair

A large leadership team in a university needs to review and agree its new five-year strategy. During the day they review personal commitments, strategic intent, formulation of a strategy, and decisions about the consequences for a revised leadership structure. They plan a very full day with an external team coach facilitating all processes.

Because of the size of the team, the coach has asked a psychoanalytically-trained colleague to observe as she herself leads the day. If there are tensions within the team, the first coach can ask her colleague to feed back directly only to her in the breaks. However, here the situation is safe and contained enough for him to be able to comment to the team and team coach directly, at regular intervals:

- *'I am struck by the number of things you seem to avoid as a team of leaders. At home you do your finances and nurture your relationships, yet here at work, you all seem to want just to do research and leave your managerial responsibility to others, such as your team's secretary.'*
- *'I can see that my colleague, your team coach, has been given a true leadership role today. You gladly leave leadership to her and seem happy to follow. I wonder what will happen the moment your coach leaves you after today?'*
- *'It seems your board secretary is leading all the subgroups he is in and those groups achieve more than other groups. Your secretariat appears more powerful and better networked than all of you formal leaders together.'*
- *(At the end) 'Now that you have a plan, you may expect resistance. And when resistance comes, my prediction is that the plan will crumble and quickly become forgotten. What realistic chance does this new strategy really have here in this organization?'*

The observing team coach is able to be relatively outspoken, because the first team coach can take over and 'hold' the team after the second coach has spoken. One team coach can have a more observing, challenging presence, while the other has a more facilitating, helping presence. Together they offer just the right amount of presence for new thinking to emerge for and from within the team and for the team itself to retain the responsibility to implement (De Haan, 2017a).

13.4: Application: recommendations for coaches

I believe that as team coaches we should maintain a 'light touch' while at the same time keeping our boldness and courage in naming what we see. We should flirt with our hypotheses but never marry them, certainly not when the whole team turns around and denies or berates us for making such a 'shocking' interpretation. Our contributions are best kept as *fleeting moments of noticing*, which will plant the seeds of some further future understanding that is as yet hidden from us – and quite possibly from the team as well.

We also need to think about our own presence in the organization and how to keep that presence as 'fleeting' as needed for independence, freedom of thinking, and good coaching results. In this regard, it has helped me to remain as clear as possible about who my client is and the 'arc' of my assignment; who am I working for and for what likely period of time. If it is different parties at the same time and a rather long period of time, say, more than a year of regular sessions, then I know I have to be much more explicit about my contribution and negotiate clearly who I am working for in every session.

Usually, the main and only client is a particular leadership team. If I were very rigid about that, I would only see the whole team together and have no one-to-one meetings with anyone, but that is very rarely the case and may make the work a lot harder, certainly at the beginning where it means long drawn-out introductions and contracting with the whole team. It is therefore more common to have one-to-one interviews before commencing a piece of team coaching work. In that way I hear about the team and how it is represented in the minds of all its members, and I also gain independent impressions of the team members themselves, with better introductions to their role and background. Even if happy to begin with such individual interviews, I am reluctant to have further one-to-one meetings when the team coaching has begun. Clearly such meetings would take the shape of individual information gathering or of individual coaching, and neither are very helpful for the journey with the team as a whole. On the contrary, they may exacerbate a lack of joint information-sharing about important team topics. It is therefore best to reduce such 'Chinese whispering' as much as possible.

What if I am asked to coach another team in the same organization, or another leader when I am already coaching one leader? Even better for me, commercially: I might be placed on a 'short list of coaches' for the organization – what to do with that? I believe all coaching is served by strict confidentiality agreements so even a single 'other client' in the same organization is not going to find the same confidential space as the first client. I believe that if a client were to know I also talk with one of their peers, say, in the organization, she would slightly change what she tells me and there will be areas where she feels less open, however small. For this reason, I imagine that a client would not want to suddenly discover that I also work with another team or another leader, and I take action to prevent that. What I normally do is first decide the two clients are sufficiently independent in the organisation, and then recognize the 'right of way' of the first client who has already built up a safe, confidential relationship. So, I ask my new client for permission to tell my 'other client' in the organization that I have had a request of working with a second client. Then I tell Client 1 about Client 2 and I make it clear that I will not take the new assignment if she has an objection, whatever that may be. This is in my experience seldom the case. Then, as a last step, I also go back to Client 2 to tell her who my Client 1 is, with Client 1's permission of course. It seems a little bit complicated and elaborate, but it works well. It also helps not to take on clients who sit on the same team or are in a hierarchical relationship with each other. One can always introduce the second client to a trusted fellow professional.

Provided some thinking has gone into working with other clients, such as in the process just described, seeing different, remote teams and individuals in one organization can be really enriching and valuable to the coaching process.

Chapter summary

The team coaching situation is much more pressurized and dense than the individual coaching setting, with many more prying eyes, many more expectations, fears, and projections. This situation can inspire even more fear than coaches are normally already exposed to, and it comes with new challenges. There is the temptation to join the team and to take some kind of leadership stance, versus the temptation to stay out of the team and follow passively. We may therefore come across either as a facilitator or 'entertrainer', or perhaps rather aloof and not really contributing to the real challenges that the team is facing. This chapter is about finding the right balance between these two evils of too much versus too little presence, and how to maintain that shifting dynamic balance within an evolving relationship with our 'coachee team'. Just like in Chapter 8, we find that love resides in the fragile and vulnerable middle of two monstrous fears, named in the classical literature as Scylla and Charybdis, two ancient sea monsters.

Note

1 This chapter is an expanded version of an article which first appeared in the January 2019 issue of *Coaching Today*. © The British Association for Counselling and Psychotherapy.

Looking back on the book – an afterword with Robin Shohet

Robin. Thank you, Erik, to agreeing to this afterword. Having read the book there was so much to comment on that I did not want to limit myself to a foreword but wanted a dialogue. So, let's start with what prompted you to want to write this book, what does it mean to you?

Erik. I started this book all the way back in 2006. I had just written a book with the title *Fearless Consulting* – and soon after it came out, I felt moved to write something about *fearless listening* (De Haan, 2006), which I am delighted to say has now found its way into this book in a much-amended version (Chapter 10). I always felt there was so much more for me to learn if I were to become more fearless or parrhesiastic (being able to use fearlessness in speech) and so this book became a decade-long work in progress, which is still in many ways unfinished …

When I look back on this book now, I feel a sense of satisfaction in that I have been able to cover so many of the experiences that make coaching truly helpful and meaningful. I feel I have come close to describing the core, basic building blocks of this magical and potent 'helping experience'. For a physicist it is a jolly good feeling to get closer to the basics and the foundations, however shaky and unknown they still are. Also, I see in the book some important ideas for solid boundaries, such as how to integrate feedback, tools, assessment, ethics, and the future of the planet.

Having found all these 'building blocks' that work, I am still in awe and puzzled by the sheer magic of the whole undertaking. The power to nurture and grow another person's reflections appears to be so strong that even if you take the helper away, it still works. People improve already by anticipating helping, by the simple fact that they have their first session in the diary. And people improve by organizing the helping within themselves, e.g. through a disciplined process of 'self-coaching'. So even if the coachee misses the perspective of the coach and helper, there is already movement and growth. We still know very little about what makes coaching helpful, but we have heard too many stories, seen too much research, not to be convinced of its intrinsic helpfulness. Conversely, when things go wrong in helping conversations, e.g. when a coach forgets something important about the client or when the coach is somehow uncaring to the client, we can also see strong adverse effects.

I re-read the beautiful ballad of *The Sorcerer's Apprentice* once or twice a year, just to remind myself of the sheer power of healing that I have in my hands, heart, and mind ('Ever new the torrents, that by him are fed, Ah, a hundred currents, Pour upon my head!'). And to remind myself to be a kind, humble, and careful professional with that power. I do not recognize myself in the 'master', the sorcerer, in that ballad – and I do not see much evidence for his magic wand anyway. It is my identification with the apprentice that makes me pick up the poem again and again, leaving me struck with awe and concern about what mess I might have (co-)created this time, in my vain efforts to help.

I am amazed and troubled by the ebbs and flow of fear and love in life generally, not just in coaching. Very frequently, at least on an hourly basis, I can feel my kindness flowing and my willingness to help – but equally frequently and often more frequently, I feel the opposing forces: mild irritation, grievances, reluctance to do simple tasks, and escapism towards drills or sensations that make me forget such frustrations, without being kind to myself or others.

I think I share with you, Robin, a deep passion for understanding the fundamental building blocks of me, or of us, but I am quite wary of oceanic feelings and mystical beliefs. I am a scientist at heart and want to demonstrate and experience all my beliefs. Even then, I remain quite sceptical of them: you can see from the book how sceptic philosophy is one of my great inspirations. As a physicist I chose the Higgs boson as my topic of study for my final dissertation, because there was still a chance that this particle did *not* exist – and that would tear down the whole, amazingly precise Standard Model of elementary particles. Now that would be super-exciting for me as we would all be baffled, astonished, and ready to learn something new about nature!

There is so much we do not know yet about the dynamics of love and fear, so I think we should pay careful attention to all sources that could shed light on the matter, including the many philosophers and spiritual teachers who have written about this. What we do know is that the dynamics run really deep inside us: deep into the unconscious. Very often we do not know what battle is going on within us, or how low we have sunk into preserving fear in the face of love, before our own gestures or a perceptive comment help us to realize some of what has been going on.

I am immensely grateful to you, Robin: over the past twenty years you kept pointing us inwards, and kept showing us the conflicting, ambivalent inclinations we all felt towards our colleagues and towards our clients. You have been a powerful supervisor to the coaches at Ashridge and showed us the way in staying true to ourselves and remaining open to what conflicting, loving and other, sinister, tendencies we admitted within ourselves. You allowed us to voice these secret wishes and concerns in the safety of your supervision groups, and also in your work with our shared clients.

Robin. Thank you, Erik. Creating safety is very important to me and I think in our work. I think my reputation in this field is partly because I have recognized how full of fear I have been in my life, and so spot it easily in others even when there is an attempt to hide it, as often happens in life and in the corporate world. And I am comfortable writing about love because there has been so much love in my life, too. I have been inspired by a book called *A Course in Miracles* which suggests there are only two emotions, love and fear. This has given me a framework for many of my ideas. *A Course in*

Miracles really goes into the nature of who we are beyond our personalities to the realm of what in Indian philosophy is called non-duality. You say you are a sceptic, but the so-called new physics with people like Heisenberg, Bohm, and of course Einstein really delve into the mystical. Perhaps you have something in common with Freud who delved deep but did not trust the so-called realm of the oceanic.

In relation to your book, I really like how committed you are to understanding the dynamics of relationship, making it key to the work of coaching. You write about transference and countertransference (in Carine Metselaar's words: we *are* the intervention), which can get overlooked in coaching. You emphasize paying close attention to beginnings; not relying on psychometrics; exploring the dependency and pitfalls of some kinds of feedback; and the need to be vigilant, especially as senior practitioners (which we both can call ourselves) and how our doubts and insecurities can get ossified into a veneer of confidence. Absolutely. And, lastly, you stress the value of supervision, which I am so glad about. I like that we share a good eye for what Jungians might call the shadow, especially in relation to power dynamics and referring to what has not been said. In a culture where achievement is prized, it is important to embrace the possibility of not knowing, and even failure. Bringing love in is a bold move. You write, 'I have long felt the role of love in the workplace has been ignored and under-explored.' And you suggest it might be too frightening a word. You describe above the work as sheer magic and want to see how some of the insights can apply beyond the coaching world, to other relationships and to the current climate crisis. These are some of the key points I got from your book. So much of it was a breath of fresh air for me.

I would like to explore a sentence on page 109 with you. You write, 'Love is not a given or a stayer, and needs to be earned with hard work'. My belief (and yes, it is a belief) is that love is who we are. All these shadow aspects of our work, like abuse of power, narcissism, even the psychopathy of leadership (which I am glad you address), are like black clouds of fear in many guises blocking the sun's love. Our job (in part, anyway) is to recognize fear in ourselves, be alert to many of its guises like criticism, blame, judgement, comparisons, core beliefs about lack and not being good enough, power grabbing, and so on. And then bring them to the table in a way that joins us. In doing so, we are showing that it is part of our humanness and there is no need to hide our fear with shame. And the essence of who we are, love, which has been hidden by fear, can emerge.

Once we talk about earning love, we are into some form of conditionality and back into a doing mode. This is important. It is not that we don't have to be careful in our work, but the idea of love having to be earnt by hard work is foreign to me. I can expand but wanted to hear your comments.

Erik. I am very grateful for your kind words, Robin, and I immediately wanted to take 'that' sentence out of the book, but then of course the afterword wouldn't work anymore so I will now be destined to keep it in.

When I read your comments and also probably when I crafted that 'hard-earned' sentence, I was thinking of the power of our minds: to choose to stay in the present, to choose to be kind, to choose to be forgiving, to be charitable and to embrace love in all that we do – or not.

Perhaps it would be helpful if you could expand a little as you suggest. I think we have great freedom here and great power. Either to engage with love and with fear, or to suppress and reject, in other words, to stay well clear of our fears. I wondered what you thought about our ability to suppress the negative, the awkward and the fearful, as well as fear itself. In this, we are sometimes egged on by positive psychologists and business coaches, who tell us to invite a version of 'love' into our work by stressing what works, what is positive, and what solutions we already have.

I was thinking about what this toughness towards fear, this active turning away from 'the problem' and from fear, will do with us. Whether it will create new fears. Fears that are perhaps less consciously accessible. I am convinced – by my dreams – that whatever we do and however loving we are, fear still has a big presence in our unconscious.

My own approach has often been to open up to fears, to stay in my own shade as long as I can and to be amazed at my shadow sides. I would rather stay with this shadow and learn from my problems, discomfort, dark sides. I think what I am often doing is pondering on those dark clouds rather than looking for the sun, or light, or love, directly. Is there something in this? Can one find love by staying with fear, by analysing fear?

After writing the book, I feel even stronger that love and fear need to be considered not only in coaching, as they are core to the ambivalences and conflicts there, but also in the context of our bigger, global, self-inflicted issues, such as climate change, race and equity, and political polarization. Even in times of crisis, love is always around us, and love is 'all you need', the only goal that matters. Even if it is sometimes very hard to see, at least coaching can remind us of this universal truth.

Robin. So much there. Let's start with the sentence 'can one find love by staying with the fear, by analysing fear?' *A Course in Miracles* is based on answering this question. It says that if we are ruthless in raising awareness about our fears which are driven by our fragile egos, they will dissolve. They are the blocks to love, a love which is who we are, or in your words, a universal truth. According to the Course, we have only the faintest glimmer of how frightened and vicious the ego is (incidentally, I see all viciousness as a form of fear). I see you sense this intuitively and from your work on yourself. And no wonder it (ego) gets acted out on the world stage. If we were to own our own shadow, we would have less need for our leaders to embody those parts of ourselves we want to disown. That, for me, is the connection between the personal and the collective, whether it is Donald Trump or climate change which you refer to. Donald Trump is part of me and vice versa. I can find the self-centred, like my own way, manipulative, divisive, abuse of power parts just for starters.

Going to coaching specifically, I agree about the false positive. We used to call it syrup on shit. I do not know the coaching world as well as you do, but I have sensed a real fear of the shadow.

You know I wrote an article 'How Green Is Your Mind?' in 1995 (reprinted in *In Love with Supervision*). I suggested that we imagine we are cars and that our brain/mind is the exhaust pipe. Every time we have a negative thought, we are polluting the planet. And to summarize the article, the negative thoughts arise from fear. We 'other' people when we are afraid of them (and do not see their humanity) and fear them when we have 'othered' them because we have made them 'the enemy'.

I am using the term 'othering' in the context that I believe we are all connected through love but deny it through othering. However, love has got many negative connotations in our work – breaking boundaries and so on and love itself has become othered. The love I am talking about is impersonal. It is at some level a kind of mini-death of the controlling personality. We often do not get to this impersonal love except in times of crisis where the fearful mind no longer dominates, and we are forced to surrender to something more. I think we can create conditions for this impersonal love in our work, although it is very hard if we are attached to results. In *In Love with Supervision* I wrote:

Inquiring into the nature of fear and sharing it brings us into connection and allows the love to shine. We see with fresh eyes. Super Vision is just that. Seeing with fresh eyes.

Another description of my work is as follows:

*To help the supervisee become more present to this other, so that he or she can join this otherness and not make it 'other". In doing so, the apparent difficulty will resolve itself, because the difficulty was not in the situation **but in the creation of otherness.***

I think the above has far-reaching implications for our work. Instead of trying to tackle the problem head on, with goal-setting, brainstorming, and such like, we ask who is the 'I' that has the problem; or how have we othered ourselves or the situation (e.g. by projection); or is there anything stopping us being in relationship right now? We come back into connection, withdraw our fear-based projections on to the story or the difficulty or the current relationship, and see with fresh eyes. We are asked to realize it is always an inside job.

One way we other is to divide things into good and bad, and your bad might be my good and vice versa. Rudyard Kipling's poem *If* speaks to this, asking us to see success and failure as the same. I would like there to be less shame around apparent failure, and less attachment to apparent success.

I get inspiration from people who have had 'awakenings', being in the world in a way that transcends their personalities. They report no longer being afraid, nor need to achieve, and a natural compassion reveals itself. They feel intimately connected to all that is. I believe the closer we get to this state, the more we can be of use to others. To go back to your question, we get closer perhaps by a ruthless honesty about our fears, and the tricks we play on ourselves (and others) to avoid feeling it. In exposing the fears, the conditions for love to flourish have been created. Your book has brought such possibilities to the foreground.

I wondered if we might end with some questions for the reader?

Erik. Yes, I like this. I just remembered that Buddha means awakening, and that the Russian word for alarm clock, *budilnik*, still shows that meaning. I agree with your idea of a few questions for meditation to end the book with.

Dear reader, here are some questions about love and fear to work through in your own time. Best to sit down for about fifteen minutes and make reflective notes.

Many coaches we work with have found this a tough but moving exercise, at the end of which they feel the warmth of their own loving self on their skins, so that they leave the exercise with a smile.

(an exploration of your fears as a coach)

1 What would you least like a coachee to say to you?
2 And you would not like to hear that because …
3 What would you least like your supervisor to know about your work?
4 And you would not want them to know because …

(an exploration of your fears today)

1 Look back on your day today and explore when you have felt something that we would call 'fearful': frustration, disappointment, grumpiness, boredom, irritation, anger, laziness, shame, guilt …
2 Make a note when this was, what the negative emotion was, and why you think it occurred.
3 What happened next, and how did you manage to move back to compassion?
4 What would you need to do differently every time this fear comes back to you? How can you embrace the fear, and make contact with the blissful feelings underneath, overcoming your fearful state of mind?

Robin Shohet and Erik de Haan, March 2022

References

Ainsworth, M.D.S., Blehar, M.C., Waters, E. and Wall, S. (1978). *Patterns of Attachment: A psychological study of the strange situation*. Hillsdale, NJ: Erlbaum.

Allen, J.G. (2003). Mentalizing. *Bulletin of the Menninger Clinic* 67 (2), 91–112.

Andersen, S. and Berk, M.S. (1998). The social-cognitive model of transference: Experiencing past relationships in the present. *Current Directions in Psychological Science* 7 (4), 109–115.

Appelbaum, S.A. (1973). Psychological-mindedness: Word, concept and essence. *International Journal of Psychoanalysis* 54 (1), 35–46.

Armstrong, D. (1997). The 'institution in the mind': Reflections on the relation of psychoanalysis to work with institutions. *Free Associations* 7 (41), 1–14.

Barber, H.F. (1992). Developing strategic leadership: The US Army War College experience. *Journal of Management Development* 11 (6), 4–12.

Barrett, F.J. (2011). Cultivating a culture of creativity and innovation: Learning from jazz improvisation (slide 17). www.slideshare.net/vlerickschool/barrett-frank (accessed 25 February 2019).

Bateson, G. (1972). *Steps to an Ecology of Mind*. Chicago, IL: University of Chicago Press.

Batey, M., Walker, A. and Hughes, D. (2012). Psychometric tools in development – do they work and how? In J. Passmore (Ed.), *Psychometrics in Coaching* (2nd ed., pp. 49–58). London: Kogan Page.

Beck, A.T. (1975). *Cognitive Therapy and the Emotional Disorders*. New York: International Universities Press.

Bennett, S. (1979). *A History of Control Engineering, 1800–1930*. Stevenage: Peregrinus, for the Institution of Electrical Engineers.

Bentz, V.M. and Shapiro, J.J. (1998). *Mindful Inquiry in Social Research*. London: Sage.

Berglas, S. (2002). The very real dangers of executive coaching. *Harvard Business Review* (June), 86–92.

Berne, E. (1966). *Principles of group treatment*. Oxford: Oxford University Press.

Bernier, T. and Kearns, A. (2018). Where there's smoke there's fire. In A. Kearns (Ed.), *The Mirror Crack'd* (pp. 107–124). London: Routledge.

Bion, W.R. (1963). *Elements of Psychoanalysis*. London: Heinemann.

Bion, W.R. (1970). *Attention and Interpretation*. London: Tavistock.

Block, P. (2008). *Community: The structure of belonging*. San Francisco, CA: Berrett-Koehler.

Bond, T. (2006). Intimacy, risk, and reciprocity in psychotherapy: Intricate ethical challenges. *Transactional Analysis Journal* 36 (2), 77–89.

Bordin, E.S. (1979). The generalizability of the psychoanalytic concept of the working alliance. *Psychotherapy: Theory, Research and Practice* 16, 252–260.

Bowlby, J. (1969). *Attachment and Loss, Vol. 1: Attachment*. London: Hogarth Press and the Institute of Psychoanalysis.

Bowlby, J. (1973). *Attachment and Loss, Vol. 2: Separation: Anxiety and anger*. London: Hogarth Press and the Institute of Psychoanalysis.

Bressan, P., and Damian, V. (2018). Fathers' eye colour sways daughters' choice of both long- and short-term partners. *Scientific Reports* 8 (1), 1–9.

Bretherton, I. (1985). Attachment theory: Retrospect and prospect. *Monographs of the Society for Research in Child Development* 50 (1/2), 3–35.

Breuer, J. and Freud, S. (1895). *Studien über Hysterie* [Studies on Hysteria]. Leipzig/ Vienna: Verlag Franz Deuticke.

Brown, D.G. (1977). Drowsiness in the countertransference. *International Review of Psycho-Analysis* 4, 481–492.

Carroll, M. and Shaw, E. (2013). *Ethical Maturity in the Helping Professions: Making difficult life and work decisions*. London: Jessica Kingsley.

Cleckley, H.M. (1941). *The Mask of Sanity: An attempt to clarify some issues about the so-called psychopathic personality*. St. Louis, MO: Mosby.

Cuijpers, P., Karyotaki, E., De Wit, L. and Ebert, D.D. (2020). The effects of fifteen evidence-supported therapies for adult depression: A meta-analytic review. *Psychotherapy Research* 30 (3), 279–293.

Czander, W.M. (1993). *The Psychodynamics of Work and Organizations*. New York: Guilford Press.

Davis, D.M. and Hayes, J.A. (2011). What are the benefits of mindfulness? A practice review of psychotherapy-related research. *Psychotherapy* 48 (2), 198–208.

Day, A., De Haan, E., Sills, C., Bertie, C. and Blass, E. (2008). Coaches' experience of critical moments in the coaching. *International Coaching Psychology Review* 3 (3), 207–218.

De Board, R. (1978). *The Psychoanalysis of Organizations*. London: Routledge.

De Haan, E. (2004). *Learning with Colleagues*. Basingstoke: Palgrave Macmillan.

De Haan, E. (2006). Fearless listening. *Ashridge 360 Journal* (July).

De Haan, E. (2008a). *Relational Coaching: Journeys towards mastering one-to-one learning*. London: Wiley.

De Haan, E. (2008b). I doubt therefore I coach – critical moments in coaching practice. *Consulting Psychology Journal: Practice and Research* 60 (1), 91–105.

De Haan, E. (2008c). I struggle and emerge – critical moments of experienced coaches. *Consulting Psychology Journal: Practice and Research* 60 (1), 106–131.

De Haan, E. (2008d). Becoming simultaneously thicker and thinner skinned: The inherent conflicts arising in the professional development of coaches. *Personnel Review* 37 (5), 526–542.

De Haan, E. (2011). Back to basics I: How the discovery of transference is relevant for coaches and consultants today. *International Coaching Psychology Review* 6 (2), 180–193.

De Haan, E. (2012). Back to basics II: How the research on attachment and reflective-self function is relevant for coaches and consultants today. *International Coaching Psychology Review* 7 (2), 194–209.

De Haan, E. (2014). Back to basics III: On inquiry, the groundwork of coaching and consulting. *International Coaching Psychology Review* 9 (1), 81–91.

De Haan, E. (2017a). *Team Coaching Pocketbook*. Alresford: Management Pocketbooks.

De Haan, E. (2017b). Trust and safety in coaching supervision: Some evidence that we are doing it right. *International Coaching Psychology Review* 12 (1), 37–48.

De Haan, E. (2018). Are you the coach you think you are? Different perspectives on coaching behaviour. *Coaching Today* (January), 6–10.

De Haan, E. (2019a). Coaching begins at hello. *The Training Journal* (July), 29–31.

De Haan, E. (2019b). Team coaching: A fleeting moment of noticing? *Coaching Today* (January), 12–19.

De Haan, E. (2019c). *Critical Moments in Executive Coaching: Understanding coaching process through research and evidence-based theory*. London: Routledge.

De Haan, E. (2020). The black-and-white magic of feedback. *Coaching Today* (July), 22–25.

De Haan, E. (2021). *What Works in Executive Coaching: Understanding outcomes through quantitative research and practice-based evidence*. London: Routledge.

De Haan, E., Baldwin, A., Carew, N., Conway, S., Elliman, J., Hazell, J., Martin, A., Mureau, S., O'Connell, P., Pounder, N., Rutherford, P. and Wanke, C. (Eds.) (2013). *Behind Closed Doors: Stories from the coaching room.* Faringdon: Libri.

De Haan, E., Bertie, C., Day, A. and Sills, C. (2010). Critical moments of clients of coaching: Towards a 'client model' of executive coaching. *Academy of Management Learning and Education* 5 (2), 109–128.

De Haan, E. and Burger, Y. (2004). *Coaching with Colleagues.* Basingstoke: Palgrave Macmillan.

De Haan, E., Culpin, V. and Curd, J. (2011). Executive coaching in practice: What determines helpfulness for clients of coaching? *Personnel Review* 40 (1), 24–44.

De Haan, E., Duckworth, A., Birch, D. and Jones, C. (2013). Executive coaching outcome research: The predictive value of common factors such as relationship, personality match and self-efficacy. *Consulting Psychology Journal: Practice and Research* 65 (1), 40–57.

De Haan, E., Grant, A., Burger, Y. and Eriksson, P.-O. (2016). A large-scale study of executive coaching outcome: The relative contributions of working relationship, personality match, and self-efficacy. *Consulting Psychology Journal: Practice and Research* 68 (3), 189–207.

De Haan, E. and Kasozi, A. (2014). *The Leadership Shadow: How to recognise and avoid derailment, hubris and overdrive.* London: Kogan Page.

De Haan, E. and Metselaar, C. (2015). Opinion: Diagnostic tools in executive coaching – more harm than good? *Coaching Today* (July), 16–17.

De Haan, E., Molyn, J. and Nilsson, V.O. (2020). New findings on the effectiveness of the coaching relationship: Time to think differently about active ingredients? *Consulting Psychology Journal: Practice and Research* 72 (3), 155–167.

De Haan, E. and Nilsson, V.O. (2017). Evaluating coaching behavior in managers, consultants and coaches: A model, questionnaire, and initial findings. *Consulting Psychology Journal* 69 (4), 315–333.

De Haan, E. and Nilsson, V.O. (2022). Does executive coaching work? A rigorous meta-analysis based only on randomized controlled trials. Submitted to *Academy of Management Learning and Education.*

Diochon, P.F. and Nizet, J. (2015) Ethical codes and executive coaches: One size does not fit all. *Journal of Applied Behavioral Science* 51 (2), 277–301.

Drake, D.B. (2009). Using attachment theory in coaching leaders: The search for a coherent narrative *International Coaching Psychology Review* 4 (1), 49–58.

Duncan, B.L., Miller, S.D. and Sparks, J.A. (2004). *The Heroic Client.* San Francisco, CA: Wiley.

Eichenberg, C., Becker-Fischer, M. and Fischer, G. (2010). Sexual assaults in therapeutic relationships: Prevalence, risk factors and consequences. *Health* 2 (9), 1018–1026.

Fairbairn, W.R.D. (1952). *Psychoanalytic Studies of the Personality.* London: Tavistock/ Routledge.

Fechner, G.T. (1860). *Elemente der Psychophysik* [Elements of Psychophysics]. Leipzig: Breitkopf and Härtel.

Fonagy, P. (2001). *Attachment Theory and Psychoanalysis.* New York: Other Press.

Fonagy, P. and Bateman, A.W. (2006). Mechanisms of change in mentalization-based treatment of BPD. *Journal of Clinical Psychology* 62 (4), 411–430.

Fonagy, P., Gergely, G., Jurist, E.L. and Target, M. (2004). *Affect Regulation, Mentalization, and the Development of the Self.* New York: Other Press.

Fonagy, P., Steele, M., Steele, H., Higgitt, A.C. and Target, M. (1994). The theory and practice of resilience. *Journal of Child Psychology and Psychiatry* 35 (2), 231–257.

Fonagy, P., Steele, M., Steele, H., Moran, G.S. and Higgitt, A.C. (1991). The capacity for understanding mental states: The reflective self in parent and child and its significance for security of attachment. *Infant Mental Health Journal* 12 (3), 201–218.

Fonagy, P. and Target, M. (1996). Playing with reality I. Theory of mind and the normal development of psychic reality. *International Journal of Psychoanalysis* 77 (2), 217–233.

Fonagy, P. and Target, M. (2000). Playing with reality III. The persistence of dual psychic reality in borderline patients. *International Journal of Psychoanalysis* 81 (5), 853–873.

Fonagy, P., Target, M., Steele, H. and Steele, M. (1998). *Reflective-Functioning Manual, version 5.0, for application to Adult Attachment Interviews*. London: University College London.

Freud, S. (1900). *Die Traumdeutung* [The Interpretation of Dreams]. Leipzig/Vienna: Verlag Franz Deuticke.

Freud, S. (1905). Bruchstück einer Hysterie-Analyse [Fragment of an Analysis of a Case of Hysteria]. *Monatsschrift für Psychiatrie und Neurologie*, Band XXVIII, Heft 4.

Freud, S. (1909). Bemerkungen über einen Fall von Zwangsneurose [Notes Upon a Case of Obsessional Neurosis]. *Jahrbuch für psychoanalytische und psychopathologische Forschungen*, Band I.

Freud, S. (1910). Die zukünftigen Chancen der psychoanalytischen Therapie [The Future Prospects of Psychoanalytical Therapy]. *Zentralblatt für Psychoanalyse*, Band I.

Freud, S. (1911). Formulierungen über die zwei Prinzipien des psychischen Geschehens [Formulations of the Two Principles of Mental Functioning]. *Jahrbuch für psychoanalytische und psychopathologische Forschungen*, Band III.

Freud, S. (1912a). Ratschläge für den Arzt bei der psychoanalytischen Behandlung [Recommendations to Physicians Practising Psycho-analysis]. *Zentralblatt für Psychoanalyse*, Band II.

Freud, S. (1912b). Zur Dynamik der Übertragung [The Dynamics of Transference]. *Zentralblatt für Psychoanalyse*, Band II.

Freud, S. (1913). Zur Einleitung der Behandlung [On Beginning the Treatment]. *Internationale Zeitschrift für ärztliche Psychoanalyse*, Band I.

Freud, S. (1914). Erinnern, Wiederholen und Durcharbeiten [Remembering, Repeating and Working-through]. *Zeitschrift für Psychoanalyse*, Band II.

Freud, S. (1915a). Bemerkungen über die Übertragungsliebe [Observations on Transference-love]. *Zeitschrift für Psychoanalyse*, Band III.

Freud, S. (1915b). Das Unbewusste (The Unconscious). *Zeitschrift für Psychoanalyse*, Band III.

Freud, S. (1917). *Vorlesungen zur Einführung in die Psychoanalyse*, Band XXVII. Vorlesung: Die Übertragung [Introductory Lecture on Psychoanalysis 27: The Transference]. Leipzig/Vienna: Verlag Hugo Heller.

Freud, S. (1920). *Jenseits des Lustprinzips* [Beyond the Pleasure Principle]. Leipzig/Vienna/Zürich: Internationaler psychoanalytischer Verlag.

Freud, S. (1923). *Das Ich und das Es* [The Ego and the Id]. Leipzig/Vienna/Zürich: Internationaler psychoanalytischer Verlag.

Freud, S. (1925). Die Verneinung. *Imago*, Band XI. Translated: "Negation". *International Journal of Psycho-Analysis* 6, 367–371.

Freud, S. (1940). Abriss der Psychoanalyse [An Outline of Psychoanalysis – Unfinished]. *Internationale Zeitschrift für Psychoanalyse und Imago* XXV (1), 7–67.

Furnham, A. (1996). The FIRO-B, the Learning Style Questionnaire, and the Five-Factor Model. *Journal of Social Behavior and Personality*, 11 (2), 285–299.

Gallese, V. and Goldman, A. (1998). Mirror neurons and the simulation theory of mind-reading. *Trends in Cognitive Science* 2 (12), 493–501.

Gardner, W.L. and Martinko, M.J. (1996). Using the Myers-Briggs Type Indicator to study managers: A literature review and research agenda. *Journal of Management* 22 (1), 45–83.

Gaudart, M. (2021). The first moments. *The Coaching Psychologist* 17 (2).

George, C., Kaplan, N. and Main, M. (1984). *Adult Attachment Interview*. Berkeley, CA: University of California at Berkeley (3rd ed., 1996).

George, E.R., Hawrusik, R., Delaney, M.M., Kara, N., Kalita, T. and Semrau, K.E. (2020). Who's your coach? The relationship between coach characteristics and birth attendants' adherence to the WHO Safe Childbirth Checklist. *Gates Open Research* 4: 111. https://doi.org/10.12688/gatesopenres.13118.1.

Gilling, S. (2013). Studying psychotherapy supported by horses. Thesis, Aarhus University, Aarhus.

Grant, A.M. (2001). Rethinking psychological mindedness: Metacognition, self-reflection, and insight. *Behaviour Change* 18 (1), 8–17.

Graßmann, C., Schölmerich, F. and Schermuly, C.C. (2020). The relationship between working alliance and client outcomes in coaching: A meta-analysis. *Human Relations* 73 (1), 35–58.

Gray, L.A., Ladany, N., Walker, J.A. and Ancis, J.R. (2001). Psychotherapy trainees' experience of counterproductive events in supervision. *Journal of Counselling Psychology* 48, 371–383.

Greene, J. and Grant, A.M. (2003). *Solution-Focused Coaching*. London: Momentum Press.

Greenson, R.R. (1965). The working alliance and the transference neuroses. *Psychoanalysis Quarterly* 34 (2), 155–181.

Grencavage, L.M. and Norcross, J.C. (1990). Where are the commonalities among the therapeutic common factors? *Professional Psychology: Research and Practice* 21 (5), 372–378.

Hackman, J.R. and Wageman, R. (2005). A theory of team coaching. *Academy of Management Review* 30 (2), 269–287.

Haeckel, E. (1866). *Generale Morphologie der Organismen* [General Morphology]. Berlin: Verlag von Georg Reimer.

Harrell, E. (2017). A brief history of personality tests. *Harvard Business Review* 95 (2), 63–63.

Harrison, R. (1963). Defenses and the need to know. *Human Relations Training News* 6 (4), 1–3.

Harrison, R. (1976). Role Negotiation: A tough-minded approach to team development. In R. Harrison, W.W. Burke and H. Hornstein (Eds.), *Social Technology of Organization Development*. La Jolla, CA: University Associates.

Hawkins, P. and Smith, N. (2006). *Coaching, Mentoring and Organisational Consultancy: Supervision and development*. Maidenhead: Open University Press.

Heimann, P. (1950). On counter-transference. *International Journal of Psychoanalysis* 31, 81–84.

Helmholtz, H. von (1867). *Handbuch der physiologischen Optik*. Leipzig: Voss.

Heron, J. (1975). *Helping the Client: A creative practical guide*. London: Sage.

Hirschhorn, L. (1988). *The Workplace Within: Psychodynamics of organizational life*. Cambridge, MA: MIT Press.

Horvath, A.O. and Greenberg, L. (1986). The development of the Working Alliance Inventory. In L. Greenberg and W. Pinsoff (Eds.), *Psychotherapeutic Processes: A research handbook*. New York: Guilford Press.

Hurley, J.R. (1990). Does FIRO-B relate better to interpersonal or intrapersonal behavior? *Journal of Clinical Psychology* 46 (4), 454–460.

Ianiro, P.M., Schermuly, C.C. and Kauffeld, S. (2013). Why interpersonal dominance and affiliation matter: An interaction analysis of the coach-client relationship. *Coaching: An International Journal of Theory, Research and Practice* 6 (1), 25–46.

IPCC (2021). *Climate Change 2021: The physical science basis*. Contribution of Working Group I to the Sixth Assessment Report of the Intergovernmental Panel on Climate

Change [Masson-Delmotte, V., P. Zhai, A. Pirani, S. L. Connors, C. Péan, S. Berger, N. Caud, Y. Chen, L. Goldfarb, M. I. Gomis, M. Huang, K. Leitzell, E. Lonnoy, J. B. R. Matthews, T. K. Maycock, T. Waterfield, O. Yelekçi, R. Yu and B. Zhou (Eds.)]. Cambridge: Cambridge University Press.

Jelley, R. B. (2021). Using personality feedback for work-related development and performance improvement: A rapid evidence assessment. *Canadian Journal of Behavioural Science/Revue canadienne des sciences du comportement* 53 (2), 175.

Joseph, S. (2006). Person-centred coaching psychology: A meta-theoretical perspective, *International Coaching Psychology Review* 1 (1), 47–54.

Keats, J. (1817). Letter 1.184 (22 December 1817). In *The Complete Poetical Works and Letters of John Keats*, Cambridge Edition. New York: Houghton Mifflin (1899, p. 277).

Klein, M. (1945). The Oedipus complex in the light of early anxieties. In *The Writings of Melanie Klein* (pp. 370–419). London: Hogarth Press (1975).

Klein, M. (1946). Note on some schizoid mechanisms. *International Journal of Psycho-Analysis* 27, 99–110.

Kohut, H. (1977). *The Restoration of the Self*. New York: International Universities Press.

Kraus, M.W. and Chen, S. (2010). Facial-feature resemblance elicits the transference effect. *Psychological Science* 21 (4), 518–522.

Lawrence, P. and Whyte, A. (2017). What do experienced team coaches do? Current practice in Australia and New Zealand. *International Journal of Evidence Based Coaching and Mentoring* 15 (1), 94–113.

Lawton, B. (2000). 'A very exposing affair'. Explorations in counsellors' supervisory relationships. In B. Lawton and C. Feltham (Eds.), *Taking Supervision Forward: Enquiries and trends in counselling and psychotherapy*. London: Sage.

Lear, J. (2005). *Freud*. Abingdon: Routledge.

Ledford, G.E., Jr. (1985). Transference and countertransference in action research relationships. *Consultation* 4 (1), 36–51.

Lewin, K. (1946) Action research and minority problems. *Journal of Social Issues* 2 (4), 34–46.

Lohser, B. and Newton, P.M. (1996). *Unorthodox Freud: The view from the couch*. New York: Guilford Press.

Luft, J. (1969). *Of Human Interaction*. Palo Alto, CA: Mayfield.

Main, M. and Goldwyn, R. (1990). Adult attachment rating and classification systems. In M. Main (Ed.), *A Typology of Human Attachment Organization Assessed in Discourse, Drawings and Interviews*. New York: Cambridge University Press.

Main, M., Kaplan, N. and Cassidy, J. (1985). Security in infancy, childhood and adulthood: A move to the level of representation. *Monographs of the Society for Research in Child Development* 50 (1/2), 66–104.

Main, M. and Solomon, J. (1990). Procedures for identifying infants as disorganized/disoriented during the Ainsworth Strange Situation. In M. Greenberg, D. Cicchetti and E.M. Cummings (Eds.), *Attachment During the Preschool Years: Theory, research and intervention* (pp. 121–160). Chicago, IL: University of Chicago Press.

Malan, D.H. (1979). *Individual Psychotherapy and the Science of Psychodynamics*. London: Butterworth Heinemann.

Mann, T.C. and Ferguson, M.J. (2015). Can we undo our first impressions? The role of reinterpretation in reversing implicit evaluations. *Journal of Personality and Social Psychology* 108 (6), 823–849.

Manné, J. (2009). *Family Constellations*. Berkeley, CA: North Atlantic Books.

Marmaros, K. (2019). The effects of counseling provider attachment style and empathy on boundary behaviors. Doctoral dissertation, Pace University, New York.

Marshall, J. (2001). Self-reflective inquiry practices. In P. Reason and H. Bradbury (Eds.), *Handbook of Action Research* (pp. 433–439). London: Sage.

McDougal, J. (1978). *Plea for a Measure of Abnormality*. New York: International Universities Press.

McDowall, A. and Redman, A. (2017). Psychological assessment – an overview of theoretical, practical and industry trends. Paper presented at the British Psychological Society Division of Occupational Annual Conference, Liverpool, January 2017.

Miller, A. (1979). *Das Drama des begabten Kindes und die Suche nach dem wahren Selbst* [The Drama of the Gifted Child]. Frankfurt am Main: Suhrkamp.

Mills, J. (2005). A critique of relational psychoanalysis. *Psychoanalytic Psychology* 22 (2), 155–188.

Minnen, A. van, Hendriks, L. and Olff, M. (2010). When do trauma experts choose exposure therapy for PTD patients? A controlled study of therapists and patient factors. *Behavior Research and Therapy* 48 (4), 312–320.

Mitchell, S.A. and Aron, L. (Eds.) (1999). *Relational Psychoanalysis: The emergence of a tradition*. Hillsdale, NJ: Analytic Press.

Nelson, E. and Hogan, R. (2009). Coaching on the Dark Side. *International Coaching Psychology Review* 4 (1), 7–19.

Nielsen, J.A., Zielinski, B.A., Ferguson, M.A., Lainhart, J.E. and Anderson, J.S. (2013). An evaluation of the left-brain vs. right-brain hypothesis with resting state functional connectivity magnetic resonance imaging. *PLoS One* 8: e71275. https://doi.org/10.1371/journal.pone.0071275.

O'Neill, M.-B. (2000). *Executive Coaching with Backbone and Heart: A systems approach to engaging leaders with their challenges*. San Francisco, CA: Jossey-Bass.

Owen, D. (2008). Hubris syndrome. *Clinical Medicine* 8 (4), 428–432.

Palmer, S. and Whybrow, A. (Eds.) (2007). *Handbook of Coaching Psychology: A guide for practitioners*. Hove: Routledge.

Passmore, J. (2012). *Psychometrics in Coaching*. London: Kogan Page.

Passmore, J. and Marianetti, O. (2007). The role of mindfulness in coaching. *The Coaching Psychologist* 3 (3), 131–137.

Patrick, C., Fowles, D. and Krueger, R. (2009). Triarchic conceptualization of psychopathy: Developmental origins of disinhibition, boldness, and meanness. *Development and Psychopathology* 21 (3), 913–938.

Patent GB130432 (1919). Improvements in or relating to electrical signalling systems.

Peltier, B. (2001). *The Psychology of Executive Coaching: Theory and application*. New York: Brunner/Routledge.

Plutarch (1st century AD). *On Listening*, trans. R. Waterfield. In *Essays*. London: Penguin Books (1992).

Premack, D.G. and Woodruff, G. (1978). Does the chimpanzee have a theory of mind? *Behavioral and Brain Sciences* 1 (4), 515–526.

Racker, H. (1968). *Transference and Countertransference*. New York: International Universities Press.

Reason, P. and Torbert, W. (2001). The action turn: Toward a transformational social science. *Concepts and Transformation* 6 (3), 1–37.

Rock, D. and Page, L.J. (2009). *Coaching with the Brain in Mind: Foundations for practice*. Hoboken, NJ: Wiley.

Rogers, C.R. (1957). Personal thoughts on teaching and learning. *Merrill-Palmer Quarterly* 3, 241–243.

Rogers, C.R. (1961). *On Becoming a Person: A therapist's view of psychotherapy*. London: Constable.

Rogers, J. (2004). *Coaching Skills: A handbook*. Maidenhead: Open University Press.

Rosenzweig, S. (1936). Some implicit common factors in diverse methods of psychotherapy: 'At last the Dodo said, "Everybody has won and all must have prizes."' *American Journal of Orthopsychiatry* 6, 412–415.

Satipatthana Sutta or 'The discourse on the establishing of mindfulness' (29 BC). Discourse 10 in *The middle-length discourses of the Buddha: A translation of the Majjhima Nikaya*, trans. Bhikku Nanamoli and Bhikku Bodhi. Boston, MA: Wisdom Publications.

Schein, E.H. (1993). How can organizations learn faster? The challenge of entering the green room. *Sloan Management Review* 34 (2), 85–92.

Schippers, M.C., Hartog, D.N.D., Koopman, P.L. and Van Knippenberg, D. (2008). The role of transformational leadership in enhancing team reflexivity. *Journal of Human Relations* 61 (11), 1593–1616.

Schippers, M.C., West M.A. and Dawson, J.F. (2015). Team reflexivity and innovation: The moderating role of team context. *Journal of Management* 41 (3), 769–788.

Schopenhauer, A. (1851). *Parerga and Paralipomena*, 2 vols. Oxford: Oxford University Press (2000).

Searles, H.F. (1955). The informational value of the supervisor's emotional experience. *Psychiatry* 18, 135–146.

Sechehaye, M.A. (1956). The transference in symbolic realization. *International Review of Psycho-Analysis* 37 (4/5), 270–277.

Sextus Empiricus (around 200 AD). *Outlines of Pyrrhonism*. I used the translations by R.G. Bury, 1933, published as Loeb Classical Library # 273, Harvard University Press (Cambridge, MA) and B. Mates, 1996, published as *The Skeptic Way* by Oxford University Press (New York and Oxford).

Sherin, J. and Caiger, L. (2004). Rational-emotive behavior therapy: A behavioral change model for executive coaching? *Consulting Psychology Journal: Practice and Research* 56 (4), 225–233.

Shohet, R. (1995). How green is your mind? *One Earth, 18*. Quoted in full in R. Shohet and J. Shohet, *In Love with Supervision*. Monmouth: PCCS Books (2020).

Shohet, R., Birch, D. and De Haan, E. (2018). Love over fear: An experience of assessment. *Coaching Today* (July), 14–18.

Steele, H., Steele, M. and Fonagy, P. (1996). Associations among attachment classifications of mothers, fathers, and their infants. *Child Development* 67 (2), 541–555.

Stern, D.N. (2004). *The Present Moment in Psychotherapy and Everyday Life*. New York: Norton.

Stiles, W.B., Barkham, M. and Wheeler, S. (2015). Duration of psychological therapy: Relation to recovery and improvement rates in UK routine practice. *British Journal of Psychiatry* 297 (2), 115–122.

Stober, D.R. and Grant, A.M. (Eds.) (2006). *Evidence Based Coaching Handbook: Putting best practices to work for your clients*. Hoboken, NJ: Wiley.

Stolorow, R.D. and Atwood, G.E. (1992). *Contexts of Being: The intersubjective foundations of psychological life*. Hillsdale, NJ: Analytic Press.

Strachey, J. (1934). The nature of the therapeutic action of psychoanalysis. *International Journal of Psychoanalysis* 15, 127–159.

Swider, B.W., Barrick, M.R. and Harris, T.B. (2016). Initial impressions: What they are, what they are not, and how they influence structured interview outcomes. *Journal of Applied Psychology* 101 (5), 625–638.

Tierney, J. and Baumeister, R.F. (2019). *The Power of Bad: And how to overcome it*. London: Penguin.

Tjosvold, D., Tang, M.M.L. and West, M. (2004). Reflexivity for team innovation in China – the contribution of goal interdependence. *Group and Organization Management* 29 (5), 540–559.

Van der Loo, E. (2007). The art of listening. In M.F.R. Kets de Vries, K. Korotov and E. Florent-Treacy (Eds.), *Coach and Couch: The psychology of making better leaders* (pp. 221–240). London: Hogarth Press.

Van IJzendoorn, M.H. (1995). Adult attachment representations, parental responsiveness, and infant attachment: A meta-analysis on the predictive validity of the Adult Attachment Interview. *Psychological Bulletin* 117 (3), 387–403.

Van IJzendoorn, M.H., Juffer, F. and Duyvesteyn, M.G.C. (1995). Breaking the intergenerational cycle of insecure attachment: A review of the effects of attachment-based interventions on maternal sensitivity and infant security. *Journal of Child Psychology and Psychiatry* 36 (2), 225–248.

Van Meurs, N. (2003). Negotiations between British and Dutch managers: Cultural values, approaches to conflict management, and perceived negotiation. PhD thesis, University of Sussex.

Vergauwe, J., Hofmans, J., Wille, B., Decuyper, M. and De Fruyt, F. (2021). Psychopathy and leadership effectiveness: Conceptualizing and testing three models of successful psychopathy. *Leadership Quarterly* 32 (6), 101536.

Wallin, D.J. (2007). *Attachment in Psychotherapy.* New York: Guilford Press.

Wampold, B.E. (2001). *The Great Psychotherapy Debate: Models, methods and findings.* Mahwah, NJ: Erlbaum.

Waters, T.E., Raby, K.L., Ruiz, S.K., Martin, J. and Roisman, G.I. (2018). Adult attachment representations and the quality of romantic and parent–child relationships: An examination of the contributions of coherence of discourse and secure base script knowledge. *Developmental Psychology* 54 (12), 2371.

Whitmore, J. (1992). *Coaching for Performance: GROWing people, performance and purpose.* London: Nicholas Brealey.

Whittington, J. (2012). *Systemic Coaching and Constellations: An introduction to the principles, practices and application.* London, Kogan Page.

Will, T., Gessnitzer, S. and Kauffeld, S. (2016). You think you are an empathic coach? Maybe you should think again. The difference between perceptions of empathy vs. empathic behaviour after a person-centred coaching training. *Coaching: An International Journal of Theory, Research and Practice* 9 (1), 53–68.

Winnicott, D.W. (1962). Ego integration and child development. In *Maturational Processes and the Facilitating Environment: Studies in the theory of emotional development.* London: Hogarth Press (1965).

Winnicott, D.W. (1965). *Maturational Processes and the Facilitating Environment: Studies in the theory of emotional development.* London: Hogarth Press.

Winnicott, D.W. (1967). Mirror-role of mother and family in child development. In P. Lomas (Ed.), *The Predicament of the Family: A psycho-analytical symposium* (pp. 26–33). London: Hogarth Press.

Wundt, W. (1862). Die Geschwindigkeit des Gedankens [The Velocity of Thought]. *Die Gartenlaube* 17, 263–265.

Zeus, P. and Skiffington, S. (2000). *The Complete Guide to Coaching at Work.* North Ryde, NSW: McGraw-Hill.

Index

Page numbers in italics are figures; with 'n' are notes.